This book offers a most interesting insight into the history of the David Cantley family. An overview of individual members is included along with several incidents which occurred in their lives. Their heritage characterizes an honest, hardworking, sharing and caring people who rely greatly on each other.

Contained is a delightful list of vocabulary terms spoken in this West Virginia territory. Word definitions shed light along with the inclusion of the words in short sentences for the reader's understanding and hearty laughter.

The love of the people, for God, and each other is much in evidence. The author has inspired us with invaluable insight into the values and principles which portray those family members who lived under the inspiration of the Scriptures. Time spent reading this book will be well worth it and I predict a most enjoyable journey will be taken.

-Dona Thornton, Ed.D.
Professor of Education Emeritus
Palm Beach Atlantic University

Rock Creek Unincorporated was written to document the Cantley family history and family stories for future generations. In so many ways, this is the story of the American journey that is repeated over and over all across America. Through Dave's narrative, we can follow the Cantley family from their pre-Revolutionary arrival through the 21st century. He highlights his formative years in West Virginia and shares the lives of his parents, brothers and sisters and the life experiences that shaped Dave Cantley, the educator.

As a parent, a school board member and community activist I was privileged to know and work closely with Dave Cantley for more than 30 years. As I read the book, I replayed many conversations we had about the importance of reading, the importance of career education, the importance of quality teachers and the value of opportunities for all students. A strong work ethic, love of family and commitment to community (all those Rock Creek values) were all shared with every student, every teacher and every educator who's lives he touched. I am one of those individuals who was fortunate to have Dave Cantley as a friend and mentor. For all the future generations who read this book, I hope that everyone who reads this book takes the time to celebrate the difference that one person can make in so many lives.

-Jody Gleason
Palm Beach County School Board Member
1992-2000

Rock Creek Unincorporated is a charming memoir, beautifully written with great style and obvious love by David D. Cantley. It tells the story of his family, the Cantleys of West Virginia–a story that spans the days of the early colonization of West Virginia to modern times. The work is remarkable in its scope. It is also remarkable for the loving manner with which it brings the characters to life–generation by generation. The book would be a welcome addition to any library wishing to chronicle the American experience. With his impressive narrative, Mr. Cantley has wonderfully bequeathed, to future generations of his family, the rich and vibrant history of their ancestors. The rest of us are fortunate observers.

-Dr. Rick Mann

ROCK CREEK
UNINCORPORATED

A Disabled Coal Miner's Son
Who Devoted His Life
to Education

DAVID DEE CANTLEY

ROCK CREEK UNINCORPORATED
A DISABLED COAL MINER'S SON WHO
DEVOTED HIS LIFE TO EDUCATION

iUniverse books may be ordered through booksellers or by contacting:

iUniverse
1663 Liberty Drive
Bloomington, IN 47403
www.iuniverse.com
844-349-9409

ISBN: 978-1-6632-1381-5 (sc)
ISBN: 978-1-6632-1380-8 (hc)
ISBN: 978-1-6632-1382-2 (e)

Print information available on the last page.

iUniverse rev. date: 12/28/2020

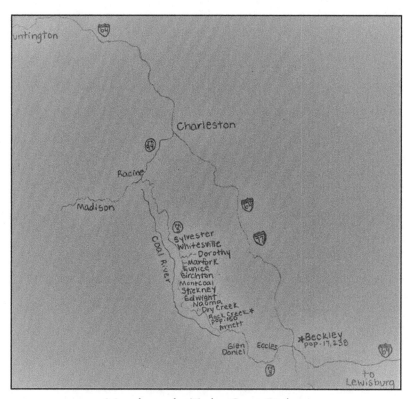

Map drawn by Taylor Grace Feulner

DEDICATION

This book is dedicated to my parents,
Hubert and Grace Lee Price Cantley.

CONTENTS

Part II

FOREWORD

This is a story about a poor boy born to a large family during World War II in the coal fields of southern West Virginia. He was one of ten children being raised by a disabled coal mining father in an area of abject poverty. David Cantley grew up in one of the most downtrodden depressed areas of Appalachia in conditions unimaginable in today's America.

The family, with strong resolve, recognized what few options were open to them and strived to make the best of limited resources. Fortuitously, they lived on a small farm and were able to grow the basic essentials which averted malnutrition. Notwithstanding what seemed like overwhelming odds, the family believed that David and his siblings would graduate from the local high school. He attained this feat in 1958.

David harbored virtually no thoughts about college attendance, given the absolute absence of the funds necessary. Education beyond high school in this region lagged behind the rest of the nation due to economic disadvantages as well as cultural outlook.

His transition from impossible to inevitable may have come about following a visit by a local college professor who doubled as a recruiter of students to discuss ways to pursue post-secondary education.

The professor remembers that his overtures to David regarding college attendance were met in an unassertive, diffident and self-effacing manner. In retrospect, David acknowledges that he was initially defensive and that his attitude was reserved, shy and somewhat humble. He recalls thinking, "How can I politely tell this man to leave and to contact other recent high school graduates who may possess the financial means required?"

Upon learning that David had played basketball, the professor, when leaving, suggested that he visit the college, talk with the president of the institution who just might offer him an athletic scholarship. Shortly thereafter David visited the college and, after meeting with the president, was, to his astonishment, given a two-year basketball scholarship which would cover the cost of tuition, books and fees.

It is often said that we underestimate the effects of randomness in our lives. David was a recipient of largely unpredictable factors. Even so, when handed the ball, one must successfully run in order to score. This he did in a most admirable way. His career path is *fait accompli*.

After enrolling for his first college classes, I am proud that David became one of my favorite students. I am that college professor who talked with him on the bridge leading to his family's farm at Rock Creek that summer afternoon sixty-one years ago.

John B. Van Dyke, Jr.
Academic Dean Emeritus
Beckley College

Mr. VanDyke in Men's Wearhouse being fitted
for a new suit on his 95th birthday.

INTRODUCTION

It was a chilly September 30, 1938 evening on the family farm, Muley Holler, at Rock Creek, West Virginia that I, the tenth of eleven children and the seventh of seven sons, was born. I was one of five to be born in that home. Six other children were born in coal camps. Although not wealthy, the Cantley family wanted for nothing; my Dad was employed as a miner and made sufficient wages to take care of his large family. However, that was to change four years later.

The Cantley family history goes back to pre-Revolutionary War days. My ancestors served in that war, The War of 1812, The Civil War and World War I. Family members also served in World War II as well as in Korea, Vietnam and Afghanistan. I am the sole survivor of eleven children and have been encouraged by some of my nephews and nieces to write the history of our family. So much history and many, many stories have been lost. I feel an obligation to write what I can research as well as what I can recall from stories that I remember my dad, aunts and uncles telling when I was a child.

Well-meaning critics have told me that "Rock Creek Unincorporated" is not the appropriate title for my book as it encompasses much more than Rock Creek. While I can understand and agree (somewhat) with their opinion, I am determined to attempt to put Rock Creek on the map.

This book is being written primarily for the benefit of my family with no hopes or plans for it to be a best seller or any seller at all for that matter. I hope to chronicle the history of my family and put this book on the shelf for future generations of the family to read so they may gain an appreciation of the contributions and hardships of their ancestors like my great grandparents Rebecca Jane and her husband James as well as my parents.

It was also my intention in writing this book to write about my career in education. I was inspired by my brother, Ronald Bee, to go to college and become an educator. It was not as much his verbal encouragement as it was the example he set for me. Having said that, this book is divided into two parts. Part One is about my ancestors, growing up in a large family living in a small house, my schools, church, and memories of the people, activities, and life in my community and the surrounding communities. Part Two centers around my education and career as an educator in West Virginia and Florida.

It is my hope that you, the reader, will enjoy reading the book as much as I have enjoyed writing it.

Right: The window on the left is where my parents stood crying, watching Junior walk down the lane to the Army and WW II. Five babies were born in that room.

Photo taken by Debby Jarrell, 12-2018

"For any American who had the great and priceless privilege of being raised in a small town there always remains with him nostalgic memories . . . and the older he grows the more he senses what he owed to the simple honesty, neighborliness, and integrity that he saw all around him in those days..."
--Dwight D. Eisenhower

PART I

PART 1

MY FORMATIVE YEARS

I was born on September 30, 1938, at Rock Creek, West Virginia. My parents were Hubert and Grace Price Cantley and I was number ten of eleven children; James, the oldest died in infancy. Eustace, Gene, Hubert, Jr., Doris, Betty, Barbara, Noel Dean, Ronald Bee, me--David Dee, and Thelma (Sugar) were the remaining children.

My Dad was a coal miner, but there is no doubt that my Mother was the parent who had the harder job. She raised ten children, cooked, washed, ironed, cleaned the house, cared for a garden and canned fruits and vegetables from the garden for our family to eat during the cold winter months. I could argue a good case for my Mother to be elevated to sainthood. She worked diligently from before dawn until late at night, and—astonishingly—never asked for anything for herself.

My Mother was an outstanding cook. My brothers, sisters, and I would frequently bring friends back to our home, and my mother would invariably insist that they eat something. Years after my Mother had died, our friends would often remark about how much they had enjoyed her meals when we had all been so much younger.

My earliest memory, at age four, was falling off the back porch into a big snowdrift. I was—literally—in over my head and had to be pulled out of the snow by one of my sisters. I also remember, at around the same time, that my Dad, at the age of 56, was injured in an accident at the Montcoal Mine, and I was taken to the hospital in Charleston to visit him. The accident occurred in the winter of 1942 when injured workers were often dismissed from their jobs without any compensation for their injuries. It was common practice for an injured miner to be examined by a board of five "neutral" doctors to determine whether he was entitled to worker compensation benefits. After examining my dad, two doctors said that he should receive 90% disability compensation, but the other three decided that he was not disabled at all. It was also common practice back then for greedy and corrupt coal companies to buy off unscrupulous doctors who would help them avoid paying workers' comp. My Dad was then told to report to the company doctor for a physical exam that would determine if he could return to work. When he was found physically unfit for work, that was the beginning of hard times for our family.

I have my Uncle Jimmy's 1942 diary and he gives us some insight into Daddy's injuries:

> *"January 19, Tuesday-Went to Charleston last night to see Hubert in hospital. Go back today and stay all night. Hubert is hurt bad, broke legs, arm, head hurt (doctors told him they took a fourth of a cup of coal from his forehead) maybe broke back. January 21-Hubert no better. January 22-Call Hospital, hear from Hubert, not good. January 23, Friday-Me, Pearl (wife) and Irene (daughter) go to see Hubert at Kanawha Valley Hospital. January 25, Sunday-Me, Pearl, Irene, June (daughter) and Chester (?) go to see Hubert. Not feeling so good. Ellen (my aunt) came back with us. February 8 Sunday-Me and Charlie Jarrell went to see Hubert. Getting along very well. February 14 Saturday-Me, Pearl and Irene went to see Hubert. February 28 Saturday-Went to Kanawha Valley Hospital to see Hubert. March 6 Friday-Went over*

to Hubert's." (It appears that Uncle Jimmy was not only visiting my Dad in the hospital but also going to our home to check on our family) *"March 7 Saturday-Went to Charleston to see Hubert. Young people's class here tonight. 45 boys and girls here."* *(The young people's class was comprised of teenage boys and girls at Rebecca Chapel)* *"March 6 Sunday went over to Hubert's. March 12 Thursday-Me, Pearl, Irene and Gracie (my Mother) went to see Hubert. Some better today. March 25 Wednesday-Hubert home from hospital. March 29 Sunday-Went over to see Hubert a couple of times. March 31 Friday-went to see Hubert me and Nelson Cooper."* *(Nelson was my uncle, married to Dad's sister Lou.)* *"April 19 Sunday-Over to see Hubert. May 5 Tuesday-Went to Mt. View School to register for sugar ration stamps. May 17 Sunday-Gracie (my Mother) was baptized. Went over to Hubert's. June 19 Saturday- Hubert fell and broke his leg again."* (I remember this and as a child of four I was very scared and thought my Daddy was not coming back home.) *"June 21 Sunday-Went to Charleston to see Hubert. Broke leg in same place. June 26 Friday-Payday. $85 plus $20,bonus."* (this would have been for two weeks of work.) *"December 5-Took Hubert to Kanawha Valley to see Okey. Operated on for piles"* *(hemorrhoids.)*

This was the end of Uncle Jimmy's entries pertaining to my dad. He made several entries on the weather. They experienced severe snow and cold in 1942 with snow accumulating to 24 inches.

My dad was not a member of the recently-formed United Mine Workers' Union and had no advocate to fight for him. I remember hearing him talk about being a private contractor hiring men to work on his crew at one point in time. I believe he later regretted not retaining a lawyer and suing the coal company, but at that place and time anyone that sued an individual or company was considered an outcast. Fortunately, my Dad had bought the farm at Rock Creek before he was injured. Our family would have been evicted had we lived in company housing as most miners did.

Back in those days, churches would give "poundings" to their preachers and to needy people in the community. The term *pounding* originated from the custom of generous parishioners donating "a pound" of food to be given to someone in need. Our church, Rebecca Chapel, gave my family a pounding when Daddy was hospitalized; I can clearly remember as a child of 4 the church members bringing their donated goods through our front door. One of the items we were given was a metal wash tub that was completely filled with food.

During those hard times my Mother was a pillar of strength. I remember coming into her and Daddy's bedroom one day while he was still in the hospital, and I saw her kneeling beside their bed on the side where my dad would have normally slept. I was too young to fully understand what she was doing, so I started crying and asked her what she was doing. She wiped away my tears and replied, "I was a prayin'." Her deep spiritual faith was the glue that held our frightened family together. My brother, Noel, once told me that Uncle Ovet, daddy's brother, and Aunt Ora came to our house one night and brought a quart of pork that Aunt Ora had canned. Afterwards, Noel said that Mommy had told him, "See, I told you that the Lord would send us something good to eat."

When Daddy was discharged from the hospital and came home only to fall and break his leg again, I was still very young and did not fully understand what was happening but I knew enough to feel frightened. When he came home the second time, he and I became so close that it was as if we were joined at the hip. Daddy was confined to his bed for a while, and during that time I would wait on him hand and foot. I slept with him at night, and remember clearly that I would use his arm for a pillow. That time with him was the most secure feeling I have ever had in my entire life. I knew that as long as I was there with him—with my head resting on that big arm—nothing in the world could harm me. When I was finally old enough to go to school, I simply—stubbornly—refused to leave Daddy. Finally, he got a job at our school as a janitor so I happily went to school the next year.

Years later, Tommy Jarrell, a friend of my two older brothers, Noel and Bee, told his daughter that our family had been poor back then, but that we simply hadn't known that we were. We didn't have the material things that other families had, but we ate better than anyone because of my Mother's great cooking. Practically everything that we ate came from our garden. We bought staple items like coffee, cornmeal, flour, lard and pinto beans. We bought pinto beans by the five-pound bag; we would have bought larger ones if they had made them. We bought flour and cornmeal in 25-lb. bags. We didn't know it at the time, but our diet was actually very nutritious.

I clearly remember that one evening I looked at our dinner table and asked Mommy where the pinto beans were. She, evidently feeling guilty for not always offering us a wide variety of different foods, explained that she thought that we should have something else to eat for a change. The next evening I noticed that—again—there were no pinto beans, so I asked, "Do you think that we could please have pinto beans for a *change* tomorrow night?" My plea really tickled Daddy.

Coal River was a great place for kids to grow up in the 1950s. My main friends and playmates were my cousins Gordon and Barry, my nephew, Ike, and Ted Jarrell. We roamed the hills and hollers, swam and fished in the river, and frequently played ball. Sometimes there would only be three of us, which was not enough to field a baseball team. I wonder how many kids today know about playing "Straight Base." When playing this game one kid would pitch, one would play outfield, and one would bat. If you hit the ball to a place where neither the fielder nor the pitcher could get you "out" before you reached base (located where second base would be in a normal field), you could either hit a home run or be stranded on base. If you were stranded, the pitcher would toss the ball into the air—and if he threw it high enough, the runner would break for home. If he didn't toss it high enough the runner would wait until he got a toss that he thought would allow him to return to home base. When the batter was finally "out" players would change position. I'm also willing to bet that not a single kid today knows about another popular game from my childhood "Rolly Bats."

My nephew, Ike, was a few years younger than the rest of us and didn't get to join in all of our boyhood activities. I do, however, remember one time when Ted, Ike and I were playing basketball at Uncle Ovet's house. Ted and I would take turns having Ike as a teammate. When it was my turn to have Ike I told him, "Get out front and get on Ted. Don't let him get around you. Get your hands in his face." Unfortunately, Ike took me literally and punched Ted in both eyes with his fingers. Ted had a hard time getting over that misunderstanding and swore that I'd told "little" Ike to punch him in the eyes.

Another memory I have of Ike is when he, Gordon, and I were swimming in the Jack Hole, our favorite swimming hole in Coal River. There was a big rock that we called the "Step Off" because if an inexperienced swimmer went beyond that point he would be in water over his head. Gordon and Ike were horsing around and accidentally went past the Step Off. Since neither of them could swim, they were both really struggling. To get his head above water, Gordon pushed Ike down so that he could dog paddle to shore. I had to go into the water and pull Ike to safety. That scary event was a big topic of conversation between Gordon and Ike for years. And every time I wanted a favor from Ike I would ask him, "Remember that time when I'd pulled your little ass out of the Jack Hole?" That approach worked for several years before he eventually decided that he had sufficiently repaid me.

During the 1940's and into the middle 1950's few people had cars but Greyhound buses had routes up and down Coal River several times a day. One of the more popular stories among locals was about how Charlie Jarrell would get aggravated with people who would come into his store and ask, "What time does that 9:30 bus come through here?" Ted and I often rode the bus to Whitesville for half fare, which was 15 cents, and for the same amount we were able to get into the movies. After the movie we would go to the drug store and buy a half-fare ticket so that we could ride the bus back home. The problem with all of this was that half-fare was for kids eleven years old and younger. At that time, Ted was about sixteen and I was about 13. One night, after we got on the bus, the driver came down the aisle collecting tickets from the passengers. When he got to Ted and me, Ted slid down in his seat, shot out his hand with the ticket and stared straight ahead at the back of the seat in front of him. The driver glanced at the ticket, looked at Ted, and asked, "How old are you, son?" Ted just kept looking at the back of the seat and replied, "Lebben." The driver said, "That's the trouble with boys on Coal River. They never get to be twelve until they are 21 years old."

In July of 2014 when I heard that Ted had only been given two to six months to live, I called him and asked if he'd like me to come up and visit him. He told me that he would really like that so my wife, Kay, and I drove to West Virginia; Ted and I spent our last night together.

Holidays were always special at our home. I can remember going onto the ridge behind the house to cut Christmas trees with Daddy or my older brothers. On occasion, we would climb a tree and cut the top out of it to get the tree we wanted. In later years, it would be my duty to "go Christmas tree hunting." I even took my daughter, Beth, hunting with me when she was about five years old. We dragged the tree home through a deep snow.

I don't know where my Dad got the money, but he always managed to get Christmas presents for us every year. One year when my sister, Sugar (Thelma), and I were older, our sister, Betty, bought us bikes for Christmas. She bought us Hawthorne bikes—a blue one for Sugar and a red one for me—from the Montgomery Ward store in Beckley. Betty was a very generous and loving sister who bought us Christmas presents and school clothes every year. Years later when I became principal at Lake Worth High School in 1980 Betty sent me a check for $100 with the notation, "For school clothes."

During my childhood, the Fourth of July was another big event for us. In the days before home freezers we would place our order for ice cream with Charlie Jarrell then we would go over to his store and wait for Oscar (the Valley Bell Dairy delivery man) to make his ice cream delivery. The ice cream came in one-gallon containers—chocolate, vanilla or strawberry were our only options—and we would have to eat all of the ice cream before it melted. A second Fourth of July treat was a watermelon which we cooled by placing it in the cold creek that ran out of the mountain.

There was always a big crowd at our house for holidays as well as for Sunday dinner. We had the usual turkey and perhaps a ham on Thanksgiving. My brothers and sisters would come to visit and bring their kids. I don't remember anyone ever bringing any food with them. Mommy and Daddy would—as my Dad used to say--"Furnish the ducks." No one ever left hungry.

Our backyard, where the cars would be parked, was a great place for car lovers on Sundays. My brothers made sure that their cars were washed and shined before they brought them to Sunday dinner. The yard often looked like today's car shows—all the hoods were raised and everyone would walk from car to car to hear each owner brag about his automobile.

We didn't have an indoor bathroom at home until about 1955 when Bee and Betty bought what was needed to install one. However, I had my first bath in a "real" bathtub as opposed to the wash-tub baths I knew at home when I was about 14 years old. I had hitchhiked to visit Noel and Mary Lou in Whitesville; when I arrived, I must have really stunk because Noel immediately took me to their bathroom. Then he filled the tub with hot soapy water, invited me to undress. and told me to hop in. I really enjoyed that bath, relaxing and soaking in the hot water. I had seen people taking baths in the movies and they were always washing their backs with a big white brush. I thought that Noel and Mary Lou must have one somewhere in their bathroom so I started to look around until I found it. I saw a white brush standing between the tub and the toilet, I grabbed it and began scrubbing my back. I had a blast pretending that I was one of those rich people in the movies. Eventually, I realized I had enthusiastically scrubbed my back with their toilet brush! Years later, in a moment of weakness, I confessed this to Kay, Noel, Mary Lou, Betty and Bobbie at a school reunion when we were staying in a motel in Beckley. As you can imagine, they all had a big laugh over that story. I now live in a house with four bedrooms and three bathrooms and I can shower anywhere I please.

Back then, there was not much for a kid to do at Rock Creek. All we had was Charlie Jarrell's store, Nona Rader's store (which included the post office), and the Rebecca Chapel. The church provided activities such as the Boy and Girl Scouts and "The Young People's Class." Opal Bradford taught the class, and we had an occasional trip to Little Beaver Lake or Grandview State Park. Jimmy and Chessie Salters started the scout groups because they had a son and daughter who wanted to be in the scouts. Many great stories came out of our boy scout experiences. I could go on and on about our week-long camp at Shanklin's Ferry Farm in Greenbrier County when my cousin, Charles, served as our scoutmaster for that week. But, as they say, "That is a whole 'nuther story."

In my younger days the radio essentially was our only entertainment. Television was still a few years away. At home our radio sat beside Daddy's chair, and it stood about four feet high; I would lie on the floor between his chair and the radio, where I would frequently fall asleep before bedtime. We listened to programs like *Amos and Andy, Our Miss Brooks, Inner Sanctum* (a scary mystery), and my favorite, *Gene Autry*. Guess who controlled the dial? The Osborne Brothers summed it up pretty well when they sang, "It was our only link to the outside world. Saturday night, Martha White, ole Lester Flatt and Earl."

One night during WW II the radio blew a tube--we were literally lost for entertainment! Without our radio, my only entertainment was listening to the tales Daddy and my uncles would tell. Uncle Ovet and Aunt Ora would come over every Sunday night and I always enjoyed those visits. One night Daddy and Uncle Ovet were talking about home remedies (my dad was born in 1888) when Daddy asked his brother if he remembered a certain remedy. Uncle Ovet replied, "Yes I do, and sheep shit tea—do you remember sheep shit tea?" To make this "cure," they would go the sheep barn, get dried sheep manure, boil it in water, and then drink it for a certain ailment.

Thanks to my sister, Doris, we finally got a tube for the radio. Doris worked at O.J. Morrison Cafeteria in Charleston and she promised to purchase the tube for us. On the designated day when Doris was supposed to bring the much-anticipated tube, we were all sitting on the front porch waiting to hear the bus from Charleston stop over at the "hard road" which was about a quarter mile away. We had a great time that night staying up late—until 9:00 P.M.—listening to the radio

For years I didn't really appreciate the fact that I came from a big family—I just took it for granted that that was the way life was supposed to be. Later in life, I would tell people about being one of eleven children and they'd consider that to be incredible. People were also astonished to hear that my grandfather was born during the Civil War.

I now know how truly blessed I was to have been part of a large, loving, and caring family.

CHILDHOOD RECOLLECTIONS
by Mary Jo Cantley Broyles

The door was always open at my grandparents' home, and the long front porch—with the swing at one end—has etched many fond memories in my mind. Sunday, when my cousins, aunts and uncles came to visit Grandpa and Grandma, was such a special blessing. Grandma was an outstanding cook (just ask anyone who ever ate her fried chicken), and Grandpa could fix anything, or so we thought. He could repair shoes, cut hair, or take a fish hook out of a poor dog's mouth. No grandparents could have been loved more than ours, and no grandparents could have loved us more than ours did.

Rock Creek was a community that didn't even have a stop sign. We had a school, a post office, two general stores, and a church. What more did we need? We have cherished memories of the school plays, the donkey basketball games which my daddy Eustace participated in, and the pony rides that Dad would give with our pony, Pepper, around and around the ball field for the school carnival.

My best memories revolve around Rebecca Chapel. Where do I start? The revivals, baptisms in the river, singing conventions, Boy and Girl Scouts, Bible School and the Christmas play, which ended with a bag of hard candy, an orange and an apple for each child. Armco, the mining company at Montcoal, also sent home Christmas goodies.

The Ladies' Aid was a group of women who met in the church on a regular basis, and among their many projects were quilting and bake sales. They would give a quilt to someone in the community, or occasionally sell one to raise money for their charity work. Easter egg hunts and other youth programs were a very important part of Rebecca Chapel's mission. My mother played the piano for church services, and my dad was the Sunday School Superintendent.

I remember—as a little girl—going to the family cemetery (which is located on the hill behind Marsh Fork Elementary School) on Memorial Day, or "Decoration Day," as it was commonly known. The adults would sing hymns, Uncle Nelson Cooper would pray, and then we would put fresh flowers from our yards and gardens on the graves. Every year, on Uncle Nelson's birthday we would have a big celebration on his and Aunt Lou's lawn. A very long table, which, to my young eyes, seemed to stretch forever, was loaded with the finest food the ladies of the church could cook. I have always considered myself fortunate to have grown up on Coal River. Some of the best people in the world lived there.

This picture was taken at one of the birthday celebrations for Uncle Nelson, on his lawn. At left (back to camera) is my Aunt Winnie. Across the table is Uncle Okey (in white shirt and tie); to his left is my brother Bee. Could that be Ike at Uncle Okey's right?

This picture was probably taken in the early 1950s at one of Uncle Nelson's birthday parties. Aunt Lou is in the center, Bill Asbury to the right. On the left, at the end of the table is Noel (left) and Junior (right).

Chapter photo: This picture was taken in 1926 when things were going pretty well for my family. Note that my siblings were very well dressed. The family lived in a coal camp at this time. They would move to the farm, which my dad purchased from my grandpa in 1929. Things would continue to go well for the family until my dad was injured in a mining accident in 1942. Picture here are: Back Row (L-R): Eustace, my mother holding Betty. Front Row (L-R): Junior, Doris, and Gene.

2

MY IMMEDIATE FAMILY

As stated earlier, during my early years I had no real appreciation for the large family of which I was privileged to be a part. I just took for granted that this was the way life was supposed to be—even though I had friends who had only one or two siblings. Ours was a closely-knit, feud-free family—except for occasional spats. I credit our Mother for (a) setting the "kindness first" tone at our house and (b) keeping everyone in check. We were not known for verbally expressing our love for each other; instead, we showed it in the way we treated each other. In fact, the only person in my family I ever heard say the words "I love you" was Betty and it was during the time when I was staying with her while her husband Bill was in the hospital.

James Cantley: The first baby born to my parents was James during the first year of Mommy and Daddy's marriage (1916). He died in infancy and was not given a middle name. Mommy did not speak of him at all until one day when Betty asked her about him; she replied, "I was young and didn't know how to take care of him." James is buried in the family cemetery at Rock Creek. Gene's son, Jerry, was mowing the cemetery one day, and said he could have sworn he heard his Grandma say, "I want some flowers on that baby's grave." You can bet that he put some flowers on that baby's grave right away! I have always told people that I am the ninth of ten children, but from now on it will be, "Tenth of eleven children-- seven boys and four girls."

Eustace Glen Cantley was born on March 6, 1917, at Marfork and died August 31, 1995. He married Thelma Cavendish on January 25, 1941; Thelma was born in 1918 and died in 2004. They had five children— Glenn Sheldon (Ike), Mary Jo, Byron Ross (Ron), Cynthia Susan and Steven Jay. The first home they owned was built on land on our farm in "the lower bottom" that Daddy gave them. Unfortunately, that house burned so they built another home in "the upper bottom." Eustace and Thelma later moved to Flat Top Lake, WV. They also had homes in Louisville, KY, as well as in both Melbourne Beach and Lake Worth, Florida.

Until the fall of 1965, mining was Eustace's primary occupation. Thelma, a teacher at Mt. View School, encouraged him to go back to school, and he graduated from Beckley College and Morris Harvey College, earning his degree in 1961. He would get up at 5 A.M. to leave for work at The Armco Mine at Montcoal, then come home, eat supper, and head for Beckley College. Oftentimes, he would put his class notes in his dinner bucket so he could study them at lunchtime.

After graduating from Beckley College, Eustace took Saturday and night classes at Morris Harvey College in Charleston. He also took classes that were offered on the radio—even though he had to drive up the hill to Mt. View School to get better reception. While working in the mine and going to school, he also found time to build a home on Flat Top Lake. Eustace worked for four years in the mine after receiving his college degree, he didn't want to take the big pay cut to become a teacher.

In the summer of 1965, when I resigned my teaching position at Marsh Fork High School to move to Florida, Eustace filled the vacancy. He served as social studies and mining teacher; he ultimately became assistant principal at his alma mater. Eustace had always told me what an easy job I had teaching school, yet Thelma said that when he came home after his first day of teaching he dragged himself upstairs, fell across the bed, and immediately went to sleep. He and Thelma had a happy life after retirement. They spent their summer months at Flat Top Lake and their winters in Florida. His hobbies were horses, playing his guitar, and running his boat on the lake.

During his last days, Eustace told Ike that he didn't have any enemies. He was a man who was known for his consideration for (and respect of) other people. He was also known for—when pushed to a point—clearly speaking his mind. Just ask Steve! "Boy, let me tell you something!" Steve refers to his dad as "E. G.," and he inherited his Daddy's sense of humor, as well as his ability to tell tall tales. I remember—at one family reunion— Betty had given me a T-Shirt that read, "PICK OF THE LITTER." Eustace looked at it and commented, "They left an 'R' out of that 'Pick'."

The last time I saw Eustace alive was when he was in the West Virginia University Hospital in Morgantown. When I shook his hand to leave, he held tightly onto my finger which turned me into mush. The memory of that moment reminds me of the Don Gibson song, *Take the Time to Touch the Morning* where he sings, "Have you ever tasted apples with the dew still on the skin. Have you ever loved somebody you'll never see again?"

Eugene Keith was born on August 5, 1918, and died February 4, 2006. He married Audrey Jarvis who was born October 7, 1920 and became an elementary teacher at Mt. View School. They had two sons— Larry Gene and Jerry Wayne. Larry graduated high school in 1961 and enrolled at Morris Harvey College in the fall; we roomed together! When Larry went home on Halloween weekend, he was killed in a car accident. Jerry became an electrician in the coal mines and is now Pastor of Glen Daniel Worship Center.

Gene tried his hand at coal mining two or three times; he never liked it! Instead, he worked in the shipyards in Baltimore, MD before WWII. I remember one time he and Audrey came home for a weekend; Gene was poking around in the smokehouse (where we kept the pork during the winter) looking for something. Finally, he found it—his hated miner's hat! He started using words I had never heard before. He headed for the chop block where Daddy always kept an axe for chores like splitting kindling wood or cutting off chickens' heads. He put that miner's hat on the chop block then came over-handed with a double-hand grip on the axe that sent pieces of the hat flying everywhere—still using words new to my tender ears. That is my earliest memory of Gene.

When our country entered World War II, Gene became one of the first members of the U.S. Army-Air Corps—known later as the U.S. Air Force. He became a sergeant stationed at Baffin Island. After the war, he again worked in the mines off and on until he and Noel landed jobs driving auto-transport trucks. Both Gene and Noel would spend the remainder of their working days hauling cars.

Gene, like Eustace, loved his guitar. They both had Gretsch Country Gentleman Chet Atkins models and played together often. The last time I visited Gene I knew I would never see him alive again. As I headed for the door I said, "Well, Gene, I'll see you later." He answered, "What do you mean later, this IS later!" I was not going to go through another heart-wrenching experience like I'd had with Eustace.

Hubert, Jr., the fourth child and our World War II hero, was born May 31, 1921. He married Lucille Fields on February 19, 1944, and they had five children—Paula Kay, Debra, Sherry, Brenda and Kevin. Hubert, Jr. died December 24, 2005.

Junior, as he was known his entire life, never showed any interest in farming. Frankly, he hated it. Instead, he tended to lean toward cars, trucks or anything with a motor in it. Daddy once said, "If I could rig it so that I could have an exhaust pipe stickin' out of that horse's rear end, maybe I could get Junior to plow."

Like Gene, Junior didn't like coal mining. As a young boy working in a mine, he'd seen a man get electrocuted from getting out on the wrong side of a "man trip" that was used to transport miners underground. At that moment he picked up his dinner bucket, walked out of the mine, and ended forever his underground mining days.

As stated earlier, Gene and Junior worked at the shipyards in Baltimore until they entered the military service. Bobbie recalls as a young girl watching Mommy and Daddy, who were in the lower bedroom, cry when they saw Junior (who had been drafted) walk down through the lane toward the swinging bridge to catch a bus to Charleston. After basic training, Junior was shipped to Germany in the closing months of the war and was assigned to the 3rd Armored Tank Division under the command of

General George Patton. I can clearly remember the pictures he sent home of piles of corpses from the concentration camps that he helped liberate.

Like most combat veterans, Junior didn't talk much about his wartime experiences until his later years. He told long-repressed stories about the Russians—our allies—whom he detested far more than the Germans. He gave me his own version of Patton after I gave him a copy of the movie *Patton*. He said that Patton, in spite of popular belief, had not been a big supporter of his men. Junior said that Patton would call a soldier up in front of his peers and proceed to unmercifully embarrass him to the point of humiliation. Junior recounted a time that he came up to the scene of an accident where a 6x6 truck reportedly had hit the staff car in which Patton was riding (injuries from this accident resulted in the general's death at the close of the war). Junior was one of many soldiers who had challenged the events surrounding that accident. He said he arrived just minutes after they had removed Patton, and that there was no 6x6 truck at the accident scene. Years later, I read Bill O'Reilly's book, *Killing Patton,* and saw a picture of Patton's staff car—a 1938 Cadillac—his car at the time of the "accident."

After the war, Junior was trained in auto mechanics and welding. For a number of years, he had his own garage at the upper end of Stickney on the river bank, and then he was employed as a heavy equipment mechanic for various coal companies. Junior always worked above ground, always had good jobs, and refused to work for, "A damn scab outfit." He enjoyed both good pay and benefits.

His retirement years were spent at his home in Joe's Creek in Boone County. He had a garage at the back of his house where he continued to work, but only as a hobby. Any time I went to visit him, I could count on a trip up to his garage where he would find something for me to take home. When I think of Tom Brokaw's book, *The Greatest Generation*, Junior and Gene automatically come to mind.

Both Junior and Gene are buried in the family cemetery at Rock Creek where years before, they had both worked extensively to make major improvements. That is where I want to be planted, where the deer and turkeys can come off the mountain at night and fertilize the grass on my grave.

Doris Lee was born December 21, 1924 and died August 5, 2002. She married Ralph Kinley Dickens on March 12, 1949, and they had two daughters—Nancy Lou and Peggy.

After she married Ralph, Doris was a housewife and didn't work outside the home. In their later years, she and Ralph bought Bobbie and Bill's house located in the lower bottom overlooking the river on the farm. Doris loved to dabble in ceramics, and she was active in our church, Rebecca Chapel, where she loved to sing. She was a constant companion and caregiver to Mommy and Daddy during their last days, something that gave all of us great comfort. It has often been said that Doris never had an enemy in the world; I believe that to be true. There had to have been a special place in Heaven awaiting "Little Dorsie."

Betty Lou was born on November 24, 1926, and died on January 6, 2009. She married Bill Billings on September 4, 1951. They were the first couple to be married in the then "new" church, Rebecca Chapel.

After graduating from high school, Betty was employed by Armco Steel Company at their Montcoal mine as a bookkeeper. Bill, also employed as a butcher at the time in Armco's company store (Standard Supply), joined the Air Force and they were married shortly thereafter. Betty remained at home until Bill completed training then she joined him when he was assigned to Wright-Patterson Air Force Base in Dayton, Ohio. His other assignments included Biloxi, Mississippi, Grand Fork, North Dakota and Orlando, Florida, where they would permanently make their home.

Like Doris, Betty didn't have an enemy in the world. She was very much like our Mother as she cared about everyone in the family. She constantly wrote letters, sent congratulatory cards for births, birthdays, anniversaries, marriages and holidays—not only to our family, but to Bill's family as well. She also, like Mommy, was not afraid to clearly state her position on an issue. Whenever she "spoke her piece" that would then be the end of the matter—there would be no further nagging or harping on the issue.

Betty was very generous to her parents and younger siblings during the tough times at home. She worked at Armco, but did not, I am sure, earn much money. Still, she always managed to have money to help out at home. She bought school clothes for Sugar and me all the way from first grade through high school. Bee recalled several times during high school when he needed money for school expenses Betty always came through. After she left home she sent checks to Mommy and Daddy on a regular basis.

When I talked my way into Beckley College—in the summer of 1958—I received a full scholarship but had no money for room and board. There were absolutely no jobs in Beckley at that time—neither part time nor full time. I needed $30 per month to pay Eustace's mother-in-law, Mrs. Grace Cavendish, for room and board from Sunday night until I would hitchhike home on Friday to have Mommy wash and iron my clothes. Betty and Bill loaned me the $30 each month to pay Mrs. Cavendish. During the summer of 1959 when the national average pay was $3.00 per hour, I worked in a steel mill in Cleveland, Ohio and made big money—$4.50 per hour. I stayed with my sister, Bobbie, and her husband, Bill, that summer (as well as three other summers), and I saved enough money to quickly repay Betty and Bill.

During the final weeks of her life, I spent a lot of time with Betty at her home and enjoyed our bonding conversations about family. At the time, Bill was in the hospital (and later a rehabilitation facility) recovering from a broken hip. She had delayed a much-needed operation to repair an aorta aneurysm and was scheduled for surgery in early January 2009. After our persuasion she finally agreed to let us bring her to our home for Christmas in 2008. She was reluctant to come because she was fearful that she might die while with us. We have always thought that this visit was a special gift from God. Typical of Betty, she delayed the procedure because of Bill's health problems. Sadly, the stress of dealing with Bill's illness proved to be too much for her to bear.

On Monday, January 6, 2009, Kay and I went to Orlando for one of our many visits after Bill's injury in mid-November. We always called Betty when we got on the turnpike to tell her we were on our way, but this time, after three or four calls with no answer, I knew I would not like what I'd find when we got to Orlando. Only days before this visit, Betty had insisted that we have a key made for her home. After knocking several times with no answer, I let myself in and found Betty lying on the floor. The aorta had ruptured, which resulted in a rapid and painless death. Although we all, including Betty, knew that it could happen at any time, I simply was not ready for what I found that day. I am so glad we'd had those earlier times together when I'd gone up to be with her during Bill's hospitalization. She was another one who had a special place in Heaven awaiting her.

Barbara Ellen "Bobbie" was the first of the clan to be born in "the lower room" on the farm at Rock Creek. Everyone before her had been born in coal camps where Daddy was employed. She was born on January 8, 1929, married Bill Asbury on August 2, 1946, and they had three children—Betty Jane, Kathy and Billy.

Bobbie was the feisty one of the girls, never taking any guff from anyone. She could be very obstinate; my mother told Bill when they got married, "I could never do anything with her, maybe you can. Good luck!" Bobbie once told Bill all her high school friends had passed away. Bill replied, "You are too damn stubborn to die." Bobbie was a housewife while Bill worked for Raleigh-Wyoming Mining Company at their Edwight mine.

As a child, I can remember seeing Bill come down the walkway to our back porch carrying bags filled with items our family could not afford to buy. He would usually bring a turkey or ham for Mommy to cook. Bill introduced me to bluegrass music. Once, while listening to a bluegrass record, I asked him, "What is that?" He replied, "That is a banjer, Fox." Fox was my nickname from early childhood. After listening to that record with Bill, I was hooked on bluegrass for life. He gave me his bluegrass record collection ten years before his death. Bill was very generous with family, friends and neighbors. I remember when a neighbor in Cleveland lost a child and couldn't afford the funeral. Bill gave Billy $600 cash and told him to take it to the family.

When the coal industry died out in the late 1950's, Bobbie and Bill moved to Cleveland where Bill worked as a welder or millwright in various factories, steel mills and foundries. Bobbie continued in her role as homemaker and loving mother to her three children. She was an excellent cook and made the best soups and cornbread of anyone. Ted Farley, an up-the-holler Rock Creek boy, told me about working with Bill in the Chevy plant in Cleveland. He told me Bill would bring some of Bobbie's cornbread to work each night, and he and Bill would go to the cafeteria at 2 a.m. to get a bowl of milk to enjoy their nightly treat.

I had a lot of fun with Bobbie, teasing her and recounting old family tales. Getting her and Betty together was like being at a circus. They kept me in stitches with laughter. One time when I visited Bobbie in Cleveland after I had moved to Florida, she told me, "There is not a single person in this neighborhood I can carry on an intelligent conversation with. This is the dumbest bunch of people I have ever seen." A few minutes later she and I were in the yard when a neighbor came strolling down the sidewalk. Bobbie said to her, "Did you know Mr. Jones' wife had a baby?" The neighbor replied, "No, was she pregnant?" Bobbie looked at me and said, "Now, do you see what I mean?"

Bobbie and I were having a phone conversation (I called her every Sunday night) one night in the early 1990's when we were discussing the family and growing up at Rock Creek when she mentioned something I had completely forgotten. She asked me if I remembered the sound of birds or something flying by our bedroom windows every night; she said they came from up the holler, circled the house then went back up the other side of the house. I told her she was crazy, nothing like that ever happened. She insisted she was not crazy, and that it did happen! A few days later I had to call her and admit that I remembered that, I had indeed heard the same sound she referenced. It sounded like a large flock of birds and their wings were fluttering very rapidly. I never knew they circled the house, but I heard them as if they had come from up the holler like Bobbie had said.

The birds, or whatever they were, were never discussed in the family. It was as if it were a taboo subject never to be "named" as my dad would say. My mother was a very religious person and prayed daily for our family. My very firm belief is that those bird-like sounds were sent by God to signify the fact that we were being protected.

In his later years, Bill again became self-employed and bought and sold scrap metals from mines in southern Ohio. He passed away after spending his last two years in an assisted living facility in the Cleveland area. Bobbie passed away on October 8, 2017 three months before her 90th birthday in an Alzheimer's care facility in Olmstead Falls, Ohio.

Noel Dean was born on February 27, 1931, and died on April 9, 2012. On December 26, 1951, he married Mary Lou Mynes (who was born on August 3, 1933). They had three sons—Noel Dean II, Randal David, and Alan Dale. Sadly, Dean passed away from cancer in December of 2001.

After graduating from high school in 1951, Noel worked for a brief time as a truck driver for a lumber company. A year or two later, he started driving for Gate City Auto Transport, hauling Chrysler products from Detroit to cities throughout the south. He remembered that his first trucks were six-cylinder Dodges and were very slow. In those days auto transport trailers only carried four cars. Take a look at how many they carry today! Because those old trucks were very slow and weak, he was forced to gear down when facing even the slightest head wind. He and Gene delivered Chrysler products in the early days and their route conveniently brought them up Coal River allowing them to spend time at home. Noel remembered Mt. View Hill as the biggest challenge they had on their entire route. Obviously, this was before interstate highways had been built.

Noel was drafted into the Army shortly after he started at Gate City; he spent nearly two years serving his country. After basic training he was sent to Nuremberg, Germany, where he served as company clerk. After he was discharged from the Army, he returned to work at Gate City where he found a brand-new truck waiting for him. Although it caused grumbling among the other drivers, someone in management must have (a) had a lot of confidence in Noel, (b) valued his work ethic, and (c) wanted to show appreciation for his service to his country.

Noel and Mary Lou moved to Perrysburg, Ohio, during the summer of 1970, primarily because Noel's job changed from hauling Chrysler products to the south to hauling Volkswagens to the Midwest. This switch eliminated his stopovers at home.

Noel and Mary Lou enjoyed a very contented retirement and, until health problems arose, they enjoyed spending winters in Florida playing golf.

Noel was another member of our family who believed in "Dancin' with them that brung you." Even while raising his own family he was always very generous and helped Mommy and Daddy—as well as Sugar and me, who were the last two to live at home. I can remember that he gave me money every time he saw me, and he even took me to Beckley and bought me a sport coat, pants, shirt and tie when I graduated from Mt. View Jr. High. On that day, he took me out to lunch at a diner on Prince Street. After we left the restaurant, I handed him some coins he'd left on the table and told him, "You forgot your change." I didn't know anything about tips.

I was grateful for the fact that while I was at Morris Harvey College Noel's company was still running gas-powered trucks. I stopped at his house in Whitesville every Sunday night on my way back to Charleston, backed my '52 Ford up to his truck, and used his siphon hose (otherwise known as a "Coal River credit card") to fill my tank. My car had a six-cylinder engine with a stick shift transmission, and that tank of gas from Noel's truck would usually last me all week. Gas was getting rather expensive back then—about 35 cents per gallon!

I love every one of my brothers and sisters equally. But there is something special about a sibling who helped you when you were in need. It is one thing to see that need, but doing something extra to fulfill that need is quite another matter. Noel, Bee, Betty, Bobbie and Junior excelled in that department.

Ronald Bee was born on November 3, 1932, and died on January 17, 2005. He married Donna Rae Allamon, and they had four children—Ronald Bee II, Mildred Jane, Rebeccah Rae, and Adam David.

Bee was an outstanding basketball player at Marsh Fork High. He graduated in 1951 and was offered a scholarship at West Virginia Wesleyan, but he didn't accept it because he would not have any spending money above and beyond his scholarship. Instead, he elected to join the Navy for four years and earn college benefits under the G. I. Bill. He spent the bulk of his time in the Navy aboard the U.S.S. Coral Sea, an aircraft carrier. Bee developed many long-lasting friendships during his Navy days. He enlisted with high school friends Eugene Pettry and Dale Dickens who would be cherished friends until his death.

One sailor, Cecil Reeves from northwest Florida, became a close friend of our family. Cecil came home with Bee several times while their ship was in port in Portsmouth, VA. I recall one time when Bee couldn't get leave to come home but Cecil had leave and came anyway. After being discharged, Bee graduated from Beckley College (where he played basketball) and Morris Harvey College, now known as the University of Charleston.

Donna had one more year at Morris Harvey when Bee graduated in 1959. He accepted a teaching position at East Bank Jr. High School to be close to the college. After Donna graduated, they moved to Beckley where Bee taught and coached at Stoco Jr. High School, and Donna taught at Shady Spring Elementary School. After several years at Stoco Jr., Bee became principal there and later the principal at Shady Spring High School. He then became assistant superintendent and later served as superintendent of the Raleigh County Schools from 1986 until his retirement in 1988.

Looking back on my own life I have come to realize that Bee was my role model. When he came out of the Navy and graduated college, college that became my goal. I thought that if Bee had done it I could do it as well. During his years in the Navy, he and Betty even paid to have a bathroom installed in our house. I believe that was in 1955. Bee also noticed that I was in dire need of dental work, and he paid for having that done. Most members of our family believed in helping each other; I thank God for that! I firmly believe it was a reflection on our home life and how our parents raised us.

Bee became a devout Christian and spent a lot of time volunteering both at his church and with civic organizations. His life was cut short at age 72, which left many family members and friends heartbroken.

I, **David Dee**, was the tenth child of the family, born on September 30, 1938. I married Gweneth Kay Jones December 27, 1964, and we have two daughters—Elizabeth Louise (born of Kay's first marriage and adopted by me after our marriage) and DeeAnne.

After graduating from high school in 1958, I had no idea about what to do with my life. The "Eisenhower Recession" was in full swing; there was no use in going north to try to get work because most workers had already been laid off. Then, one day in July, a representative from Beckley College—John B. "Jack" Van Dyke, Jr.—came to see me. I was crossing the bridge to go to the store, or perhaps the post office, when I met him in the middle of the bridge. Long story short, this man—whom I consider to be Heaven sent and to have been the answer to my prayers—was instrumental in getting me a scholarship to attend Beckley College. Around the time I graduated from Beckley College in 1960, President John F. Kennedy continued The National Defense Student Loan Program established by President Eisenhower which enabled needy students to complete college. Another miracle at just the right time! This program and my summer jobs enabled me to graduate Morris Harvey College in 1962.

After graduating Morris Harvey in the summer of '62, I went back home and started teaching social studies at Marsh Fork High. Kay and I were married on December 27, 1964. We did not see much of a future for us within the West Virginia school system. Our salary for the 1964-1965 school year was $3,800, which was only $800 above the amount required to qualify for President Johnson's poverty program. We immediately began looking elsewhere for teaching jobs. During the summer of 1965, while I was in Cleveland working at Chrysler and building tanks for The U.S. Army, Kay was sending out applications for teaching jobs. She sent three to Florida school districts—one each to Palm Beach, Orange (Orlando) and Monroe (The Keys). I received a letter from the Palm Beach County system that—sight unseen—offered me a job teaching elementary physical education. I called the director of physical education, Jim Pigott, right away and accepted the position.

We have absolutely no regrets about our decision to move to Florida because it was a great opportunity for us. I retired in 1999 after 34 years in Palm Beach County schools--my last 19 years with the district were spent as principal of Lake Worth High School. Kay retired in 1998 as a business education teacher at John I. Leonard High School in Lake Worth.

Thelma Mae. "Sugar Foot" (or "Sugar" for short) was born on February 20, 1940 and died on August 24, 1997. She married Leo Boggs shortly after high school, and after their divorce, she married Joe Briguglio. She had two daughters, Karen Elaine Boggs and Angela Grace Briguglio.

Sugar lived in Orlando during the last 15 years of her life where she worked in housekeeping at an Orlando hotel. She and Betty were constant companions, and Sugar took great pride in hosting Betty's 70th birthday party in her backyard. She was so happy to do something for Betty who had done so much for all of us since childhood.

Karen remembers her mother (Sugar) for the love and nurturing she provided for her daughters. Times were always hard for Sugar but she never complained—instead she just kept on providing as well as she could for her girls. Karen firmly believed that Sugar loved and was proud of all her brothers and sisters while, at the same time, feeling that she had fallen short in life. She never questioned why unfortunate things had happened to her in life but—in Karen's words—she just kept on squeezing that lemon to make more lemonade.

Health problems plagued Sugar for the last ten years of her life. Eventually, she had to resign from her job with the hotel because she was not physically able to do the work she loved so much and was so proud of. Unfortunately, she had kidney disease and was on dialysis for the last few years of her life.

At her request, her body was returned to the family cemetery and buried "beside Mommy and Daddy."

My Dad was born during the horse and buggy days (1888) and lived to see a man walk on the moon. A horse figured prominently in his life from birth until he became too old to farm. During his boyhood days the family depended on their horses not only for farming but transportation as well. He was always proud of his horses and took excellent care of them. Every horse he ever owned was, "The best that ever peeped through a collar. Not a knot nor a blemish on her, gentle as a dog." And then gesturing toward either me or one of my brothers he would say, "That boy could crawl under her belly and she would never even kick at a fly." My brother Bee said, "I am glad he never put one of us dummies under that horse's belly to prove his point." Note the pipe in his hand. He smoked one from early youth until he died. When he was taken to the hospital his pipe was filled and tamped, ready to light.

My Siblings (left to right, top to bottom): Eustace; Gene; Jr.; Betty; Doris (pictured with daughters Nancy and Peggy); Bobbie (pictured with Betty).

My Siblings (left to right, top to bottom): Noel, with Mary Lou; Ronald Bee; Me (David Dee); Thelma (Sugar).

50th wedding anniversary in 1965. Left to right, back to front): Eustace, Noel, Gene, Bobbie, Jr., Betty, Doris, David Dee, Grace and Hubert, Ronald Bee

Upper Left: Bee and Sugar. House in the background was Eustace and Thelma's house which burned down. Later, Bobbie and Bill built a home on that site; Doris and Ralph later purchased the home. **Upper Right:** My sisters, Betty (L) and Bobbie (R) and Sugar coming down the steps in the background, circa 1945. **Bottom Left:** My Daddy, circa 1920. Notice his pipe in his right hand. **Bottom Right:** Betty on the Swinging Bridge, 1956.

Upper Left: Raleigh County Rambers—Gene is pictured front left and Eustace, front right. **Upper Right:** My father, Hubert Cantley. **Middle Left:** I am pictured here with my parents coming home from my first teaching job at Marsh Fork High School in 1962. **Middle Right:** I am pictured with my siblings, Betty and Eustace. The shirt I am wearing is a gift from Betty. **Bottom Left:** at Marsh Fork High School with (L-R) Noel, Bobbie, Bee, Junior, David, Gene and Betty. Circa late 1980s. **Bottom Right:** Me, my first year teaching, 1962.

Top picture: My brothers, Junior and Eustace at a family reunion

Middle picture: My mother's 80th birthday. L-R: Bee, Junior, Betty Eustace, Gene Bobbie, David (back), Mommy, Sugar, Doris, Noel. **Bottom picture:** Here we are at a motel in Beckley at a family reunion L-R: Betty, Kay, Bobbie, Mary Lou, and Noel

Top: Mommy and Daddy at their 50th wedding anniversary. After his death, Kay overheard my mother say, *"I love my kids. God knows I love every one of them. But, the love I feel for them, all rolled together and multiplied by thousands, couldn't touch the love I felt for Hubert."*

Middle: Pictured with my brothers at a family reunion, (L-R) Bee, Gene, David, and Junior.

Below: The Cooper Home—the home of my Uncle Nelson and Aunt Lou Cooper. Photo taken by Jo Alice Bradley Heck.

Above: This is what was left of the old cellar in the mid 90's. My mother filled it with canned food every summer and fall. We also had a "tater" bin in the back.

Bottom: Bee and Eugene Pettry celebrating Bee's 71st birthday in 2003 at Millie's home. Bee and Eugene were close friends from the first grade at Mt. View School, until Bee's death. They served together in the Navy and Eugene visited Bee every day he was hospitalized in Beckley. That was a 50-mile drive round trip.

Chapter photo: My siblings and me at Eustace and Thelma's home on Flat Top Lake.

JAMES ADAM CANTLEY, MY GRANDPA

(1861--1930)

James Adam "Big Jim" Cantley, my grandpa, was born at Dry Creek, West Virginia on August 12, 1861 and died on January 12, 1930. His father, James Alexander Cantley, was a casualty of The Civil War, and his mother was Rebecca Jane Clay Cantley. On August 18, 1882, my grandpa married Celia B. Hunter, who died on January 2, 1932.

Big Jim could not afford the luxury of attending school because he had to become the man of the house at an early age. Thus, he stayed home and learned the art of farming from his grandfather, Alexander James Cantley, who was my great, great grandfather. Anyone named Alexander was referred to as "Elec." "The old man, Elec" had received the original 60 acres of the farm from the government for his services rendered in The War of 1812.

The lack of a formal education didn't hold Big Jim back. After all, how much book-based schooling did a man need to learn to plow, plant and harvest crops, cut timber, be a blacksmith, be a miller, care for animals, and complete all the other chores associated with farming? Big Jim managed to grow the farm from the original 60 acres his grandfather, "Elec" had started out with and owned over 180 acres at his death. The farm was completely self-sufficient and the family cultivated every fruit and vegetable that would grow in the area. They also raised cattle, chickens, sheep and horses which were used not only for farm work but for transportation as well.

My grandmother, Celia Belle Hunter Cantley, was like most women of her generation—a hard-working woman who contributed whatever she could to her family. Grandma Celia, like my Mother, saw to it that anyone visiting her home had plenty to eat. There was no shortage of homeless men during her time; instead of being "left to the streets" as is done today, people would take these men in, give them a place to sleep and a good meal. One story my Dad told many times was about "Old John," a homeless guy who came around from time to time. Of course Grandma knew what he was coming for. One morning when he walked in she asked, "John, have you had anything to eat today?" He replied, "No, Seely, I ain't had a bite." When she said she would fix him something he replied, "Now Seely, don't go to a big lot of trouble for me. Just fix me two or three eggs, some gravy, biscuits, a piece of ham, and a cup of coffee. That will do me."

Grandpa Jim built small buildings alongside the road that led to the "up the holler" area where the homeless and people passing through could sleep. My brother, Eustace, said those buildings had reminded him of the slave quarters at Mount Vernon. One of those cabin-like structures was still standing when I was a boy. My cousin, Myrtle Lemon, told me a story about a black man who came into Grandpa Jim's yard one evening and wanted to know if he could sleep in the barn for the night. She said Grandpa told him, "No, you can't sleep in the barn. That is where we keep the cows, horses and sheep. We have a bed for you to sleep in." Myrtle said Grandpa put him in one of those cabins for the night and she, being just a little girl, was scared to death all night; she had just seen a black person for the first time in her life.

Occasionally, Grandpa would try to get some of his star boarders to work. One day he put one guy out in a field and instructed him to dig a tree stump out of the ground. Apparently, Grandpa knew the guy wouldn't do much and, sure enough, around noon—just in time for dinner—as the noon meal was called, the guy came in and said, "Jim, I couldn't do much today on that stump. My hell-fired wrist went back on me." Another time, Grandma sent one guy to the store at Dry Creek to get a spool of thread. He came back two months later. He evidently just decided to keep walking—to God only knows where.

Big Jim's family was apparently of better-than-average means for their time and place. The farm even boasted a coal mine at the top of the mountain where they mined coal by hand for cooking and heating the home as opposed to using wood. Big Jim also owned the only grist mill for miles around which was located down by the river just upstream from the current bridge that leads to Jarrell Bottom. People came from surrounding communities to have their shelled corn ground into cornmeal. The charge or "toll" for milling the corn was a peck (approximately two gallons' worth) out of each bushel. The Cantleys had the luxury of having iced drinks through most of the summer because they had built an underground icehouse near the river. During cold winter months--when Coal River froze over—the men would go to the river with saws, cut large blocks of ice, and carry them to the icehouse. Saw dust served as insulation between the blocks of ice. Icicles were taken from the cliff on the opposite side of the river and added to the icehouse.

It appears that Big Jim was an intelligent, hard-working man who provided well for his family in spite of the fact that he did not have a formal education. Although he was illiterate, he had a deep respect for education. Big Jim saw to it that all his children received the maximum education (probably six years) that was available on Coal River at that time. And even though he couldn't read or write, he served as Chairman of The Marsh Fork District School Board for twelve years. My dad often said, "When you saw Pa with his little black mare hitched to the buggy and wearing his good hat, you knew he was on school board business." Although I never had the honor of knowing him—he died eight years before I was born—I am proud of his achievements and contributions to the community.

Chapter photo: My grandpa, James Adam Cantley inherited a farm of approximately 60 acres from his father, James Alexander Cantley. He expanded the farm over a period of years to well over 200 acres. His wife, my grandmother, Celia B. Hunter Cantley, was always by his side doing her part in raising a family and doing chores that were common for women during her time.

JAMES ALEXANDER AND REBECCA JANE CLAY CANTLEY

The Civil War was an epic event in American history--it was the cause of the greatest upheaval in our country's history. It resulted in over 600,000 deaths, which represents more casualties than any other war in which our country has been engaged. Historians still debate the cause of the war—the struggle over slavery, civil rights, tariffs or, some say, all three. The South was overwhelmingly Anglo-Saxon-Celtic and agricultural while the North was more cosmopolitan and industrial.

The Republican Party was formed on July 6, 1854 by the Abolitionist wing of the old Whig Party. Their first presidential candidate, John C. Fremont, was unsuccessful in 1856. Abraham Lincoln was elected in 1860, winning about 40% of the popular vote. By the time he was inaugurated in 1861 six Southern (Democratic) states—seeing the handwriting on the wall—had seceded. On April 12, 1861, the first shots of the Civil War were fired at Fort Sumter, South Carolina. Not only were the Democrats the party of slavery and secession, they then formed a terrorist wing known as the Ku Klux Klan. This upheld their rule over blacks with Jim Crow Laws and segregated public facilities.

When Lincoln issued a call for troops to serve the Union cause, my great-grandfather, James Alexander Cantley, was among the first to answer the call. James left his wife, Rebecca, and their children and was sworn in on November 2, 1861 at Charleston, Virginia. He was assigned to Company H, Eighth Regiment of The Virginia Volunteers, later to become a West Virginia unit. He was mustered into service on November 20, 1861, at the time of his enlistment Army records describe James as being 5'8" tall, having dark hair, a dark complexion and hazel eyes. His Army record states he was, "Born about 1826 in Raleigh County, VA, the son of Alex and Mary Scott Cantley."

James returned on a furlough (date unknown) only to learn that his third child—four-year-old Ellen—had died. The story (as passed down by family members) recalls him walking into their cabin and seeing boards missing from the ceiling. He knew those boards could have been used for only one purpose—to make a casket.

On another furlough home, James was able to witness the birth of his only son, James Adam, my grandfather. He hid out on the mountain behind the home because rebel troops were reported to be in the area. When Rebecca started to go into labor, she waved a tablecloth to signal that the coast was clear. He saw his son for only a few minutes before he had to return to his unit. It is my understanding that this was the only time he saw his son.

In 1863, James was wounded in the Battle of Cross Keys, Virginia, and was transported to an army "hospital" which was—for most Civil War soldiers—a place to die. Army records indicate he had been "shot in the left breast, afflicting the left lung." Medical care was practically nonexistent; most deaths were a result of disease and gangrene poisoning caused by gunshot wounds. Penicillin—not discovered until 1928—could have saved untold thousands of lives.

Army records indicate that James was "sent homeward" in the accompaniment of his brother-in-law, James Clay; he died enroute and was buried at Antietam Cemetery. My late nephew, Noel Dean Cantley II, had a keen interest in our family's history and researched James' military record. He even went to the cemetery at Antietam where he saw the plot where the Army said James was buried—only to discover that no one was buried there. I remember my Uncle Okey saying that James Clay reported he and James Alexander Cantley took refuge in a barn loft somewhere between Maryland and Dry Creek; James died that night and was buried in an unmarked grave on the farm. Uncle Okey said that Rebecca was never told of Clay's accounting of her husband's death. She apparently died thinking that her husband had been given a Christian burial and was interred in a government cemetery. I have been told that the old long-abandoned Clay Chapel located at Dameron and burned in 2018 was named for James Clay, Rebecca's brother.

The U.S. Government is known today to manipulate the facts and tell its citizens only what they want them to know. It is my firm belief that the same was true during the trying days of the Civil War. I do not believe James Clay would have fabricated the story he told the men folk of the family. Why would he? What would he have to gain? I leave it to the reader to make up his or her own mind as to the burial site of James Alexander Cantley.

The Civil War, in my opinion, represents the darkest and most shameful days of our history, pitting neighbor against neighbor and brother against brother. Historians write that boys as young as 14 years old paid the ultimate price. I have read of young boys dying late into the night at Gettysburg crying for their mothers while creeks ran red with blood. I am very proud of my great-grandfather and his contribution to our country. My impossible dream is to locate his body and to have it buried near his father, Alexander James, in the family cemetery at Rock Creek.

While doing research for this book, it did not take long for me to develop a deep respect for and admiration of my great grandmother, Rebecca. I consider her to be the grand matriarch of our family. During the Civil War she was left alone to provide for her children, operate the farm, and fend off raiding rebel soldiers while her husband served in the Union Army.

Her obituary states that Rebecca was born in Pike County, Kentucky on June 25th, 1828. Her family left Kentucky and moved to Wyoming

County, Virginia (now West Virginia) when she was a baby. From there the family moved to Breckenridge, a community that no longer exists. It is my understanding that Breckenridge was located within The Marsh Fork District. During this time, Rebecca married James Alexander Cantley.

Rebecca and James spent the first two years of their married life at The Cottle Place now known as Saxon. Here their children, Janetta and Nancy Jane were born. From Cottle Place they moved to the farm we know as "the home place" most recently owned by my Uncle Ovet Cantley and later by his son, Barry Ned Cantley. It is the present site of Marsh Fork Elementary School. The first home was across the creek (now in an underground culvert) from where the school sets. Cousins Barry and Peggy remember that their Mother, Ora, said the "new" home was built about 1898. The original home was, in all probability, a basic log home located on a nice flat piece of land near a spring and creek because easy access to water was one of the criteria when selecting a home site. Two more children, Ellen and James Adam (my grandpa—later known as "Big Jim"), were born in this home.

Rebecca, forced to hold down the home front, was subjected to raids, thefts, intimidation, and threats by marauding rebel soldiers both during the time her husband was deployed as well as after his death. I heard Uncle Okey tell the following story several times (Uncle Okey would forget that he had told you the same story a dozen times, but his stories never changed). He said that on one occasion the Rebels came to the farm on one of their many trips through the area. Rebecca had been forewarned by a lady at Dry Creek who went to the edge of a cliff or rock and signaled with her apron that trouble was on the way.

The rebel officers—I understood there were three or four—came to Rebecca and asked where her husband was. She replied that he was away fighting with Union soldiers. The officer in charge promised that nothing on the farm would be disturbed if she would prepare a meal for the officers. She complied with his request and during the preparation of the meal the officer in charge looked out the window and saw a soldier raising the lid on a bee hive. He admonished the soldier by telling him, "This lady's husband is away fighting for his country and we will not take or disturb anything on this farm."

According to Uncle Okey's account, one of the officers—trying to intimidate Rebecca—walked to my Grandpa James' cradle and looked menacingly at him. Rebecca, wanting to distract the soldier from her baby, asked him what he would like to eat. He looked at her with a large knife in his hand replied, "baby meat." She said she then saw tears come to his eyes while telling her that he had a baby at home the same age as James.

One officer asked Rebecca what the baby's name was, she replied that it was James. The officer then asked what his middle name was and she replied that he had no middle name. The officer then said, "Give him my name, call him Adam." That is how my grandpa became James Adam. My Daddy, Hubert, James Adam's first son said, "If you wanted to make Pa mad, all you had to do was call him Adam." Big Jim said he didn't appreciate being named after "a dad-blamed Democrat Rebel."

On one occasion Rebecca had butchered a pig; knowing Rebels were in the area, she hid the meat in the attic wrapped in a petticoat. The Rebels found the pork and took it along with a mare that had just foaled. They left the colt in the barn. After leaving the farm the squad moved to Arnett where they camped on property owned by John Surratt, who was friendly with both the Rebel and Union forces. Surratt recognized the mare as belonging to the Cantley family, so he convinced the Rebels to turn her loose and she returned home at 2 A.M. I am told this was taken from a story published in *The Beckley Post-Herald*.

Following the end of the war, Congress passed "The War Widow and Children's Act of 1867." Rebecca applied for benefits for herself and children, Janetta, Nancy, and James Adam. Dealing with the government was no easier in 1867 than it is today. Records show that Rebecca made several trips to Charleston to plead her case for benefits.

She could not produce a marriage certificate; she stated in her application that, "All the records in the courthouse in Beckley had been either burned or carried off by the Rebels." She took witnesses with her to testify that they were present at her wedding to James Alexander Cantley conducted by "One Felix Ellison, now departed this earth." I have heard my Daddy say in order to travel from Rock Creek to Charleston in those days you had to cross streams about 20 times, many times being forced to wait until the waters receded before attempting to cross. Rebecca's trips to Charleston with witnesses were, no doubt, by horse and wagon during winter months. While the winter months were probably very cold, it would also be the time of the year when the streams were low. Spring snow melts and summer rains would have made for a more difficult journey.

After much red tape and government hassle, Rebecca was awarded a pension of $8 per month and $2 per month for each of her three children until they reached the age of 16. James Alexander's file then was inactive until Rebecca's death on May 26, 1910. After Rebecca's death, her son, James Adam (Big Jim) applied for reimbursement for burial expenses in the amount of $37.57. The expenses were as follows: Physicians' Bills—$25.00 from Dr. P. J. Hurst, "Burial Goods"—$2.22 from Massey Brothers, and Livery charge—$10.35. The charge of $10.35 also shows in another document as being for "burial goods" purchased from R. E. Barrett. Barrett was the owner of the general store at Dry Creek, which is still in operation at the time of this writing, and is the oldest retail business in Raleigh County.

There are stories in nearly every community of women who had to step up and assume not only her duties, but those of a deceased or disabled husband. Rebecca was such a woman. In my research, I read she had had six miscarriages. This was never spoken of by anyone in the family. After reading this, I visited her grave on my next visit to the cemetery; sure enough, there are six little graves marked by field stones standing upright. I am sure there was a special place awaiting my great-grandmother, Rebecca, in Heaven.

Rebecca Jane Clay Cantley's Obituary

Rebecca Jane Clay, daughter of Charles L. and Awry Clay, was born in Pike County, Kentucky, June 25, 1828. When but a baby her parents left their Kentucky home and came to Wyoming County, Va. to make a new home in the Mountain State, and as this home was being built, one by one, sisters and brothers were added to the family until there were four boys and six girls.

During this home life in Wyoming County the subject of this sketch, then a little girl of twelve years, at a camp meeting held in their community heard and heeded the call of Jesus Christ to "Follow Me," and then and there accepted and publicly confessed him as her Savior, and united with the Methodist church and began the Christian life.

After living in Wyoming County some eighteen years, her parents sought a new home coming into Raleigh County and locating at Breckinridge. While living there another sister and brother came into the home. Breckenridge was their home but four years when they moved to Sand Lick where they made home until death, August 1, 1852.

While living at Breckenridge, the subject of this sketch, Rebecca the oldest daughter was married to James Cantley, and they spent the first two years of their married life at the Cottle Place, now better known as Saxon. While here their first child, Nettie J. was born. They lived the next four years at what is now known as the Old Flats, and during their brief stay there they were blessed with the second baby, Nancy Jane.

From that place they removed to the present home, where Mrs. Cantley spent the rest of her days. Two other children came to live in this little family Ellen and James. Ellen, however, after four years, went to live with Him who said, "Suffer the Little Children to Come unto Me."

When Lincoln issued the call for 75,000 volunteers in 1861, James Cantley responded to that call, left his faithful wife and beloved little ones to go out never to return, for in the battle of Cross Keys, Shenandoah Valley, Va., he received a wound that soon proved fatal. He was taken to the Harrisburg hospital and after ten days started for home, getting as far as Cumberland, Maryland, where his strength failed, and he departed this life and was buried at that place.

Mrs. Cantley, now a widow with three little ones, took up the battle of life with its toils, and bravely met the responsibilities, doing as best she could—trusting always in Him to whom she had yielded her life as a child. Her friends and neighbors pay her the splendid tribute of calling her a good kind Christian woman. She departed this life "looking unto Jesus, the Beginner and Finisher of her faith," on May 26, 1910, aged 81 years, eleven months, and one day, leaving to mourn their loss, two daughters, one son, sisters, brothers, 20 grand-children, 31 great grand-children and many other relatives, as well as a great host of friends.----from *The Register-Herald*

Chapter photo: I consider my great grandmother, Rebecca, to be the grand matriarch of the family. She had to endure many hardships including raising a family, running the farm, and warding off raiding rebel soldiers. She is pictured here with her brand new, store-bought dress.

ALEXANDER JAMES CANTLEY

(1794--1884)

Alexander James Cantley, my great. great grandfather, was the son of Samuel and Rebecca Clark Cantley. He, Alexander James, was born in Greenbrier County, Virginia on 22 February 1794 and died in Raleigh County, West Virginia on 2 March 1884. He married in Monroe County, Virginia, 1816, to Mary "Polly"Scott, who was born in Monroe County, Virginia about 1797 and died in RaleighCounty, West Virginia, 20 November 1875, daughter of John Scott. Alexander married a second time in Raleigh County, West Virginia, 24 August 1876, the widow Tempay (Ball) Hopkins, born in Monroe County, Virginia about 1827, died in Lewiston, Kanawha County, West Virginia, 8 December 1903.

Alexander's childhood years were spent on a homestead on the waters of Indian Creek, a branch of the New River in what is today Monroe County, West Virginia. His siblings included Eleanor, John, Sally, James, Rebecca, Mary and William. When his father, Samuel, died without leaving a will, his mother, Rebecca, became an administrator of his estate. The appraisal of Samuel's estate shows a thriving farm with livestock that included many hogs, cattle, horses, sheep and geese.

Alexander was drafted into military service in Monroe County during the War of 1812. Under Lieutenant William McDaniel's command, he soldiered in the 5th Virginia Militia as a private from 13 September to 9 October 1813. At that time anyone drafted could pay another man to serve in his place. He offered a horse and twelve dollars to someone to take his place but the man turned down the offer only to overtake "Elec" after he had left his home. Elec, however, refused the deal saying, "I have already left my family, that was the hard part." He was then transferred to serve in Captain James R. Nemoe's company from 10 Oct 1813 to 10 Mar 1814. He was discharged in Norfolk, Virginia in March, 1814.

After the war, Alexander married Polly Scott and they lived in Logan County, Virginia. About 1830 Alexander moved his family to new land in the Marsh Fork of Coal River area. He was not alone in his quest for better land; many other settlers increased the population of southwestern Virginia. This soon led to changes in boundary lines. In 1831 the Cantley property was encompassed by the new county of Fayette. By 1850 the county boundaries had changed again placing Alexander's family under the governance of Raleigh County.

When Congress acted to bestow bounty lands to veterans in 1850, Alexander had the opportunity to move out of Virginia. He applied for and received two bounty land warrants for his service. The first was for land in Ionia County, Michigan which he signed over to Truman P. Allen in Raleigh County, Virginia on 26 July 1856. The second for land in Genesee County, Michigan, was signed over to Rodney D. Hill on the same day and in the same place. Apparently Alexander was content in his surroundings even after the outbreak of the Civil War created the new state of West Virginia around him. His son, James Alexander, served with the Union Army in the Civil War, and died of wounds sustained in the battle of Cross Keys, Virginia. Beginning in 1851, Alexander appears on the Raleigh County tax rolls throughout the remainder of his life.

Over the years of their marriage, Alexander and Polly faced more than the usual challenges of parenthood. Their daughter Elizabeth's blindness and the visual and psychological impairment of their sons John, Jordan, and Richard must have placed additional stress on the family. The census records show these unmarried adult children remaining in Alexander's household for quite some time. The county court system provided some limited relief. Alexander was paid $26.50 from the Overseer of the Poor in 1865 plus an allowance of $20 for Richard was made in 1866. Alexander remained active in caring for his family. Upon the death of his daughter Caroline's husband, Steele Massey, in 1869 Alexander obtained letters of administration to settle his estate.

After Polly's death in 1875, Alexander married Tempay (Ball) Hopkins. However, a few years into their marriage the couple separated. Tempay moved to Lewiston, Kanawha County, West Virginia, while Alexander lived the final years of his life in the Raleigh County home of his youngest daughter, Ladocia, and her husband, James Mandeville Clay. Alexander died on 2 March 1884 aged 90 years and 9 days and was buried in the Cantley Cemetery in Rock Creek, Raleigh County, West Virginia. His gravestone commemorates his service in the War of 1812.

Uncle Ovet once told me that he ordered the grave marker for "Eleck" from the government and went to the railroad depot in Edwight in a Model T Ford to get it. He said he drove up the hill, unloaded it and placed it. There are two field stones beside the marker, presumably that of his two sons who were blind. Uncle Jimmy told me that although blind, they could hear someone lift the lid on their snuff box from across the cabin. In my research I found the boys were good singers.

Chapter photo: Great, great grandfather, Alexander James Cantley's tombstone

REBECCA CHAPEL

The Rebecca Chapel, located alongside Route 3 in Rock Creek, WV is the result of Rebecca Jane Clay Cantley's resolve. She has been described as being a very devout Christian and shortly after her husband's (James) death she decided that the area needed a church. She was of the Methodist persuasion and Rebecca Chapel had, until 2018, always been Methodist. There is no record of the date when the original church was built although it would probably date in the 1890s.

The **first site** of the church was on the old wagon road above the convenience store at Rock Creek. The wagon road was the predecessor to "the hard road," as we used to call it, and ran under the hill behind Mt. View School down by the entrance to the Miller Cemetery. It crossed the creek (Rock Creek), ran behind what was Bernard Green's home, and within site of the store. It continued on between what is now known as Uncle Ovet's and Uncle Okey's farms, then ran downstream toward "The Lick Point" overlooking Friendly View.

In addition to donating land for the **original** church, I would bet my last dollar that Rebecca also donated the timber to be sawn into lumber for the chapel. While the church was being built, Rebecca rode throughout the countryside gathering donations for the church bell. Uncle Okey said that the bell cost $12, and that Rebecca took a team and wagon to the railroad depot at Mordue (near Whitesville) to take delivery of it.

According to my brother, Gene, the church I remember attending as a young child was actually the **second** church built on that site. He said that the original building had very high ceilings, was drafty, and difficult to heat. Jodie Heck is in possession of a newspaper clipping from *The Raleigh Register* which states the **rebuilt church** was dedicated June 30, 1937.

I can remember going to all-day meetings and dinner on the church grounds at the old church. Men built long tables that appeared to me to be as long as a river barge and the ladies covered them with food fit for a king! There were many large beech trees down from the church near the old road; the tables were built there in the shade of the trees. Since grass would not grow under those trees, I remember that the ground was covered—instead—with velvety green moss. That building is still standing, but it has been converted to a residence.

Rebecca Chapel volunteers also built and maintained a parsonage which was a home for the pastor and his family to live in. I know nothing about the history of the parsonage which has long since been demolished. The parsonage was the center of notoriety when, sometime in the 1940's, the preacher who lived in the house shot and killed his wife. I don't recall any details; little conversation was heard on the subject. However, I do remember the preacher was acquitted. He claimed that he fired the gun accidentally. This—naturally—created a lot of controversy among the locals.

I remember I was about 12 years old when the "new" (**current**) church was built with volunteer labor. Rebecca's bell was moved from the second church building site and was in place in the current church in time for the official dedication in 1951. My sister, Betty, claimed that she and her husband, Bill Billings, were the first couple to be married in the new church.

The effort to build the new church was led by our pastor, The Rev. Henry Boley, who was a true man of God. He was an old country preacher and farmer from Nicholas County and he did whatever was needed to serve his flock. When my dad was injured in a mining accident, in 1942, Preacher Boley plowed and helped harvest crops until Daddy was able to get back in the fields.

After the new church was finished a few influential members of the church decided that they needed a new preacher to go with their new church. Apparently, they felt that Preacher Boley no longer met their needs. After he left, Rebecca Chapel saw a long string of pastors who never seemed to work out. They came and went every few years with none of them really making an appreciable change or contribution to the church or community. My dad felt that this happened because of, "the way they treated poor 'ol Preacher Boley."

Rebecca Chapel still stands proud and stately beside the road at Rock Creek and continues to be maintained in pristine condition. It has seen its ups and downs throughout the years with attendance dipping to as few as 12-15 people, and pastors coming and going.

Rebecca Chapel underwent a massive resurgence in 2015, which saw attendance increase tenfold. The lion's share of the credit should be given to Jim and Bobbie Kay Webb Farley who were raised at Rock Creek and were married in the church. Jim came from his home in Cincinnati several times to assist church trustees in the reorganization of chapel business. Jim and Bobbie found the answer to many people's prayers in mid-2015 when they convinced Steven Smith to be the new pastor of Rebecca Chapel. Pastor Smith immediately set about building attendance and organizing programs for children. Unfortunately Pastor Smith resigned his position, came back again and resigned again in the summer of 2019.

The church had not been paying dues to the Methodist Conference for several years and was led to believe that if the church folded the Conference would assume ownership of the church and sell it. Fortunately, Bobbie Farley is an attorney who loves Rebecca Chapel. She began researching West Virginia church law and discovered that the church does not belong to the Conference, but to the trustees of the church. When confronted with this information, the Conference told church trustees that they could sever ties with them by paying $1,113. Part of the deal required a name change for the church. It had previously been known as Rebecca Chapel United Methodist Church, but is now simply called Rebecca Chapel.

Rebecca Chapel continues to have its ups and downs as they strive to find a pastor that will lead the flock. Lynn Halstead is serving as pastor, leading efforts by Edsel Dickens and others to remodel the basement. I am confident that the church will one day be restored to its golden years as long as the Farleys, my dear friend Lonnie Burnside, the Cantley family and others continue their support.

The following classified ad appeared in The Register-Herald after the church property was assigned to the Rebecca Chapel Board of Trustees by The Conference of The United Methodist Church Conference in exchange of $1,113.00.

NOTICE OF PROPOSED CONVEYANCE OF UNITED METHODIST CHURCH PROPERTY (REBECCA CHAPEL UNITED METHODIST CHURCH PROPERTY)

Notice is hereby given that the Board of Trustees of the West Virginia Annual Conference of the United Methodist Church will, on or after December 31, 2015 upon the sum of One Thousand One Hundred Thirteen Dollars ($1,113.00) in cast, Quitclaim, sell and convey to Trustees of Rebecca Chapel Church of Rock Creek, West Virginia, all of their right, title and interest, and to the following tracts of parcels of land situate in Marsh Fork District, County of Raleigh and State of West Virginia, and more particularly described as follows:

Tract One: The surface of Lot No. 32 of the Clay Farm Subdivision No. 2, Marsh Fork Tax District, Raleigh County, West Virginia, and Subdivision is shown of a corrected map of record in the Office of the Clerk of the County Commission of Raleigh County, West Virginia, in Map 10, page 62.

And being the same property conveyed from Macie L. Clay widow, to Dewey O'Dell, Bill Blankenship, Chris Linville, and Arley Clay, Trustees for the Rebecca Chapel Methodist Church of Rock Creek by Deed dated the 17th day of January, 1980 and of record in the Office of the Clerk of the County Commission of Raleigh County, West Virginia in Deed Book 623, at page 528, referenced to which is here-by made.

Tract Two: The following described tract of land, situate, lying and being in Marsh Fork District of Raleigh County, West Virginia, and being a part of the Clay Farm Subdivision Number Two is as follows: Lot Number 25 (twenty five), 26 (twenty six), 27 (twenty seven), 28 (twenty eight), 29 (twenty nine), 30 (thirty), 31 (thirty one) as shown on a map in the Raleigh County Clerk's Office in Beckley, West Virginia, listed as Clay Farm Subdivision Number Two, located on Marsh Fork District, Raleigh County, West Virginia.

And being the same property conveyed from W. L. Clay and Macie L. Clay, to Dewey L, J.L. Bradford, Bill Blankenship, Chris Linville, Marvin Dickens, and Charles Jarrell, Trustees for the Rebecca Chapel Methodist Church of Rock Creek, West Virginia by Deed dated the 3rd day of June

1971 and of record in the aforesaid Clerk's Office in Deed Book 499, at page 167, referenced to which is hereby made.

Tract Three: The surface on of the following described tract or boundary of land, situate lying and being in Marsh Fork District of Raleigh County, West Virginia, and being a part of the "Clay Farm Subdivision Number Two," bounded and described as follows: Beginning at an iron stake in the center of Rock Creek in the North right-of-way line on State Route No. 3, and a corner between land owned by Rome Rader and land owned by W. L. Clay; thence leaving said Rock Creek with said right-of-way line in a Western direction, a long chord or which bears N. 46 08 W. 47.6 feet to an iron stake at the East Side of the road; thence with the East side of said road N. 34 48' E. 154.6 feet to an iron stake at the corner of Lot Nos. 3 and 4 of "Rock Creek Subdivision No. 1"; thence with the division line of said lots S. 55 12' E 119.3 feet to a point in Rock Creek in a line of said Rome Rader; thence down Rock Creek with a line of said Rome Rader S. 59 04 W. 177.0 feet to the place of beginning; and containing .295 acre; and being Lot Nos. 1, 2 and 3 of said "Clay Farm Subdivision Number Two."

And being the same property conveyed from W. L. Clay, his wife, to Okey R. Cantley, J. Lewis Bradford, Charles E. Jarrell, Hubert Cantley, Dewey O'Dell, J. W. Acord and Mrs. J. L. Clay, Trustees from the Rebecca Chapel Methodist Church of Rock Creek, West Virginia, by Deed dated the 15th day of March, 1948 and of record in the aforesaid Clerk's Office in Deed Book 276, at page 339, referenced to which is hereby made.

Said Church having been declared discontinued and/or abandoned by the regular 2015 session of the West Virginia Annual Conference of the United Methodist Church.

Date the 23rd day of December, 2015
BOARD OF TRUSTEES OF THE WEST VIRGINIA ANNUAL CONFERENCE OF THE UNITED METHODIST CHURCH,
By: Robert N. File, Chancellor
130 Main Street Beckley, West Virginia 25801
(304) 253-3358 12-30-WED-2-RH:3814

Little White Church in the Valley
*Written by: Karen Fairchild, Kimberly Schlapman, Wayne
Kirkpatrick, Philip Sweet, James Lee Westbrook*

*There's a little white church in the valley
That stands in my memory each day
And it seems I can hear the bells now ringing
Though I am many miles away*

*And many times in church on Sunday morning
That whole countryside would gather there
They would all kneel down by the altar
As they lifted up their voice in prayer*

*Oh the church in the valley that little white church
Is the place I love so well
Now I'm sad and lonely, yes I'm sad and lonely
For that little white church in the dell*

*They would sing the old song Rock of Ages
Oh Christ let me hide myself in thee
And I know some of them are now waiting
Just o'er the dark and stormy sea*

*I know that their troubles are ended
And happy forever they will be
They are waiting and watching up yonder
For the coming home of you and me*

When I hear this song, I always think of the Rebecca Chapel, "The little white church in The Coal River Valley." It was here that the basis of my faith was formed. In that little country church where we sang "Rock of Ages," "In the Garden," or "Gyarden," as my dad used to say, "Bringing in the Sheaves" and other good songs you don't hear in today's modern churches. We had youth activities including wiener roasts, trips to state and county parks and Scout Troops.

Rebecca Chapel of Rock Creek, West Virginia
Photo taken by: Charles Bradford

Family gathering on the church steps following
sister Doris' funeral in 2002,

Rebecca Chapel Family
Early 1950's

First Row: Glenn Cantley, Earl Underwood, Barry Cantley, Rodney Jarrell, Mike Lewis, Norman Underwood (don't know child behind Norman to the right of him) Duane Acord, Randall Webb, David Webb, David Green, Peggy Cantley **Second Row:** Jack Lemon, Bill Blankenship, Andrew Burnside, Jo Alice Bradley, Hulda Lane, Norma Bartrum, Lewis Bradford, Shirley Bartrum, Betty Underwood, Carol Blankenship, Sharon Peters Darlene Accord, Kay Marshall, **Third Row:** Bob Williams, Dewey Odell, Nelson Cooper, Charles Clay, Ruby Marshall, Lou Cooper, Betty Burnside, Ellen Pettry, Laura Accord, Eliza Jane Clay, Mary Jarrell, Shirley Blankenship **Back Row:** Ovet Cantley, Ora Cantley, Mathel Odell, Myrtle Lemon Willa Jo Bradley, Paul Lemon, Opal Bradford, Carl Bradford, Margaret Accord, John L. Clay, Deana Bartrum, George Aliff,, Ruth Underwood and Minnie Aliff, Ovet Cantley and Mary Jarrell. *Photo taken by C.E. "Charlie" Jarrell, 1946.*

Rebecca Chapel *Photo by Charles E. "Charlie" Jarrell 1946.*

Chapter photo: The following was written on the back of the picture, "You should have seen that crane trying to lift the steeple in place." Homer Webb from Arnett purchased this steeple for Rebecca Chapel. He also purchased one for the Arnett church.

THE HUNTERS

My grandmother Celia's maiden name was Hunter. Uncle Okey left us with a brief history of the Hunter family. I have learned from his notes that the name Hunter originated in England during the 15th century. There was a family who kept to themselves in a section of the country in England and followed hunting and marksmanship with care. It was said that they could take a long bow and split a thin twig at 40 yards. Being impressed by this talent, the King at that time, gave the family the name of Hunter and appointed them to provide meat for his court. Members of the Hunter family sailed to America sometime in the 17th century and settled in Giles County, VA.

William Hunter was born on October 13, 1813, in Giles County, VA and was married to Mahala Pettry in Raleigh County. They resided on Peach Tree (Pine Knob) and reared a family of eight children—Lewis, Jacob, Elizabeth, Robert, Nancy, Celia (my grandmother), James and Letha.

Uncle Okey wrote, "William Hunter came to (no date given) what is now Edwight and started working for Jacob Pettry. Jacob Pettry was a man of considerable wealth in those days and owned, among other properties, a race track at Edwight that was nearly a mile long."

William Hunter started working for Jacob Pettry. Hunter was a carpenter and developed a trade as a tanner of leather and builder of grist mills. Pettry had three beautiful daughters, one of whom was Mahala, and Hunter soon fell in love with her. One evening, Mr. Pettry was sitting on his porch reading when Hunter walked up to him and said, "Mr. Pettry?" "Yes, William, what can I do for you?" Hunter replied, "Mr. Pettry, I would like your daughter's hand in marriage and $500." Mr. Pettry replied, "William, any man would want a pretty girl but what would you do with $500?" He said, "Mr. Pettry, I have bought a tract of land on Peach Tree and I want to build a house as well as put in a tanning yard and a grist mill." Mr. Pettry hung his head for a minute and finally said, "You shall have both, William."

According to Uncle Okey's notes, Lewis—the oldest child of William and Mahala Hunter—raised eight children, four of whom became doctors. R. Robert Hunter practiced in Whitesville and Edwight, Dr. Byrd Hunter practiced in Coral Gables, Florida, Dr. Hubert Hunter was a dentist in Whitesville, and Dr. Harve was a dentist in Beckley. Uncle Okey's notes state that three of the doctor sons are buried "Way up on Peach Tree," all except Robert. He wanted to be buried there, but his wife had him buried in Huntington instead.

I found a short note at the bottom of one of Uncle Okey's pages that read as follows: "Aunt Nancy, Ma's (Celia's) sister, married Jim Acord. Jim was the brother of Jack Acord who claimed he'd met a man in the Red Bud Holler with no head. I have walked through there many nights and was ready to shoot anything I saw."

Chapter photo: My grandparents, Celia Hunter Cantley and James Adam Cantley

THE PRICES

My mother, Grace Lee Price, (whose parents were Lightburn Hayes and Viola Workman Price) was born at Barrett in Boone County, West Virginia on March 18, 1898 and died January 3, 1979. She remembers having lived in a log house as a child and riding in a horse-drawn wagon while her family was moving. She had two sisters, Emmer and Bertha, as well as one brother, Bethel, who was a World War I veteran. Aunt Emmer and Uncle Mont Massey lived at Packsville and would often come to our home for a Sunday visit. Aunt Bertha married Arthur Pierce and they lived in Greenup, Kentucky. I remember Aunt Bertha's letters to my mother, which always began with "Just a few lyons to let you know how we are doing." Uncle Bethel and Aunt Effie lived in a big house on the hill above the road that was below Horse Creek.

I always knew that my mother had a sister who was killed by a runaway log train as a young child, but I never knew details of the accident until I read a book written by Rick Bradford, a resident of Edwight and a graduate of Marsh

Fork High School. In his book, *I Want to Paint a Picture,* Rick writes of events of Coal River and other areas of Raleigh County. Rick gives the following account of the accident that took the young girl's life taken from The Raleigh Register on Thursday, March 14, 1910: "On March 5, 1910 Jack "Cricket" Johnson climbed aboard his engine and went up Sycamore Creek Hollow (near Ameagle) to get a load of logs. His young son, Cecil, was on board. Johnson's flatcars were loaded, but on his way back down the mountain he found he could not stop because frost was on the tracks. His locomotive with an estimated speed of 100 miles per hour crashed through the trestle killing him, his son and seven-year-old Effie Price. Daughter of Lightburn Price. Effie was playing in a log barn which the train struck. Her body was returned to Bald Knob in Boone County from where her family had recently moved. I believe this had an indelible effect on my Mother throughout her life because she always harbored a great fear that one of her children would be harmed. She slept very little while waiting for the last "youngun" to come home at night.

As a young girl my mother's dream was to become a teacher. Presbyterian Missionaries offered to pay to further her education, presumably at a boarding school in Charleston. Her mother, however, refused to grant permission because she felt that it would not be fair to the other girls. If she had become a teacher, there is no doubt in my mind that she would have put the same passion into her role as an educator that she put into raising her family; she would have become a great teacher.

My mother, Grace (middle), pictured with her sisters Bertha (left) and Emmer (right). This photo was taken at my parent's 50th anniversary celebration in July of 1965.

Chapter photo: The Price Family—(Left to Right, Back to Front) Aunt Bertha; Uncle Bethel; my mother, Grace; my grandmother, Viola Workman Price; and Aunt Emmer.

STORIES MY DAD AND UNCLES TOLD

Many people seem surprised when I tell them that my Dad was born in 1888 and that my Grandpa Cantley was born during The Civil War. Even though Daddy was born during the era of horse and buggy days, he lived to see Neil Armstrong walk on the moon. Horses figured prominently in his life from birth until he became too old to work his farm. In his youth, when he became old enough to handle the responsibilities of working and caring for a team of horses and a wagon, he and a friend loaded the wagon with vegetables and fruit and hit the road to peddle them to people who did not have gardens. These sales were probably the primary source of cash for the family.

The trip to peddle the load would mean overnight stays of two or three nights. In those days it was common practice to stop at the home of a stranger for a meal. Daddy told us about how he and his companion stopped at a home where the family invited them for dinner (lunch) when he saw "a big table was full of 'younguns.' " All they had on the table was squirrel meat and cornbread. While the father of the family was saying grace, Daddy said he heard a slight movement around the table and when he looked up he saw that each kid has his/her fork cocked over the squirrel plate. As soon as that family's father said "Amen," each fork speared a choice piece of the meat. Daddy said the old man reprimanded the kids, made them put the meat back, apologized and then passed the plate to Daddy and his buddy asking them to help themselves.

Another time Daddy and his friend (probably the same one as mentioned above, but I have forgotten his name) stopped at a farm for dinner and were directed to the wash basin. When they went to wash their hands Daddy's friend said, "They ain't doing too good, air they? They ain't got no soap."

Whenever they stopped for the night, Daddy and his friend looked for a place near a stream where they could water the horses and have a good place to sleep or as Daddy would say, "lay out." He said they used a "wagon sheet" (probably a tarp) to spread on the ground where they would make their bed. One night they found the perfect spot to camp and were just getting settled in when they heard a party of revelers nearby. Daddy said they were getting drunk and raising quite a ruckus. Fearing for their safety, remember they were only teenagers, they packed up and moved on to find another spot.

Daddy told another tale about "laying out" on a peddling trip when he couldn't sleep. He could hear his buddy snoring away so he thought he would pull a trick on him. Daddy kicked a hot ember from the campfire in the direction of his snoring friend but the ember hit the guy's blanket and it started smoking so much that he was afraid the guy was going to get burned. Finally, the guy—coughing from all the smoke—woke up. Knowing my dad and his propensity for pulling pranks, he came over to see if dad was awake. Daddy said the guy got so close to his face that he could feel his breath. Finally, the guy muttered "By God, you'd better been asleep." Daddy said he had to stuff his blanket into his mouth to keep from laughing.

In my dad's day (the early 1900s), young boys had to provide their own entertainment. One story I remember him telling centered around a mean old ram they kept in a corral. Boys would go into the corral, hold the ram by the horns, twist his head, and generally torment him. When one boy would get tired, another one would go in and relieve him to make sure that the ram was always held so he could not attack. Dad said they let one guy go in, but no one would relieve him—everyone just sat on the fence and watched him sweat while he tried to get close enough to the fence to jump up to safety.

Daddy said they had a homemade boat that they kept at the jack hole (a swimming hole) for recreation and fishing. One Sunday afternoon, the river was up and a guy was paddling around in the boat, rowing to the upper end of the hole where the current was strong. He'd then ride it to the lower end before rowing back. Dad said he begged the guy to let him ride but he said, "No, Jim told me not to let you in this boat because you can't swim." Dad said he waited until the guy got close to the big rock under the cliff where he was standing he then dropped a heavy rock into the boat. The rock knocked a board loose in the bottom of the boat and it promptly sank. The guy in the boat was wearing his Sunday suit (probably wool,) and he was having trouble staying afloat. Eventually he was swept to the lower end and he reached up and grabbed a tree limb that was hanging over the current. Daddy said that when he got out of the water his pants legs had shrunk halfway to his knees and his jacket sleeves were half way to his elbows. He looked at his suit, then at Daddy, and said, "Now, By God, ain't I purty?"

The only Christmas story I ever heard my dad tell was about when he was a little boy. An old man who was a friend of the family would come to their home every Christmas Eve. He would fill his pockets with candy before stopping by the river to cut evergreens which he used to cover his entire body. When the old gent came into the house (this was the old log home that had been built by Eleck years earlier), all the kids would jump on him, pull the evergreens off and get into his pockets. Daddy said the visitor would cackle and laugh. It was something both he and all the kids looked forward to each year.

As stated earlier, people had to provide their own recreation "back in the day" sometimes it involved a certain amount of danger. Dad told a story about how he and another boy took .22 caliber bullets and put them in the split end of a five or six feet long switch then threw the bullets at the side of the barn. There was not enough power to propel the bullet like it was in a rifle, but if the bullet hit the barn just right it would go off. Dad said sometimes they could hear the bullets whizzing overhead. When he heard one heading toward his buddy he asked, "Where did that bullet go?" The guy replied, "It went into my damn mouth." For that particular day his comment stopped the action.

Uncle Okey told a story —he had a million— about one cold snowy winter day when he and three or four other boys had nothing to do so they decided they would build a sled to ride down the hills. They took tools and went to the hill east of the cemetery above a paw-paw patch which I believe is still there. We used to get paw paws there when I was a kid. Okey said they worked the better part of the day making the sled with wood. He described in great detail how they cut runners, made the bed, and bored holes into the runners for standards to hold onto. When it was finished Uncle Okey said, "Now, I will go first." He told me there was no way he was going to get on that sled on top of that ridge but he knew this one boy, the bully of the group, would insist on going first. The bully said, "Like hell you will, I'm going first." Okey said they pushed the sled off the top of that steep ridge and it took off like a rocket—headed for the paw-paw patch a flyin' with that guy holding on for dear life. He said that when the sled hit the patch it flew into splinters knocking the rider unconscious. He was—literally—banged and bruised all over.

Uncle Okey often told a story about approaching the bridge at the mouth of Rock Creek on a bright moonlit night. As he approached the bridge he could see four figures sitting on the bridge. All four figures had the body of a man but the head of a hog as he got close to them he was "mad and scared, too." When he got even closer, the figures looked at him and jumped off the bridge into the creek. The creek had just gone dry and there was only fresh mud where the water had been. Uncle Okey was sure he would find tracks in the mud the next morning but when he went to inspect he found the mud to be undisturbed.

Young men of my dad's generation often carried a pistol—supposedly for protection. Uncle Okey once told me that when he was a young man he carried a pistol. One night as he was undressing for bed the weight of the pistol in his pants pocket caused them to drop to the floor and the pistol made a distinct "thud" when it struck the floor directly over "Pa and Ma's bedroom." He said there was a blue hole in the middle of the mill pond and "Pa told me the next morning, 'Son, take your pistol and put it in the blue hole and no one will know about it but you and me." His dad knew that sound could have been nothing but a pistol.

My mother found out (God only knows how) that one of my older brothers was carrying a pistol. She went into their room one morning, got the pistol, took it out in the backyard, laid it on a big flat rock and pounded it to pieces with a hammer. The pistol was loaded but, luckily, none of the shells were detonated.

As stated earlier, Uncle Okey was a great storyteller. The only problem was that he never remembered that he had told you the same story a dozen times. One of my favorite stories he told was about the haunted section of The Eunice Coal Mine. He said there was a certain area where a miner had been killed and men refused to work in that area because they felt it was haunted. Men who had tried to work there reported hearing a series of three whistles. "Whew, whew, whew" and then the same three whistles again. A new guy named Harrison Vanderpool came to work at the mine; he bragged that he would "Fight any damn man, dead or alive. I ain't afraid to fight any sumbitch." Uncle Okey was a blacksmith which meant that he worked with fire and had to work on the outside of the mine. One morning Vanderpool was shown the haunted area where he resolutely went to work. Uncle Okey said that about mid-day, Vanderpool came walking by him carrying his tools and was white as a sheet. When he asked why he was not working, he told Uncle Okey, "Blacksmith, I will fight any sumbitch on earth. I was in two or three cutting scrapes in Kentucky and I didn't come out second best on any of them. I listened to that damn whistling all morning and put up with it, but when a sumbitch coughed within three damn feet of my face and I couldn't see him-- that was enough."

Ironically, as principal of Lake Worth High School, I interviewed a young teacher whose last name was Vanderpool and he was from Kentucky. Since I couldn't resist, I told him about Harrison Vanderpool from Kentucky and the haunted mine at Eunice. He replied, "That sounds like Uncle Harry. Mom said he got into trouble in Kentucky and had to go to West Virginia to work in a mine there." What are the odds!

My dad and his siblings always started a story with "One Time," and then they would go into the story. So, in keeping with tradition, "One time" Kay, our girls, and I went back home for a summer visit. I took Beth and DeeAnne over to visit Uncle Ovet. They were very young; Uncle Ovet was looking at them, and I knew something was going on in his mind. He and Aunt Ora were empty nesters at the time and finally he said, "Dave, they are going to grow up and break your heart someday. I swear to God, they are." When they each got married I remembered what he had told me and I felt his pain.

I never heard Uncle Okey tell this story but his grandson, Robert Holt, told it to me. When he was stationed in Germany during the First World War Uncle Okey had a day off and was hitting the bottle to pass the time of day when he decided to get a haircut. When he walked into the barber shop the barber told him to have a seat because he was going to take a short lunch break. He told Okey that if anyone came in to tell them they would be second in line. Shortly, another soldier walked in thinking Okey was the barber told Okey how he wanted his hair cut. Okey told him to have a seat and he put the apron on the soldier and proceeded to cut away. When the real barber returned the soldier looked in the mirror and saw that a butcher job had been done on his head and proceeded to start punching Okey. He must have done a pretty good job because Okey told Robert, "I had a big tusk and he took care of that." The two were reported for the fracas and went before a hearing officer. When the officer heard the full story he had a big laugh and declared the case closed. Okey said the next day at roll call when the sergeant came to his name he said, "And the barber?"

Okey was assigned to guard Beethoven's piano when he was in Europe during WWI. He told Robert that the room's acoustics were so perfect you could drop a penny on the floor and hear it all over the house. He also took the liberty to play the piano. Remembering him playing in Rebecca Chapel, I know Beethoven's piano got a workout like it had never had before.

Uncle Okey deserves an entire chapter dedicated solely to him. He was a very colorful storyteller. He had a very sharp mind with a great memory. I loved his stories and remember many of them. He had a habit of elbowing you to make sure he had your undivided attention and would stick his tongue out the corner of his mouth when "tellin' a big'un." I was talking with Uncle Ovet one day about Uncle Okey sticking his tongue out and elbowing whomever he was talking with, or better still, talking to. Uncle Ovet, being aggravated with Okey's actions said, "You think about a man getting his self in such a damn shape."

Uncle Okey once told my brother-in-law, Bill Asbury, about a strange-acting man he worked with in the Republic Steel Mill in Cleveland, OH. Bill asked Uncle Okey, "What kinda damn feller is he anyway?" Uncle Okey replied emphatically, as he usually did, "I'll tell you what kinda man he is. He's never owned a fishin' pole. He's never owned a shotgun. Now you make up your own mind."

I suppose I have been blessed with a great memory dating back to my early childhood although Kay would tell you that I remember only what I want to remember. I have a couple more of Uncle Okey stories I would like to "share" with you.

Uncle Ovet always owned a Chevy pickup truck and it was not uncommon for family and friends to ride to the big town of Whitesville on Saturday in the back of the truck. I was in the truck returning from town along with Uncle Okey and others when we passed a gentleman riding a horse between Horse Creek Road and the beginning of the Flats (Naoma) Hill. The gentleman's only means of transportation must have been that horse. When sighted on the road people would yell, "Hi Yo, Silver" which elicited a tirade of profanity from the rider. (For those too young to know, the Lone Ranger was a popular cowboy movie star and Silver was his horse.) As we passed the rider, Uncle Okey yelled, "Hi Yo Silver" and that prompted a very loud, "Go to hellll, you old gray-headed son of a bitch." Uncle Okey bent over laughing so hard I was afraid he would fall out of the truck. That made his day!

One day Uncle Okey was ranting about something that had gone wrong in his life. He was complaining about the bad luck he was having and stated, "I could touch the tip of my little finger in a barrel of honey and come out with %$@& up to my elbow." To fully appreciate Uncle Okey's stories, you had to have known him.

Uncle Ovet's nickname was "Polecat," another name for a skunk. He was a fisherman, hunter and trapper. He could never understand or accept the concept of golf. He once told me that he was fishing one day at a lake near Hinton and while fishing he also watched activity on a nearby golf course. He said, "I watched a man rear back and hit a golf ball as far as he could and then hunt forever for it and then hit it again. He then hunted it up and hit it again."

He got the nickname "Polecat" from a trap he set on the mountain of Montcoal mine where he worked. He told his boss if he would go to the spot where the trap was set he would probably find a fox or raccoon in the trap. When the boss reached the spot he found a skunk spraying everything in sight, including the boss. Uncle Ovet was "Polecat" the rest of his life.

My Uncle Jimmy, James W. had a personality completely different from my Dad and his siblings. I never saw him with socks on his feet and although he could discuss the Bible with any Biblical scholar, he could say very few sentences without cursing. Uncle Ovet worked at the same mine with Jimmy; I heard him say one day that Jimmy's actions were embarrassing to him. Ovet said that he had seen Jimmy at the mine "talking Bible" with men who knew the Bible well and at least one of them was a preacher. He said Uncle Jimmy was holding his own in the discussion and when he was ready to leave he said, "Well, I'll be damned if I don't have to get the hell outta here." He then took off whistling loudly. Whistling was another of Jimmy's trademarks.

Charlie Jarrell, owner of the general store at Rock Creek, said to me one day, "The damnedest thing I have ever seen in my life just happened here. Jimmy Cantley came in, went over to where I have my winter caps on display, tried on a couple until he found one that fit, laid down his old dirty worn-out cap and walked out with my new one on his head."

While I was away in college, Uncle Jimmy was painting the metal roof on our house. My Mother said that the whole time he was on the roof he was either cursing or whistling very loudly. She said, "I was scared to death that the Lord was gonna knock him off this roof." Bobby Lovely told me when he was a kid he was sitting on a rock outside Rader's General Store one day and, "Jimmy Cantley was going home after work when he stopped, rolled down the window on his truck and said, 'Hello, you little bastard' then proceeded to drive on up the holler."

Dad's sister, my Aunt Ellen told a story about Uncle Jimmy being in the hospital when the doctor pronounced him dead and ordered him taken to the morgue. She said, "Jimmy opened his eyes and cursed them." I asked Jimmy about that and he only gave his trademark laugh, "Poh-haa-haa."

I never saw Uncle Jimmy wear socks and I am 100% certain that he never wore a necktie in his life. His job in mining required him to work with fire as a blacksmith, welder and other duties. This caused black marks to form on his eye glasses. Cousins Nelson and Margaret told me they asked their dad, my Uncle Okey, what those black marks on Uncle Jimmy's glasses were. Their dad replied, "Fly shit!" The term "colorful" could be used to describe my Dad and his siblings.

Dad's sisters, my Aunts Lou and Ellen, had their own brand of Cantley personality. In their youth, they hunted and fished right alongside the men of the family. Aunt Ellen took in Uncle Okey's grandson, Michael Lewis, and raised him from infancy until he left home for college. She was very active in the church and community life. You will read elsewhere that Mike became one of the most renowned physicians in West Virginia.

Aunt Lou was a big baseball fan and loved her Cincinnati Reds or "Red Legs" as she called them. She told me once, "Vadey (Vada) Pinson has done been give up to be the fastest man in the National League." She bought one of the first color televisions in the area and had a new antenna and wire installed. She told me, "David Dee, the picture is so clear you can see 'em spit when they come to bat." She took great pleasure in going on her front porch at night and throwing firecrackers into the yard at Christmas time. I will never forget her opening line when she was ready to ask you as question, "Now, now, now tell me somethin!" Aunt Lou lived well into her 90's and was bed ridden in her later years with "that damned Cantley arthritis" as my cousin Guy Rumberg once said. At my Uncle Ovet's burial site the funeral director announced, 'That concludes the service. You may leave now." Aunt Lou remained seated prompting the funeral director to lean near Aunt Lou and say in a louder voice, "THAT CONCLUDES THE SERVICE, MRS. COOPER. YOU MAY LEAVE NOW." "Well I will if Ellen will get off my damn walker." My Aunt Lou was a real character.

My aunts and uncles were very different in some ways, yet very much alike in other ways. They all played important roles in my upbringing, and I loved each and every one of them.

It was common practice in the old days for volunteers to help dig graves for the deceased. I remember volunteer grave diggers in the early 1960s. The cemeteries were family owned and families took great pride in maintaining their cemeteries as my family does today, thanks to nephew, Jerry. I remember Uncle Ovet telling about going to work one Monday morning when a fellow miner asked, "Polecat, what did you do this weekend?" He replied that he had helped dig Dan Rumberg's grave, whereupon the friend asked, "Did he die?" Uncle Ovet said that he replied, "No, we buried him alive." I remember helping dig that grave when I was a senior in high school.

My dad told a story about a scoundrel of a man that passed away and was held in such low esteem that no one would serve as pallbearer or grave digger. Dad said that while the hired grave diggers were performing their duties the preacher went up to the cemetery, "Didn't even take off his big black hat and looked at the diggers and said 'gentlemen, he drinketh of a bitter cup. He has gone to receive his just reward. Proceed with the burying' and walked away.

Photo taken at our home on my dad's 80th birthday party. Standing left to right, Aunt Ellen, Daddy and Uncle Ovet. Seated left to right, Uncle Jimmy, Aunt Lou and Uncle Okey.

Chapter photo: Back row (L-R): Daddy, Uncle Mont Massey, Uncle Jimmy. Front row (L-R): Aunt Lou, Aunt Ellen and Uncle Okey.

UNCLE OKEY'S DONKEY, JIM
AS TOLD BY OKEY R. CANTLEY

When I was a twelve-year-old boy, horse traders used to come through the countryside on a regular basis. They sold and traded farm horses, saddle horses as well as mules. Since my Dad was friends with most of the traders, they would sometimes spend the night with us. There was one man who was particularly friendly with Paw, and he came through on one trip with a little donkey that I immediately fell in love with. I begged Paw to buy the donkey for me, but my pleading fell on deaf ears. The trader, aware that I wanted the donkey said, "Jim, the boy really wants that donkey. Tell you what I'll do. For ten dollars I will give you the donkey and throw in the saddle and bridle." Miraculously, Paw accepted the deal and it was the happiest day of my life.

I named my donkey "Jim" and we became close buddies. The Post Office and store were one mile away and I rode him there every day. I also rode him to school, where I'd let him roam free until it was time to go home in the afternoon. Jim would follow me around the farm just like my dog, Bruno, would.

One summer in May, a man who lived about 15 miles away wanted to buy Jim for $20. Paw said I had owned him long enough and I could use the money to buy a nice suit and a pair of slippers. I watched with a heavy heart as the man led Jim away; I didn't sleep well that night because I missed my friend so much. Summer passed, fall came and went, and winter set in. One very cold snowy night in March I heard Jim at the gate calling for me. I ran downstairs to wake Paw and tell him that Jim was home. We lit a lantern, went to the gate to meet Jim, and took him to the barn. When we brushed and curried his coat to get rid of the snow and ice, we could see that he was a half-starved pitiful sight. I put Jim in his little stall with plenty of hay and grain. He had travelled many miles to reach where he knew he would be fed and loved. Over breakfast the next morning Paw said, "Jim will never leave here again."

Chapter photo: Uncle Okey in his WWI Army uniform. The two children are unknown, possibly Eustace and Gene.

HELL IN THE HOLLER

This chapter is a collection of sayings that I remember hearing as a boy growing up on Coal River. A few of these phrases were coined by my Daddy, who had his own way of expressing himself. If he accidentally pronounced something correctly, he would back up and make it right.

- *If nuthin' don't happen* - Barring unforeseen circumstances. "If nuthin' don't happen I will be goin' up there Saturday."
- *Thusevening* - This evening. "I can't go thusmorning, so I reckon I will have to go thusevening."
- *Doin' any count* - Doing any good. "I ain't been feeling like nuthin', and I ain't been doin' no count for quite a spell." When someone asked Daddy how he was doing, his reply was usually "I ain't cuttin' much of a shine."

- *Hell in the Holler* - Trouble big time. I first heard this one from my brother Hubert, Jr. "If that 'ol boy's wife ever finds out what he has been up to, there's gonna be hell in the holler."
- *Howl'n growl, lob lolly and knock 'em stiff* - Words my dad used to refer to dishes he didn't like. "Dee, pass me some of that knock 'em stiff down here."
- *A fixin' to* - Preparing for. Used throughout the south even today. I like to use this one myself when speaking with gullible flat landers and Yankees. It messes with their minds. "I'm a fixin' to plow that corn tomorrow."
- *A thoat latch* - Another of Daddy's sayings, meaning to grab someone by the throat. I heard brother Bee say that when he was principal at Stoco Jr. High School—a drunk toughy was trying to get into a dance and that he (Bee) "Got around behind him, got a thoat latch on him, and dragged him out of the gym."
- *Ferninth* - Across from or adjacent to. Daddy pulled this one on Noel and me when we were fishing on one of our many trips to New River. We were sitting around the campfire after supper when Noel asked Daddy where he wanted to fish tomorrow. He said he wanted to fish "fernint (his pronunciation) that island tomorrow." When I got home I looked it up in the dictionary and verified the word. It is no longer in the current Webster's Collegiate Dictionary.
- *Dauncy* - Light-headed or dizzy. My mother used this term often, and we thought it was something she had come up with. I looked it up in the dictionary years ago and verified it as a word. This one is also not in my Webster's Collegiate Dictionary. "I have to lie down and rest a while. I am feeling dauncy."
- *Payin' the Preacher* - Having good luck. "Hey, you got a good parking spot. You must be payin' the preacher."
- *Masterest Feller That Ever Wuz* - I don't know where Daddy got this one, but he used it to describe someone who was a great guy. "Ol' Joe was the masterest feller that ever wuz."
- *Tarpin* - We pronounced terrapin as "tarpin." "There is a tarpin in the garden, and it is eating everything in sight." I didn't know

any better until I read in the Sports pages about the University of Maryland Terrapins.

- *Evaleen* - Evelyn. I always thought she was "Evaleen Burnside" until I heard my sister, Betty, call her Evelyn.
- *Gyarden*—This is how my dad pronounced the word "garden." My brother, Eustace, once told me about Daddy singing the hymn, *In The Gyarden*. Bobbie, my sister, told me, "Daddy tried to see how many words he could mispronounce, but he was the only one in our family to pronounce "radish" correctly. Everyone else called it "reddish."
- *Poke* - A paper bag. "She carried her school lunch in a poke."
- *Idey* - Idea. I ain't got no idey what is goin' on up there, do you?"
- *Skin a gnat* - Another one invented by my dad. "That feller is so tight he would skin a gnat for its hide and towler (tallow)."
- *Hit a lick at a snake* - Used to describe a lazy person. That feller is so lazy he wouldn't hit a lick at a snake."
- *He's as tight as bark on a beech* – Used to describe a stingy person. I am sure you know how tightly bark clings to a beech tree. If you don't, try debarking one.
- *Goin down to Charleston* – Coal River is one of the few rivers in the world that runs northward. Among others being the Nile, the New and the St. Johns in Florida. Because we would travel "down the river" to get to Charleston, the state capitol, we were actually traveling northward, but we said we were going "down to Charleston" instead of "up to Charleston." When we went "up to Beckley," the county seat 25 miles from Rock Creek, we were actually traveling south.
- *Right Smart Number* – A considerable amount. "That guy owns a right smart number of acres of land."
- *A Mess of Beans* – Just enough for a meal. "I will pick enough beans for a mess."
- *Set it Down* – Put it in writing. "Give me his phone number and I will set it down so I won't forget it." Another one of my dad's sayings.
- *Get Shut of* – Get rid of. "That old dog won't hunt so I think I will just get shut of him." I have a lot of fun with people using this one.

Chapter photo: Bringing in the coal for my mother to cook another great meal. Note that he has that ever present pipe in his mouth, He started smoking the pipe as a teenager and it was tamped and ready to light when he was taken to the hospital, where he would later die.

SCOTT T. JARRELL

His family and friends on Coal River call him Teddy, but he has always been Ted to me. He once told me to refer to him as Teddy when talking with his friends because they wouldn't know who Ted Jarrell was. Ted didn't know he had a first name until he had to produce a birth certificate to join the Navy. We have been close friends for as long as I can remember. Before his death in 2014, we often visited each other and exchanged Christmas gifts—I would send him Florida oranges and he would send me his homemade apple butter and honey.

As kids, Ted and I had great times growing up at Rock Creek. We hunted and fished together, played "baxetball," as Ted would say and baseball, ran trap lines, as well as roamed the hills, hollers and creeks as boys should do as a part of growing up. He was a few years older than I and he made sure that I didn't go wrong—like drinking Pepsi instead of RC Cola. Pepsi was "too sweet." He also made me a NY Yankee fan (instead of The Cleveland Indians) and he steered me to The NY Giants (instead of the Cincinnati Reds). Ted could hit a baseball left-handed farther than I could point.

The area across the bridge from the new Marsh Fork Elementary School is Ted's birthplace; it's where he lived until he died. It is now known as Jarrell Bottom—as nearly all the area's residents are Jarrells—but it didn't always have that name. Cecil D. Cooke, the principal at Mt. View School, lived in the house on the left after crossing the bridge. In those days, the 1940's, the only way of crossing the river was via a swinging bridge. That must have been pretty hard for a city boy to take so Mr. Cooke called the community "Misery Bottom." In later years Ted was given the honorary title of "Mayor of Misery Bottom." He probably blamed me for that. I wonder why?

There were absolutely no jobs for a kid when we were growing up on Coal River in the 1950s. The only opportunity to earn a few dollars was to do odd jobs working around people's homes or, in season, work for farmers in corn and hay for 50 cents per hour. Eight hours, got you four dollars and a trip to Charlie Jarrell's store. We would feast on a pint of ice cream, honey bun cake, and an RC Cola to reward ourselves for a hard day's toil in the hot sun. We would usually top it off with a five-cent blue tip cigar. All of that only cost about 75 cents. We were really living it up!

When Ted reached 16 he dropped out of school and went north to find work. He lived in Chicago for a while before joining the Navy. He was injured while on duty and was given a medical discharge. He then returned home and got a job with a mining company at Montcoal where he worked until he retired. Ted's son, Tommy, and his daughter, Marsha, now live on Ted's Dad's farm. Ted was very serious about his religion, was active in his church, and always volunteered to help anyone in need of a helping hand.

During the winter months Ted would check on snowbound neighbors to make sure they had food, heat, water and their mail. He would even make soup and deliver it to people whom he felt might need a hot meal. Most cities have shelters that house and feed people who are unable to care for themselves. Because of good-hearted people like Ted, residents of Coal River (and other rural areas) take care of their own by making sure their neighbors receive assistance so they can remain in their homes.

Scott T. Jarrell could always be counted on to help anyone in need ...

unless it was the first day of deer season. Or the first day of bow season. Or the first day of turkey season. Or the first day of bear season. Or if the state had just stocked Coal River with trout. Or if there was a NASCAR or Indy 500 race within 300 miles of home.

When I heard—in July of 2014—that Ted had stage-four-lung cancer, I called his daughter Marsha to schedule a visit. Kay and I drove to West Virginia and I spent the night with him. Marsha and Tommy cooked both a country dinner and breakfast to die for. Ted and I had a great visit and talked about old times, both fully aware that this would be our last visit. Before I left the next morning, I told him that I loved him and hugged him. As I was walking out the door I could hear him crying. Two weeks later, he was gone.

If the system were to collapse and the country came to a screeching halt with no goods or services, I would want to live right next door to Scott T. Jarrell. Ted could repair anything and he could also grow, can or freeze his own vegetables, kill game to provide for himself, his family and friends. To say he was resourceful is a pitiful understatement. Hank, Jr. sang, "He can skin a buck and run a trotline. A country boy can survive." Ted was an invaluable asset to his community and church; he is deeply missed by many. I was proud to call him my friend. He would be "tickled plumb to death" to know that his picture and story are in this book.

WANTED, WANTED!

WANTED: David Dee Cantley (Lft.) and Scott Teddy Jarrell (Rt.) for stealing chickens, hunting and fishing out of season, illegal trapping, exceeding the limit on all fish and game, spotlighting deer, running other people's trotlines, lying and breaking every game and fish law in the state of West Virginia. Cantley was a pretty good old boy until he was led astray by Tom and Ada's little darlin'.

REWARD: A big cold RC, a honey bun, one pint of Pet ice cream and a blue tip cigar.

These subjects are dangerous and armed with tall tales and the most outrageous lies known to mankind.

I mailed the above spoof to Ted after returning home from my final visit with him. Unfortunately, it arrived on the day of his death. I am sorry he didn't get to see this. The above picture was taken on his front porch the day before I left him.

Chapter photo: Ted in his sailor uniform

HOG KILLING TIME

Warning: Not for the Faint of Heart

One of my most vivid memories of growing up on the farm back in the 1940s and '50s centered around hog-killing time. We fed the hogs grain and a product called "Larro" which came in a 100-lb sack and had to be mixed with water in a 5-gallon bucket, then stirred. We would occasionally pull what we called "hog weeds" and throw into the lot because the pigs loved to eat them. In the fall when the weather got colder, the hogs (we usually had two) would be put in the pen and not allowed to be in the lot. That was also when we would step up the amount of grain we fed them. The grain process, ears of field corn on the cob, was called, "fattening up for the kill."

There was an old saying, "If it gets any colder, I'm gonna go home and kill a hog." This originated from the need to wait for cold weather to kill hogs because we had no home freezers in those days. Much of preparation went into getting everything ready for the big day. As I recall, one of the first things we did was have a tub of boiling water waiting where the hog would be dressed. The fire had to be started under the tub early in the morning so that the water would be boiling and ready to scald the hog before scraping the hair off.

Our hog pen and lot were about 200 yards from where the hog would be dressed. My Dad or my brothers would harness the horse and take the sled to the lot where it would await loading the hog. The horse would then be unhooked from the sled and removed from the immediate area. The hog had to be coaxed out of the pen as he usually sensed something was up. The hog would be shot between the eyes with a .22 caliber rifle and, generally, would fall over on the spot. He would then be stuck with a sharp knife, to sever the jugular vein. This was necessary because if all or most of the animal's blood wasn't drained, the meat "would taste strong." Thus, the saying, "bleeding like a stuck hog."

When the bleeding stopped, the dead hog was dragged or lifted onto the sled. I can remember horses smelling the blood and snorting and prancing nervously with their ears pinned back when they were hooked back to the sled. The sled was pulled above the house to a spot under a big walnut tree where there was a heavy chain hanging from a limb. We would hang a block and tackle from the chain. A hook from a short singletree (I know you don't know what a singletree is, so look it up) was hooked through the tendon on each hind leg the hog was then hoisted above the sled with its head pointed downward in preparation for removal of the entrails.

The sled was then cleaned and scalded in preparation for the hog carcass to be laid on it for butchering. We usually had a couple of neighboring farmers help with the job, each helper would get a bucket or dish pan of fresh meat to take home with them. I remember either Daddy or Tom Jarrell would start the process of removing the entrails by starting with a sharp knife at the top of the hanging animal's body between the hind legs. A wash tub was placed under the hog's head and the entrails would fall into the tub. We never ate the "chitlins" and the tub's contents were always taken out and buried where dogs or varmints couldn't dig them up.

After the entrails were removed the carcass was lowered to the cleaned sled and splashed with boiling water. It was then that the hair was removed then the meat was cut into hams, ribs, pork chops, "middlings," etc. The meat was kept in what we called the smokehouse though we never smoked meat to preserve it as past generations had done. Daddy would season or cure the meat by rubbing it with salt. My sisters, of course, were squeamish and couldn't get near the work on hog killing day. I remember one year my Mother removed the meat from the hog's head and cooked or baked up something that was delicious. My sister, Bobbie, and her friend, Virginia Jarrell, ate a big bait of it. They were complimenting Mommy on how good it tasted when Daddy came in. He said, "How did you like the hog's head, girls?" Bobbie cried out, "Oh my God, Daddy, don't tell me I just ate a hog's head!"

Looking back on it all now, killing hogs does sound morbid—but that was part of our family's livelihood. Everything we ate was grown on that little farm, and we were glad to get fresh meat. In our leaner years pork, chicken and wild game were our only sources of meat.

To this day, I would love to make a meal out of one of the rabbits Daddy shot and a few of Mommy's biscuits. That would knock your hat in the creek!

Chapter photo: Daddy taking Pepper from the barn to the watering trough in creek.

CARS

by Glenn S. "Ike" Cantley

Cars and trucks have always been synonymous with the Cantley boys. The picture above is what remains of my Uncle Gene's (E.K) 1953 Dodge cab-over-engine tractor. He and his brother, Noel, drove trucks like this in the early 1950s for Gate City Transport while hauling Chrysler products from Detroit throughout the Carolinas. The trucks were very weak, powered by a six-cylinder engine that necessitated slow and painful climbs up the mountains. Noel and Gene said that their most challenging hill climb on their entire route was Mt. View Hill at Rock Creek.

Gene owned his own truck—as opposed to driving a company-owned vehicle. Note his name on the door above the company name. He and another uncle, Hubert Jr. who was an excellent mechanic decided to tackle what Chrysler engineers dared not attempt. After many measurements and calculations, they decided that they could fit a large V-8 engine into the cramped engine cavity that previously could only house a six-cylinder engine. Gene, Jr. and some friends successfully made the conversion, and Gene became the talk of the truckers as he passed them on the highway— both on flat land and on hills! No one dreamed that there was a hot V-8 engine in that old Dodge. Talk of their success soon reached Chrysler engineers who wanted to inspect the truck to see how it had been done. Gene, being Gene, refused to permit the inspection by saying, "Let them get some tools and try it. They are engineers, they should be able to figure it out."

Ike at a car show looking over a nice old Ford.

Chapter photo: What is left of Gene's (E.K) 1953 Dodge cab-over-engine tractor

15

ROCK CREEK PEOPLE OF NOTE

Raleigh County School Board Member, Richard Snuffer, once stated publicly in a board meeting that Marsh Fork High School had graduated as many doctors and lawyers as any school in Raleigh County. Referring to a rural mining community where students' parents were, for the most part, blue-collar workers—that was a pretty bold statement. Mr. Snuffer's claim could be verified by simply looking at the makeup of the residents of Coal River. While many were not regular church goers, they did have a deep faith and a strong work ethic which they instilled in their children. We were taught that we could become whatever we wanted to become if we set our goals, then worked hard to achieve them.

Marsh Fork High produced many top performers in accounting, business, education, law, medicine and other professions. Plus, there were hundreds of graduates who entered the workforce after school, and worked hard to raise families, pay taxes and become good citizens who made contributions to their community. Many grads joined the armed forces in service to our country.

Let's look at Marsh Fork High grads who were raised in the tiny hamlet of Rock Creek, the title of this book. When unsuspecting folks ask me where I am from in West Virginia, I proudly tell them that I am from Rock Creek, which will prompt another question, "Where is Rock Creek?" Then, when I tell them that it is one mile upstream from Dry Creek they usually give up. During my day (the '40s and '50s), Rock Creek could be identified by the post office that was housed in Rader's General Store, Charles E. "Charlie" Jarrell's General Store, and Rebecca Chapel. Rader's Store is gone now, the building houses only the post office. Charlie's store is now a convenience store but Rebecca Chapel is still going strong. Rock Creek probably never had more than 500 residents in a good year, that number includes folks who lived along Route 3 and "up the holler." The misinformed would say "hollow."

Dr. Michael Lewis

Dr. Michael Lewis was one of the most outstanding graduates of Marsh Fork High. Mike was my second cousin and the son of June, Uncle Okey's daughter. He was raised in Mt. View Bottom at Rock Creek by my Aunt Ellen Pettry, my dad's sister. If there had been gifted classes in Mike's day he would have been at the head of the class. Aunt Ellen taught him to read by using comic books and Sunday School literature before he started school. She taught Mike to practically recite the Bible from cover to cover. My cousin, Gordon, and I were jealous of Mike whenever Aunt Ellen would "put him on the stump" to recite The Books of the Bible and other passages to the oohs and ahhs of his audience. I remember Mike wearing a coonskin hat as a young boy during the Davy Crockett TV show days and going squirrel hunting with it on his head. I always worried that he would be mistaken for a squirrel. He suffered from asthma during his youth, and this lead many of us to believe that his illness inspired Mike to study medicine.

Mike graduated high school in 1961, earned his Bachelor of Science in chemical engineering in 1965, and a Master of Science in chemical engineering in 1968 from West Virginia Institute of Technology. Then, in 1969, he earned a Ph.D. in chemical engineering from Virginia Tech in Blacksburg, VA. Upon graduation, he was employed by Union Carbide in Charleston, WV to conduct research. I am told that Mike actually designed and supervised the construction of chemical plants for Carbide.

Mike soon realized that medicine was his true calling and enrolled at West Virginia University School of Medicine from 1971 to 1974 to earn his Doctor of Medicine Degree. After graduating medical school he opened a family practice in St. Marys, West Virginia serving that community for ten years. He then joined the medical school faculty at West Virginia University as second chair of The Department of Family Medicine. Mike then served as Vice Chancellor for Health Sciences and Associate Dean of Charleston Division of the West Virginia University School of Medicine. After that, he served as Vice Chancellor for The Higher Education Policy Commission.

In 2002, Mike accepted an appointment as Vice Chancellor for Health Sciences at East Carolina University at Greensboro, North Carolina. Governor Earl Ray Tomlin invited him to return to West Virginia to serve as cabinet secretary of the West Virginia Department of Health and Human Resources; Mike held that position from 2011 until health issues caused his resignation in 2012.

Mike received many honors, awards and accolades during his career. He was cited in Who's Who in America, 2010; Distinguished West Virginian Award, 2002; and the Family Doctor of the Year Award, West

Virginia Academy of Family Physicians, 2002. Mike was a credit to his profession, during his "days off" he volunteered to treat indigent patients.

My sister-in-law, Audrey, once told her doctor in Beckley that she had taught Mike at Mt. View School. The astonished doctor gasped, "You mean Dr. Michael Lewis from West Virginia University School of Medicine is from Coal River?" Yes, Doc, some of us actually learned to read and write!

Dr. Michael Justin Lewis died from brain cancer at the age of 70 in Charleston, West Virginia on August 10, 2013.

Ronald Bee Cantley

My brother, Bee, graduated Marsh Fork High School in 1951. He was an outstanding basketball player, another Rock Creek boy, Gene Wills, once proclaimed that if Bee had been one foot taller he would have played in the pros. After graduating high school Bee joined the Navy and served on The USS Coral Sea, an aircraft carrier. Upon being discharged from the Navy he enrolled at Beckley College where he played basketball for two years. After he graduated Beckley College (a two-year institution), he enrolled at Morris Harvey College, now the University of Charleston, where he majored in education. He taught at East Bank Jr. High School for one year before moving to Raleigh County for a teaching job at Stoco Jr. High. He became principal at Stoco Jr. High before being promoted to principal at Shady Spring High. Bee then became assistant Superintendent of Raleigh County Schools and was finally appointed by the school board to be the only Marsh Fork High grad to serve as Superintendent of Schools.

Nelson Lee Cantley

Nelson also graduated in 1951 and played with Bee on the basketball team. He joined the Army after his high school graduation, served as an MP, and continued to play basketball with his base team as well as in an industrial league. After being discharged from the Army with the rank of sergeant he trained to become a court reporter in Jacksonville Beach, Florida and worked in the field for a period of five years in Columbus, Ohio. He then moved to California where he became "florist to the stars." Among his many clients were Victor Mature, Patti Page, Desi Arnaz, Jimmy Durante, Robert Young, Mary Tyler Moore, Milton Berle and Carol Burnett. In 1974, he spent a week decorating the White House at Christmas time for President Ford. Nelson was twice voted florist of the year in FTD 10 A/B District (comprised of southern California and Nevada) he served as president of that same district for two years. The Academy Award in the floral industry is having a plant or flower named after you. Nelson was honored by having a cymbidium orchid named for him--"Mstr Lee." His floral shop was voted best in the San Diego area in 2000. Nissan sent Nelson to Hong Kong where he boarded the luxury cruise liner, the Golden Odyssey, and sailed the China Seas for 16 days giving lectures and demonstrations as well as doing floral designs for certain parts of the ship.

Nelson appeared on television many times for interviews and many articles appeared in local newspapers about his shop which was twice voted in the top five flower shops in Southern California. And to think that he got his start by stoking the furnace at Rebecca Chapel for six dollars a month!

James F. "Jim" Farley

Jim and Bobbie Farley with Coach Doc Holliday Jim and Bobbie, Marshall University graduates had seats reserved on the ill-fated Marshall flight that crashed at the Huntington Airport returning from a game at East Carolina on November 14, 1970 killing all 75 people on board including the team, coaches and staff, community members, flight crews and alums. Jim had to cancel their reservations because they could not arrange for a babysitter. Their seats were taken by another husband and wife.

"Jimmy," as he was known growing up, was an "up-the-holler" Rock Creek boy. He eventually made his mark in the field of nursing care. Jim graduated Marsh Fork High in 1960, where he lettered in every sport the school offered—football, basketball, baseball and track. He also served as President of the Student Council.

Jim received his bachelor's degree in business administration from Marshall University where he attended school on an academic scholarship and a Masters of Health Administration from the Medical College of Virginia. Jim is president, managing partner and co-founder of Nursing Care Management, Inc. He is the recipient of many professional and civic awards including Marshall's prestigious Distinguished Alumnus Award.

Governor Jim Justice appointed Jim to the Marshall University Board of Governors in July of 2017.

When our alma mater, Marsh Fork, was closed (and later burned by vandals), Jim spearheaded a drive to obtain the site where the school had been and turn it into a park. Jim recruited several volunteers to create a much-needed facility for the residents of Coal River. He and his wife, Bobbie (also a Rock Creek native), always remembered to "dance with them that brung you," and helped save Rebecca Chapel from extinction. There is no doubt in my mind that without their intervention, time, and money, there would be no Rebecca Chapel today.

Jim was selected as a recipient of the Cincinnati Tennis Club's Founders and Guardians Award, which is the club's highest honor and recognizes those members whose leadership and service over many years have contributed in advancing the goals, traditions, programs and the sport of tennis at Cincinnati Tennis Club. Jim was presented with the award May 21, 2017. He, his wife, Bobbie, and their two daughters, Angela and Andrea, have been very active in the sport of tennis and all are members of The Cincinnati Tennis Hall of Fame. Jim was elected vice-chairman of the Marshall University Board of Governors in June of 2020.

Bobbie Webb Farley

Rock Creek—Looking Back and Forward--A Woman's Perspective *by Bobbie Webb Farley*

My family moved to Rock Creek in 1950 after living in the nearby community of Naoma. Our home was on a hill overlooking the community Methodist Church, and the only businesses in the community—two general stores, one of which housed the local post office. Miller Cemetery was on the hill behind our home. The house had been recently built and consisted of just four rooms—a living room, a kitchen, and two bedrooms—one for my parents, Kermit and Inez Webb, and a second one for my two brothers, David and Randall, and me. The house was built on the side of the hill. There was no basement. The back side of the house basically set on the ground, and the front half rested on large timbers placed on each corner . For my parents, it was a major step to purchase a home. I was six years old at the time, and David and Randall, were five and four, respectively. We were each one year apart in age, and had August, August and September birthdays in consecutive years.

Our father quickly began a project to enlarge our home by increasing the size of the living area, adding a third bedroom—one for me—and one for David and Randall to share, and our first bathroom. The improvement included enclosing the half basement. This was a great place for me to play. I made my playhouse in the basement, and remember making "butter" with soap suds in a small wooden churn that my grandfather had made for me.

We had a well and a pump for our water supply. On one occasion, my dad had to dig up all the drain pipes from the kitchen sink and found the pipes were filled with coffee grounds. My mother had been putting coffee grounds down the sink drain and they had totally clogged the pipes. I also remember my father coming home from the mines, with his face totally black from coal dust, and I remember how much he enjoyed fall trips to the mountains of eastern West Virginia to squirrel hunt. My mother would pack boxes of supplies and food for these annual trips, and the boxes were scattered around the kitchen for days while they were being filled for these treasured hunting trips.

I never heard my parents express why they chose to live at Rock Creek; however, I am certain that it must have been in large part because Mt. View Elementary and Junior High School was located in the community; and the school had an excellent reputation. Both my parents had attended Mt. View Junior High and completed their elementary education in Pine Knob schools. I loved Mt. View School and all my teachers. I had a great desire to learn and I enjoyed the fun activities, too. I loved to play hopscotch on the school sidewalks and to jump rope. I learned to jump rope and play jacks in third grade with my left hand after I broke my right wrist playing in the woods with my best friend and next door neighbor, Ann Lovely. My friends and I would also set up playhouses in the woods around the school filling the separate rooms in the houses with items we would bring from our homes. As soon as the bell rang for recess, we would run as fast as we could to our playhouses.

There were "blue laws" in those days that kept most retail businesses closed on Sunday. On most Sunday mornings my mother would fry chicken, make potato salad, baked beans, and similar dishes for a picnic lunch; then our family would travel to parts of southern West Virginia to enjoy a picnic lunch at one of the state parks or at a table along one of the narrow highways. On one particular Sunday I recall that we had my mother's parents with us. My grandmother had never been out of the state of West Virginia, so my father drove us over the state line to another state. On another Sunday, my dad drove us to Beckley and we got on a new highway, called a turnpike, that connected Beckley with Charleston, the state capital. There was a beautiful tunnel along the turnpike that fascinated us.

My mother's ambition had been to become a nurse, and while she was in high school she wrote to several nursing schools for catalogs and information regarding admission. One of the major requirements was that every student had to be 18 or approaching her eighteenth birthday. At the age of 16, when she graduated from high school, she was much too young to enroll in nursing school. She tried to convince my grandmother to let her work in one of the local company stores until she became 18. But her mother argued that if she began making money on her own, she would not want to quit and would therefore not go on to college. She enrolled in Morris Harvey College just shy of her seventeenth birthday, and two years later she got a job teaching in a one-room school. She wrote in her autobiography that she had never felt so insecure.

In my mother's second year of teaching at Edwight, she and my father were married. Our father was a coal miner, and mining jobs in the 1950's did not provide secure employment. There were continuous layoffs at the Edwight mine where he worked. During one of the layoffs after we had moved to Rock Creek, my father operated a Keystone service station at Stickney, and we lived in an apartment in the same building at the service station. After he was called back to the mines, we moved back to our new home in Rock Creek.

Following another layoff in 1954 at the Edwight mine, my father took a job driving a car transport tractor trailer with a company based in Huntington. It was an exciting time for our family living in what we considered a big city after all the years living in Rock Creek and its rural surroundings. After several months as a transport car driver, my father received a call that the Edwight mine was reopening and he was offered a job. He returned to work in the mine and following just his eighth day on the job, tragedy struck and he was killed leaving my mother to raise my two younger brothers, who were nine and eight at the time, and me. I will never forget that day when I was called out of class, stood at the bottom of the steps leading to the second floor and was told about my father's death. As my mother said in her autobiography, "There was no warning. He simply went to work well and happy and never came back."

The days following our father's death were very dark days for our family, yet it was not easy for us young children to grasp entirely the gravity of the situation. We survived primarily on the strength of our mother with help from her parents, other family members, and her many teacher and community friends. Following our mother's death in 2004, I found a number of short poems and quotes that she had collected, and to the best of my knowledge, had not shared with anyone. As I read one of the poems, entitled *Widow*, by Maureen Cannon, the words spoke volumes about our mother and how, in the words of the last line of the poem--"... she...rearranged her life."

I do not recall Mother's outwardly showing much grief in front of us children. I think she wanted to protect us and that gave her the will to be strong and move along—one step at a time. She did an amazing job of ensuring our school and community connections were strong, and she began to "rearrange" her life.

With three children to raise alone, she then "dug in her heels" and began to work on completing her college degree. She knew that if she could graduate from college with a higher teaching certificate she would be able to make a better living for her family. Since she had begun her college studies at Morris Harvey College in Charleston, she decided to pursue completing her degree there, which she did by taking night classes on campus and by extension and by going to summer school full-time on campus. I was frightened to stay by myself or with just my brothers, so her brother, our Uncle Ted, would come home from work and stay with us when my mother drove to Charleston—generally with other teachers—to take a night class. It was not until years later that I realized how difficult those days must have been for her—taking care of three young children, teaching school all day with lesson plans to make, and papers to grade outside of class, and taking college classes at night.

It is said that it "takes a village" to raise a child. Although our mother was amazingly strong and independent, she had help from neighborhood friends in addition to the help she received from her family and our father's family. There was a great sense of community spirit in our small Rock Creek community, and neighbors were always willing to help out when needed. One of the neighborhood girls, Betty Underwood—a few years older than my brothers and I—stayed with us during part of the time while our mother was continuing to pursue her college degree. I thought it was great to hang out with Betty—a high school student at the time.

Mother took on the role of our mother and our father. I remember my brother David saying in later years that he would send Mother and Father's Day card. She was really the only father we ever knew. There was hardly anything that she would not undertake for the benefit of us children.

We were so proud of the fact that our mother was a teacher. Each day we would travel the short distance to Mt. View School together and return home together. Our neighbor, Mrs. Lovely, got a television before we did; and each weekday afternoon during the school year we would go over to her house and watch television for one to two hours. We loved the novelty of television, and this gave Mother time to fix our dinner, grade papers, and perhaps get in some study for her ongoing college classes. Ann Lovely was my good friend and in my grade at school so she and the three of us loved watching Howdy Doody and other afternoon shows. With the introduction of rock and roll, American Bandstand became one of our favorite shows.

Although we had little extra money growing up in Rock Creek, Mother made certain that we had many of the advantages of children in more urban areas. Shortly after we moved to Rock Creek, she began a Girl Scout Brownie Troop. She also organized Intermediate and Senior Girl Scout troops. Each summer, with assistance from a staff person in the Girl Scout office in Beckley, she would direct a summer day camp in the Dry Creek area on the road to Peach Tree Falls. Girls from several of the Coal River communities would participate in the day camp. I remember how much fun we had setting up camp and making out "kaper" charts. We learned a lot about organization and teamwork during those summer camps. Mother also became a camp counselor at Camp Beckwith, which gave me the opportunity to spend a week at camp in a log cabin and meet girls from all over Raleigh County.

Mother also helped with the formation of Babe Ruth and Little League teams and in the summers she organized and manned a concession stand at Mt. View School to raise funds for the baseball teams. It was fun for me to help her operate the concession. Mother did the ordering of products, and we sold the concessions in the "white building" on the grounds of Mt. View. It was one of my first "volunteer" jobs.

There was little opportunity for any kind of paying jobs for young girls in Rock Creek. I did manage to get some small pay for babysitting, and my first real job to substitute for the post mistress while she was on vacation for one week.

Because David, Randall, and I were so close in age, we enjoyed many of the same activities. We would play Indian trapper with friends among the trees of our property, shoot basketball at a goal Mother had installed in our front yard, and play softball in an open field beside the Green's house in Rock Creek bottom—all the time managing to stay safely away from the Green's dog, Rex, when a ball would go into their yard. Weekends would find us around the kitchen table playing our favorite board games—Monopoly, Chinese Checkers, and Sorry.

One of our chores each spring was to pick up all the limbs and twigs that had fallen over the winter from the many large poplar trees on our property. Cleaning the property was followed by making a "camp" each summer out under the trees a few hundred feet from our house. We would frequently sit around campfires with neighborhood friends and make s'mores—still today one of my favorite treats.

Life was not, however, all fun and games. I took on the job of cleaning the house every Saturday, and David and Randall helped get coal from the coal pile to the furnace located in the basement. It was a wonderful day when Mother had electric heat installed in the house, and there was no longer the requirement to wheelbarrow coal to the basement.

I took piano lessons every week and dance classes on Saturday in Whitesville. Our family friend, Betty Salters, was one of the best dancers at the dance studio. She was a few years older than I was, and my goal was to become as good a dancer as she was. I loved the costumes we got to wear in recitals. Mother bought an upright piano, and David and Randall and I would play "Stop the Music," a popular television show. I would play a few bars on the piano, and they would try to guess the name of the song. David played a flute in the band, and I played a clarinet. We worked at learning to play duets with our band instruments. Randall would sometimes join in on his trumpet.

We were active in the Rebecca Chapel Methodist Church. Mother's Grandfather Workman had been a Methodist circuit rider during the early part of the 20th century, so it was normal that we would follow in the family tradition of attending a Methodist church. I read recently that Grandpa Workman married a lot of couples as he traveled around from community to community, and he became known as "the Marrying Parson."

Mother taught Sunday school, and Doris and Novie Marshall were our youth group leaders. "Aunt" Ellen Pettry, Michael Lewis' aunt, was our Sunday school teacher. Each week our youth group would meet at the church, and at Christmastime we performed in the annual Christmas programs. Sue Jarrell was the church pianist. After she graduated from high school, I began to play the piano on Sunday mornings. There were only a few songs I felt proficient enough to play—and these were always hymns with flats—no sharps. I was always able to fall back on playing *What a Friend We Have in Jesus.* It had just one flat!

I always knew I would go to college after high school. Following my father's death, my brothers and I received small amounts of Social Security benefits each month until we were 18. Mother set up separate accounts for each of us, and deposited the benefits she received into the accounts. These were our college funds. She could have easily used those funds for fancier clothes and cars, yet I knew those funds were there to provide opportunities for us to go to college or get other training after high school.

Growing up in Rock Creek, I was destined to be a school teacher. Not only was my mother a teacher, one of her sisters was also a teacher, too. Also, my grandmother, who had never had the opportunity to attend college, was a teacher in the 1930's and 40's, and many of our neighbors and family friends were teachers. Many elementary and high school teachers resided in the tiny village of Rock Creek. These men and women—mostly women—were the professionals in our community and were our role models. The only other professional person was the local doctor—Dr. John Lee—who worked with his nurse to take care of the minor illnesses of the folks in the community.

In addition to my mother, our next-door neighbor, although a few hundred yards away from our house, was a teacher—Grace Tabor. In 1959 when the Tabor family moved to a house across from Mt. View School, another teacher, Ramona Jarrell, and her family moved into the Tabor home and became close family friends. Across the hill from our home, another of our neighbors and friends was Maude Parolari. And there were many others—Betty Jarrell; my first grade teacher, Margaret Miller, and her sister, Reba; my fourth grade teacher, Thelma Cantley; my high school chemistry teacher and the part-time high school guidance counselor, Shelby Webb, and his wife, Mabel; and my high school algebra and geometry teacher, Bernard Green, and his wife, Alberta. For a village whose name could not be found on a road map, our community was filled with learned professionals, whom I admired greatly. I do believe we had the most "sophisticated and learned" community on Coal River.

During high school years, my brother, David, and I were more likely to be found at home every school evening doing our homework. Our brother, Randall, on the other hand, would more likely be exploring with his many friends all that Rock Creek had to offer—riding bikes and taking trips up Rock Creek Hollow frequently to visit the Price family—an elderly gentleman and his son, who many described as hermits. Randall also had a knack for fixing things, and even before he could drive, Mother bought him an old car to work on. The first thing he did was to chop the top off of the car. He called it "Chop Top." I heard him say many times he could not envision growing up anywhere except Rock Creek.

After graduating from high school as valedictorian in 1962, I enrolled in Marshall University's Teachers' College and that year I became better acquainted with Jim Farley, whom I had known in high school and whose family also lived at Rock Creek a short distance up the hollow from Route 3. At the end of my second year of college, we were married at Rebecca Chapel and continued to live in Huntington to continue our schooling. Our first daughter, Angela, was born in December 1964, and Jim began a graduate program in hospital administration in Richmond the next year. I worked full-time as a secretary during Jim's two years in graduate school.

After completing my degree at Marshall University, I taught high school for six years—three years at Huntington High School in Huntington and three years at Point Pleasant High School in Point Pleasant. Our second daughter, Andrea, was born just after we moved to Point Pleasant in 1971.

It was the 1970's, and women were branching out into the non-traditional fields of business, law and medicine. My brother, David, who was also valedictorian of his high school class the year after I graduated from Marsh Fork, had an engineering degree from West Virginia University, as well as a law degree. I began to think I would like a career in law, too.

I secretly studied for the LSAT exam and took it in Charleston. I would go to my husband's hospital office, and study for hours preparing for the exam. I applied to the law school at West Virginia University; however, I told no one. I did not want to explain if I did not get accepted. The good news was that I did get accepted; the bad news was that if I went to law school in Morgantown, the two girls and I would be living away from Point Pleasant for portions of three years. After much discussion with Jim, I decided to give law school a try. We surveyed the accommodations for students in Morgantown, and decided that the purchase of a mobile home would be a wise investment for the three years. It turned out we were right; we sold the mobile home after three years for the same price we had paid for it. If Mother felt insecure when she faced a group of students in grades one to six in a one-room school at the age of 18, I felt completely frightened at the prospect of tackling law school with two children.

And then there were those who said it would never work—that I was breaking up the family—that it was unfair to my husband and my children. I remember vividly a male lawyer friend of ours who asked when he heard I had been accepted to law school, "What do you call a female barrister?" At that time it was still somewhat of a novelty for women to be lawyers. Oh, there had always been women lawyers; however, many of them were daughters or granddaughters of male lawyers or judges. It was not until the 1970's that large numbers of women began to study law. In my freshman class of 1975, one third of the class of about 100 were women, many more than any prior year.

In high school, it had never occurred to me that being a lawyer was a career choice. Shelby Webb was our part-time high school guidance counselor. It was common in the early 1960's when I graduated from high school for boys who were good in math to be directed to engineering in college and for girls, who were going to college, to be directed into teaching. For girls to be directed towards law, medicine or business was unheard of in those days, and it was no different at Marsh Fork High School than it was around the county. This was about to change.

The 1960's brought about many social changes, and women benefited greatly from the strides made by the leaders of the women's movement, as well as the strides made by the leaders of the civil rights movement. I consider myself lucky to have been part of the transformation that was taking place in our society, and I am grateful for all those who were at the forefront of the transformation. In some respects, it seemed natural for me to take on a role that had been previously been held primarily by men. After all, my mother had been both mother and father to my brothers and me. If she could take on a man's role, then perhaps I could do that, too.

After graduation from law school in 1978, I joined a law firm in Point Pleasant with two male lawyers. I had read John Molloy's book, *Dress for Success*, in which he encouraged women to emulate the dress of men—dark suites and small ties. The idea was if you were going to be part of what was considered at the time "a man's world," you should dress like a man. I was unsure as to how I would be accepted as the only female lawyer in town. I felt the same insecurity my mother must have felt when she at the age of 18 faced a group of 23 students in one-room school in Pine Knob. Somewhat to my surprise, from the beginning I was welcomed as a member of the Mason County Bar and I never experienced any discrimination. It was a big step for me.

After two years with the firm of Shaw & Stein, our family moved to Cincinnati, Ohio, where Jim had an opportunity to start a new company. He had been tremendously successful in turning around a failing hospital in Point Pleasant, and he was chosen to lead a new company in the field of long-term care. My career path took an abrupt change with the move. While it was relatively easy for me to practice law in Point Pleasant and still maintain the extracurricular activities involved in family life, this was not possible in our new life in Cincinnati. I hung out my shingle as a sole practitioner, which afforded me flexibility to manage family life in a new community. I worked with Jim's fledgling new company to navigate the increasing number of federal and state regulations affecting nursing homes and to assist them in the expansion of the company.

As Gail Collins wrote in her book, *When Everything Changed—The Amazing Journey of Women from 1960 to the Present*, published in 2009, in less than a decade—from 1964 to 1972 or 1973—women became equal under the law, applications to graduate school, law school, and medical school shot up, and the vision of what women could do was transformed. Yet it was my elementary and high school teachers—both men and women—and especially my mother, who were my role models and who had given me the belief that I could achieve anything I set out to do. Many of my teachers, who had been raised in the rural and secluded communities of Coal River, had overcome financial hardships and had perservered to secure college educations and become teachers. They were strong and smart and found a way to get an education during tough economic times.

I am grateful for the strong work ethic of the professional teachers, including my sixth grade teacher—my mother—who motivated me to learn and to work diligently during my school years. I was also fortunate to have opportunities made possible by the strong and smart women who were the leaders of the women's movement of the 1960's. This was the decade in my life when I worked full-time to help my husband complete his education, completed my college education and became a high school teacher following in the footsteps of my mother and other educators in my family and in the community of Rock Creek and surrounding communities and with my husband's help managed the family-work issues involved in raising our young daughters.

As a woman, I was fortunate to come in at just the exact time when—to quote Gail Collins--,"The windows were all thrown open by women who were about three seconds older than I was. They did all the suffering, the filing of the suits, the protest, the challenging of employers. I got all the benefits. I stand on their shoulders." I was lucky to have lived in a time period that opened up amazing opportunities so that I could become the first woman to practice law in Mason County, West Virginia; the first woman president of the Ohio Valley Tennis Association; and the first woman to chair the United States Tennis Association's Constitution and Rules Committee.

Through the hardships of my husband's and my completing our college education after marriage with our young daughter and later embarking on three years of legal study with two children in tow to a new career in law and more than 20 years of tennis volunteerism that took me from Rock

Creek to the national arena, I always had the notion with perseverance I could achieve anything I set out to do. This notion to succeed resulted in my being, to the best of my knowledge, the only woman in the history of Marsh Fork High School to become a lawyer. One of the benefits I derived from the accomplishment was to be invited to be the high school commencement speaker in the early 2000's. My mother—also a Marsh Fork High School graduate—had set the model for me—both mother and father—and a "can do" attitude that provided both inspiration and motivation.

Dr. Jim Wills

An up-the-holler country boy who rose from poverty to become a successful radiologist, engineer, and pilot. *By Jim Willis*

I was the youngest of five children—Eugene, Joann, Bob, John, and me. The first four children were well-spaced—according to the plan for a fertile woman of the forties who had no birth control available other than breast feeding. There was an eleven-year gap between my nearest brother and me—I guess I was a bit of a surprise. My mother was Donna nee Williams, my father, Clarence Wills.

Early years were pretty normal for a kid in up-the-holler Rock Creek, except that—having no playmates or siblings my age and two now-old people who worked incessantly as my parents, I was bored much of the time and spent a great portion of my day "looking for something to get into," as they say.

I girded my loins for school, starting in first grade. Kindergarten had just started in those days, but I think my parents had to provide transportation, and I began my career in Mrs. Miller's first grade. The thing I remember most was that it was so easy; there must be a trick lurking somewhere. I never found it.

In second grade, I made friends with Joey Jarrell, Jr. His mother had a college degree and worked outside the home! My mother always said that they were rich; all I knew was that here was a kid with a battery, a nail, and a bulb that he had brought to school for show-and-tell, and he could make it do stuff. Him—a kid. Wow! We became fast friends; he was too short and uncoordinated to play any sports, so academics was his thing. Joey was a part of an academic family, and that seemed to be what I wanted to do, rather than mine coal. We became "oldest and best friends" and stayed that way all through high school and college. We remain friends to this day.

When I was about ten, the Johnsons—desperately poor folks—moved just down the holler. The Johnson family had moved from California. There were nine or ten of them; the woman made a welfare-living by producing children and then being "abandoned" by the father, who sneaked back and lived with them when the coast was clear. No welfare queen she, though; I remember one particularly hard winter when they ran out of coal for the stove and huddled up in the kitchen with quilts covering the doorways to keep heat in, warming themselves by running the electric stove and hoping their power wouldn't be cut off. By the next spring they were pretty desperate. I remember standing in the yard and hearing one of the kids say, "Mommy! I found a quarter!" The quarter was then brought to the mother, who held it up in front of her as if it were the Hope Diamond, wondering out loud if they should buy milk for the baby or buy a bag of beans so everybody could eat.

Like all kids, I was oblivious to their poverty. The Johnson boys and I amused ourselves by running telegraph lines between our homes, the wire gleaned from balls of tangled "shootin' wire"—recovered from the remnants of dynamiting coal seams. We patiently untangled the ten-foot lengths, skinned them, twisted the bare ends together, and had reasonably reliable telegraph between us for several years. Then we discovered that, if we used speakers instead of homemade telegraph instruments, we could shout into one and be heard on the other end, so it became our erstwhile telephone line.

Then they moved away; I've not heard from the Johnsons since.

Joey and I mentored each other through grade school, always friendly competitors—doing projects for Science Fair, making "shockers" out of car ignition coils, and exploring the chemistry of things that exploded. I made friends with another fellow, Deward Scott, and we learned of motorcycles, girls, and—as usual—things that exploded—a recurring theme, you see. We lost our virginity on the same night on the same bed, although not at the same time—in his recently—deceased grandmother's house, so as you see, we were good friends. (Unfortunately, when the mine at Montcoal exploded in 2010, he was one of the first they pulled out).

Inexpensive dirt bikes were just coming over from Japan, and I managed to talk my father into allowing me to buy one. It transformed my world. Although my Suzuki 90 was tremendously underpowered, it meant I didn't have to walk or ride a bicycle to get where I was going and opened up the hundreds of miles of steep (jeep) mountain trails.

My high school was a tremendous letdown. My grade school (Mt. View Elementary) was a marvel of efficiency and discipline; Joey and I tested between 96th and 99th percentile nationwide on standardized achievement tests; this dropped to 50th percentile by the time we graduated Marsh Fork High. Discipline was nonexistent; my buddies and I traveled together for mutual protection from the older boys, who would line up in the hallway at noon, punching underclassmen in the shoulders as they passed. I was happy to get out of there.

College was quite a culture shock. My high school class graduated 58, incoming freshman class at WVU was nearly 5,000. I was dazzled but delighted by the change, and immediately plugged into the system. I had won a scholarship from Armco Steel, which owned a local mine near my high school, and I spent my summers working in the mines to make money for fall terms. I enrolled in the mining engineering curriculum at WVU; my future was set.

What a jar that turned out to be! The minimal effort high school had required netted me "C's" the first year and "F's" the second year as I got into the more advanced classes in my major. My high school mathematics left me completely unprepared—firstly, for the level of difficulty, secondly—and more importantly—the level of work required.

By the end of the first semester of my sophomore year, I was in a bad place. My nearly worn-out car required constant repair, attention and expense, and both Joey—now my roommate—and I were flunking out. It was an extremely depressing and guilt-ridden time, and I felt especially guilty about my father, who had expected so much from me. Many of his sisters' sons had become doctors; he'd had the same hopes for my eldest brother, who had dashed them in a flurry of drinking, gambling, and general carousing—terminating in a disfiguring drunken auto wreck. Gene had subsequently joined the service and announced his exit from college via a letter from an army base in Germany; my father was deeply wounded.

One cold December night, Joey and I had a long, sobering talk until about 4 a.m. about our sad state of affairs. We decided we had to "shit or get off the pot," as they say. He decided to quit school; I thought about my old Dad—especially about how old he was and that I was his last hope, and I just couldn't quit. I just couldn't do it. I had to make something of myself. The next morning I looked out the window at the WVU Medical Center in the distance and decided that, with my grades, the toughest thing I could do would be to get into med school.

And that is how the decision was made. Just like that. I quit engineering and enrolled in the biology curriculum.

Now I had a goal. I worked hard; I organized my time; I studied between classes. My grades went up; I eliminated distractions. My girlfriend and I scheduled our time together, but miraculously I had more time than ever—and when I was off, I was really off because I knew everything had been taken care of ahead of time. I was working harder than ever, but my stress level was almost non-existent. I don't remember a happier time. What a lesson in discipline!

Medical school came and went. The intensity was very high; many coped via depression and anxiety, but—Hillbilly to the core—I coped through anger, and because I never let "them" get the better of me, I became sort of counselor to my classmates. None had much experience beyond the classroom; I had worked as a surveyor and coal miner, rode motorcycles (horrors!), built off-road buggies from cast-off Volkswagens, and was a generally irascible fellow who would tell the egghead professor exactly what I thought. Probably not that smart, but I did survive the process.

My father died during my last year of medical school, so he never saw me graduate. I had also been restoring his mother's mantel clock, finishing it two days before he died, so he never saw that, either. It sets on my own mantel now and keeps good time. He died 35 years ago; hardly a day passes that I don't think of him.

Then came a four-year residency in Radiology. I had married between my second and third year of med school. We lived in a trailer, but it was nice and clean, in a small mobile-home park that catered exclusively to med students, and we were extremely happy. Since I was small, I had been fascinated by flying; during that time I built an ultralight airplane and powered it with a cast-off snowmobile engine. I have since graduated to "real" airplanes, and fly my 1962 Cessna on long trips.

The perennial student, after only ten years of private practice, I became bored and decided to finish my engineering education. Always an electronics enthusiast, I closed my medical practice in 1995 and enrolled at West Virginia Tech in electrical engineering. During that time, I became involved in a robotics competition, and our school won the grand prize in head-to-head completion with regional colleges, including our "parent" school, West Virginia University. They were not amused.

There's not much else to tell. I have two wonderful sons, one of whom is a computer programmer in Washington State, and a second who is studying accounting at a local university. I have officially retired, but I keep my "hand in" by reading X-rays for a cancer clinic in West Virginia via the Internet. I live on ten acres in Farmville, Virginia, and spend my time flying, reading X-rays, general tinkering, and working on aircraft.

David Hamilton Webb
by David Hamilton Webb

My sister's (Bobbie Kay Webb Farley) chapter on Rock Creek captured the essentials about our family's arrival and our growing up in Rock Creek. I appreciate her contribution, which saved me a lot of effort. For that and for many other things, I am grateful to my older sister.

In fact, because Bobbie was such a good older sister, I have remarked that the filial position of siblings should begin with an older sister—especially if they could be like Bobbie.

Bobbie captured the essence of our Mother, a person who accomplished a lot without ever giving the impression of having suffered through life. Inez Bone Webb truly led "a life well and fully lived." Special thanks to our relatives on both sides of the family for the support we received from them.

I am grateful that men who worked in the mines all day found the time to be Little League baseball coaches and Boy Scout leaders. Thank you, Jim Salters, Jimmy Vaughn, and others. Thanks, too, for the people who bought Grit papers from me and our brother Randall (God rest his soul), and who gave us rides to events when Mom could not be in two places at once.

We could roam Rock Creek all day in the summer, and Mom knew we were safe—even if she did not know exactly where we were at all times. Countless hours were spent in the swimming hole behind the Richard Henderson home, playing basketball or badminton at Mt. View School, and pitching horseshoes. We did things then that kids do not think of today—playing marbles, cowboys and Indians (where are you Larry Bartram and Sonny Scarboro?) and other lost activities. Bobbie mentioned board games, and those are ancient history, too.

Bobbie was on point about the teaching professionals in Rock Creek, as well as those in our family. These folks instilled the value of education. Although Bobbie headed toward Marshall University for her higher education, I majored in civil engineering at West Virginia University, after which I graduated from the WVU College of Law. I was an editor on the law review and received an award as the "outstanding editor."

After law school at WVU in 1971, I earned a Masters of Law in environmental law at George Washington University on a Corps of Engineers fellowship. This expanded education took my wife, Mary Kaye Staggers, and me to Mobile, Alabama, where I was legal counsel to the District Engineer. The civil engineering degree meshed well with the law degree during my tenure with the Corps of Engineers. I received the Corps "District Outstanding Employee Award" for my creation of a Litigation Management Unit to handle complex litigation. I presented a paper on the idea in Chicago, and the Navy borrowed the concept for litigation against the military branch.

In a break from my service with the Corps, Mary Kaye and I spent nearly a year in Europe traveling and freelancing as our own travel guides, and we have traveled a good bit since then. On two separate occasions, Randall and I spent two weeks riding motorcycles in the Rockies—from Montana to Arizona and from Kansas to Death Valley.

Family politics brought us back to West Virginia. We helped Mary Kaye's brother win a seat in the U.S. House of Representatives, and we decided to put down roots in Mineral County. I served in the Prosecuting Attorney's office handling grand juries, juvenile cases, misdemeanor cases, and trial work. (Interestingly, one fellow whom I prosecuted for murder and who went to prison and another who served time on a sex offense charge came to me for legal service after being released from prison). Afterward, I developed a private practice, from which I retired in 2012. In 2014, when the assistant prosecuting attorney became very ill, the Prosecutor called me out of retirement for a few months to take over the caseload.

The aforementioned individuals are, but a few, who come to mind when I think of Rock Creek individuals. Dr. Jim Wills became a doctor who treated cancer patients and practiced in Beckley. Bobbie Farley's brother, David Webb, became an attorney, and Ed Scarbro was a highly decorated soldier in World War II. Read Bobbie Farley's life story, *"Rock Creek—Looking Back and Forward: A Woman's Perspective."* These individuals were all from tiny Rock Creek. Stories like these could be repeated many times by young people raised in other hills, hollers, and hamlets along Coal River—all graduates of Marsh Fork High School.

Chapter photo: DeeAnne and me in front of the Rock Creek Post Office.

16

COAL TOWNS

During World War II and into the mid-1950s, coal mines located on Coal River were operating full blast—they employed hundreds of men and ran three shifts per day. The economy was booming and Whitesville, our only town of any size, was bustling with business. At Christmastime —as a small boy—the town looked to me the way Disney World must look to a kid today. Christmas lights were strung across the street, (there was only one, Boone) store windows were decorated, and shoppers crowded both sides of the street forcing them to elbow their way to their next destination.

Miners were paid twice per month and many of them spent their paychecks within a week. Beer joints were crowded with miners on weekends as they celebrated the end of yet another week of hard labor. There were three or four beer joints in Whitesville, going up Coal River, there was one at Edwight, Sundial, Jack's Place at Naoma, Mt. View Tavern at Rock Creek, and The Sandlick Tavern, which was located "up the way" from Arnett. It was common practice for celebrants to "have a few" at each establishment. Road races and car wrecks were a common occurrence on payday weekends and, of course, fights were a very popular sport when the conditions were right. Kay's uncle, Maurice Flowers, told a story about driving up Coal River with some other guys when they decided they would go to The Mt. View Tavern and listen to the Joe Louis boxing match on the radio. (They obviously did not have a radio in their 1930s or 1940s model car.) Maurice said that as he walked through the front door of the tavern Bob Wills and His Texas Playboys were cranking out "San Antonio Rose" at full volume on the jukebox. Just as soon as he cleared the door, a pistol shot was fired into the wall directly above the door. Maurice said he kept right on walking through the joint, into the kitchen, and straight out the back door.

Hundreds of miners were employed at mines located at Edwight, Stickney, Montcoal, Birchton, Blue Pennant, Red Dragon (below Whitesville) and Eunice. Rick Bradford still lives in his family home at Edwight and gave me the following "guesstimates." He estimates Edwight had approximately 600 residents in its heyday. Rick says that only 6 people live in what is left of Edwight, Hazy and Shumate Branch. Stickney had a population of 450 but only about 35 people live there today. He estimates Montcoal had 600 residents in the "golden years," but only one person lives there today. I spoke with Jim Peters (known as James in his '56 Marsh Fork High School class) about his hometown of Birchton. He said approximately 200 people lived in Birchton during the 40s and early 50s. Four families have held steadfastly in what is left. I was surprised to hear this as the only homes I remembered were along Route 3 with the river, railroad and mountain only allowing for a dozen or so homes. Jim said there were 20 homes including those across the river accessible only by a swinging bridge and four homes up the holler behind the Jack Cooper home. He said some of the homes had as many as 7 or 8 kids. Jim is a pretty good source as he was the newsboy for his neighborhood.

The communities in which the mines were located were commonly referred to as "coal camps," a name probably derived from the days when miners had to literally camp in tents in order to get work. Eventually, coal companies built housing for their employees and their families. A typical house usually consisted of two bedrooms, a living room, dining room, a kitchen and "a path." My sister, Barbara, and her husband, Bill, were married in 1946, and had to wait several months for a house. They lived with Bill's parents in Edwight until a house finally became available, it was probably the worst one in the "camp" as it was located in "Stringtown," directly in front of the coal tipple—the coal processing plant, which operated 24-7. The noise was deafening--coal dust persistently entered the house in spite of all efforts to keep cracks sealed. Stringtown was named because all the houses were built in straight lines on both sides of the street.

For the most part, Coal Camps were usually self-contained. Each had its own store which usually sold anything the miner's family might need. The store was owned by the coal company and was known as "The Company Store." Prices were usually higher than what "outside" stores charged, but miners' families could draw advances on their paycheck by "drawing scrip," i.e., using brass coins that could be spent only at the company store. It was common for some miners to never receive a check on payday because either they or their family members had already depleted their would-be earnings by drawing scrip. When Kentuckian Merle Travis wrote the hit song "Sixteen Tons" later recorded by Tennessee Ernie Ford he got the line "I owe my soul to the company store" from a saying his dad used whenever someone asked how he was doing. Travis' dad would reply, "I have to keep working, 'cause I owe my soul to the company store." It was an obvious referral to the debt he owed the store, which had probably been incurred by cutting scrip.

Coal companies usually rented space in their company store buildings to the U.S. Postal Service to house the Post Office. My dad told a story that dated back to his early days of mining in the 1920's when catalogs from Sears and Roebuck were delivered to the post office. The company had one of their employees drive a horse and wagon to the back of the post office, throw all the catalogs onto the wagon, and haul them to the dump where they would be burned. It wasn't enough to make a profit off the backs of hard-working miners working in deplorably dangerous conditions, greedy coal operators also tried to squeeze every nickel from the men by controlling where their families spent their money.

Rick Bradford graduated Marsh Fork High School in '61 and remains steadfast in his family's home at Edwight refusing to be intimidated by the coal company that gobbled up most of the privately owned homes.

Rick has written several books on Edwight, Hazy and Coal river. In his 2008 book EDWIGHT NEAR THE MOUTH OF HAZY he does a good job telling what the area was like before coal died. Rick did a superb job researching the history of the Edwight camp and Hazy. He has gone through many sources to list the names of miners killed in the Edwight mine.

The deaths are as follows: December 21, 1920--John Peters, a Russian immigrant died in a slate fall; April 8, 1926--Hilliard Raines died in a slate fall; November 1, 1927--Lee Hill and John Hitchcock cause of death was slate fall; April 28, 1924--John Lilly was killed by a falling "Kettlkebotom," a petrified stump; November 1, 1927--Lee Hill and John Hitchcock in a slate fall; December 29, 1928--Willie Williams and Tom McNee in a slate fall; December 27, 1929--February 27, 1927--William King, slate fall; July 31, 1929--Frank Strother in a slate fall; August 16 1929--Robert More in a slate fall; October 16-- 1929--Howard Carlisle in a slate fall; September 15, 1030--Charley Stanley was electrocuted; December 20 1930 Arthur Jarrell in a slate fall; September 2, 1930--Paul Jone was crushed by slate; Winter of 1929--Earl Tucker, preacher of the gospel was killed by a falling rock; January 27, 1920--Charles Frederick Perry in a slate fall; January 27 1930--Ashby Manuel, slate fall; December 27, 193--Creed Adams was electrocuted; July 11 1932 Pete Simpson electrocuted; June 22, 1935--Lenox Robertson died from" maceration, or softening of the skull." ; June 20, 1941--William Cheek from a heart attack; October 31, 1941--Eddie Tucker in a slate fall; December 26, 1941--Woodrow way in a slate fall; February 11, 1942--Curtis Jenkins no cause of death; June 27, 1942--Ernest Smith, no cause of death; July 16, 1942--Clarence Miller, no cause of death; March 16, 1942--Guy Wright, no cause of death; November 23, 1943--Alpha McMillon, no cause of death; December 15--Tommy Hill from a slate fall; June 30, 1945--Criss George; July 16 1945--Arnett Miller; August 22, 1945--Lee Clay; August 11, 1946--Tommy Lockhart; October 15, 1945--Jack Frost, an Englishman: June 15, 1947--Russell Payne when he became entangled in a conveyor belt: August 12, 1947--Van Williams in a slate fall; August 9, 1948--JohnWinbush crushed by equipment; June 20, 1948--Steve Stockton in a slate fall; January 20, 1949--Cecil Peters' head was crushed by a rock rolling off a feeder belt; February 16, 1949--Ern Wills was scalded to death by a boiler explosion; January 17,

1950--Arnold Ash in a slate fall: May 3, 1950--Kelly Combs in a slate fall; August 5, 1950--Willie Harmonand and Leonard "Cookie" Bartrum were electrocuted (I remember this happening when I was 12 years old); August 11, 1952 Alva Robertswas crushed by a shuttle car; October 10, 1952--Alva Roberts was crushed by a shuttle car; October 10, 1952--Ed Jenkins crushed by a shuttle car on his last day on what was to be his last day working in the mine: April 30, 1953--Tommy Holly fractured skull: November 26, 1953--Kyle Jarrell; April 28, 1955--Kermit Webb was killed when caught between a shuttle car and mine wall (read about how this affected his family in Bobbie Webb Farley's chapter); July 16, 1956--Lester Price was run over by a mine motor.

At noon, November 26, 1958 the whistle at the Edwight blew for the very last time putting a skeleton crew of 76 men out of work. The few families that were left scattered followed those before them to northern cities seeking work. Raleigh-Wyoming Mining Company awarded dismantling mine machinery and equipment to the Joe Fish Company. Dexter Doss was working for Fish junking the number one mine. He was standing on the back of a steel-bedded truck when it accidentally backed into a live trolley car killing Doss instantly. I was in the Rock Creek Post Office when Buddy Richmond came in and announced Doss' death.

As stated earlier, larger coal camps were mostly self-contained. Some had restaurants, movie theaters, barber shops, beauty parlors and pool rooms. The Montcoal mine (owned by The Colcord family—and later by Armco Steel), actually had a YMCA, the first in Raleigh County.

My friend, John Vergis, was raised at Edwight and graduated Marsh Fork High School, class of 1952. I hitched many rides with John when we both attended Beckley College as he commuted from his home at Naoma. I was always glad to see him and his '56 Chevy coming up the road.

John wrote an account of having been raised in a coal town entitled, *I Remember a Small Coal Mining Town in Southern West Virginia*. He graciously consented to allow me to include it in this book (Chapter 17). This story also appeared in the Spring, 1993, issue of *Golden Seal Magazine*. I chose to include John's story in this book so that younger generations could get an understanding what a coal mining town was like in the glory days.

Eunice coal camp houses at the height of coal production. This picture was probably taken during the early-mid 1940s. Photo provided by Rick Bradford.

Chapter photo: My father-in-law, Damon Jones, at work in Van, West Virginia coal mine. Circa late 1930's.

I REMEMBER A SMALL COAL MINING TOWN IN SOUTHERN WEST VIRGINIA

by Johnny M. Vergis

As I sit here in Shreveport, LA, fingering through my coin box, what are these strange coins with a small hole in them? Let's see! I remember now! This stuff called scrip was a private currency issued by coal companies as wages to West Virginia coal miners. The inscription reads, "Raleigh-Wyoming Mining Company." These ugly pieces of metal could buy anything at the company store. You name it. If you wanted a fountain coke, clothing, toys, or to fill up the family car with gasoline, it could be done with this medium of exchange.

As I stare at this handful of scrip, my mind wanders back through the years and I can see myself descending through clouds over my beloved state of West Virginia. I land on a mountain overlooking a small town below and clearly recognize my boyhood home. I remember climbing this mountain many times as a youngster. Most people probably don't know what we call the huge rock on the very top of this mountain. I really don't know how its name originated, but for history's sake, we called it Turkey Rock. Look down there, it looks like ants crawling through town. No, they are coal miners walking to and fro between the bathhouse and company store. What a bustling and booming town! With this much activity going on, the setting must be sometime in the 1940s.

I don't know the mine superintendent's name, but a fellow by the name of T. S. Ray was the superintendent of operations here in 1920 (p. 36, Vol. 17, No. 2 *Golden Seal Magazine*, Summer 1991). The name of the town? Oh yes, I am looking at Edwight, West Virginia, located just off State Highway 3, approximately seven miles south of Whitesville. Let's drop down and take a closer look at the intersection of State Highway 3 and a dirt road that leads across a steel girder bridge into the town. But first, what are those two business establishments on either side of the intersection? One is a gas station with a large oval sign that reads "Esso." Look at those gas pumps where the gas floats to the top enclosed in a glass container. I remember now, this is the garage owned and operated by Clyde Montgomery, whose house is built on the back of the business. On the other side of the business is The Coffee Pot Café, which will become a teenage hangout in later years.

As cars run across the wooden planks that run the length of the bridge, they cause a rumbling and clapping noise. Look below, that is Coal River. The water is greenish and clear except where Hazy Creek meets The Big Coal River. Here the water becomes black as a result of the coal dust being washed off the coal at the tipple. The tipple is located at the base of the mountain and is the final destination of the coal before it is loaded into railroad cars. I used to lean over that bridge and spit between my teeth. Look there on the side of the mountain. That repugnant smelling blue smoke is coming from slate, a discard of coal that has ignited after years of exposure. At night the slate produces a simmering glow and will burn uncontrolled for years to come.

The largest building in town is the company store. It is constructed of red brick and is surrounded on three sides by a wooden porch, with intermittent wooden steps. My favorite part of the store is on the south end where you could get honest to goodness fountain cokes and comic books. My choices are cherry coke and Superman comics. The other end of the store houses the offices where the miners go inside to the teller's window and draw scrip, which is debited against their future wages. The miner's lament: "Saint Peter, don't call me 'cause I can't go, I own my soul to the company store," was a very popular song with miners in the 1950s.

The man who works in the office and always wears a hat and smokes a cigar is called "Big Tom." Those other two clerks are Arthur "Shorty" Jarrell, brother to the town barber, and Reginald Deitz, father of Gene and Bob, two of my playmates. To your right is another teller-like window where you could buy stamps for your letters. Yes, Edwight has a post office to locate eligible candidates. As you leave this office and enter the middle door on the outside of the store, you go past the soda fountain on the right. Straight ahead are steps that lead up to the store offices. On the lower floor there are meat, clothing, toys and many articles for sale. In the dry goods section is a lady named Ruth Foster, and in the meat department is Mr. Sharp, the butcher. The store manager is Aubrey Ward, whose son, Sonny, is one of my playmates.

The bathhouse is the responsibility of Ray "Shorty" Williams, the father of two of my friends, Billy and Harry. As I help Billy assist his father in cleaning up the bathhouse, I notice the strangest thing. The miners' clothes and personal belongings are hanging on the ceiling, hoisted by a chain and secured by a lock. I have never seen anything like that before, but everyone else thinks it is normal and no big deal. I still think it looks strange.

Across the street from the company store is the town poolroom operated by Claude Robinson and later, by Kenneth Eskins and Bill Parsons. Some form of segregation is practiced because there is a center island dividing the pool room into two sections, one for the "whites" and one for the "colored" folks. This is a busy place, but when they try to get into the hamburger business, they fail miserably. The hamburgers are too small! The best hamburgers still come from "Mike's Place," a successful privately owned restaurant and beer joint.

On one end of the poolroom building is the town doctor's office. Dr. Ford, our doctor, will later move to Beckley to continue his practice. In later years a new doctor's office made of cinder block will be built just across the street and will be operated by kindly Dr. John D. Lee, ably assisted by Mary Brown.

In addition to playing poker and pool, the miners have another pastime, playing baseball. On the mound today is an awesome left hander, Glenn Rutledge, a giant of a man, whose stare alone causes many a batter to tremble. Catching for Glenn is the versatile and talkative Don Lamb, whose chatter can unnerve any batter, especially when combined with Glenn's stare. Johnny Holley's premature gray hair masquerades his agility and responsiveness as he quickly turns a double play to retire the side. Assisting him is Bill Smith, also the manager who easily makes each play as if there's nothing to it. Other outstanding players are Bunny Hudson and Eddie "Jack" Soulsby.

The main street, a dirt road with potholes from each new rain, runs parallel to Coal River. Both sides of the streets are lined with wooden sidewalks, company houses and a few business establishments not owned by the coal company. The homes, wood frame houses, are painted either dull gray or white. Some of the porches are screened and generally include a squeaky wooden slat swing. Some have picket or chain link fences. An occasional white-washed fence or tree brightens the homes and represents the occupants' attempts to personalize their surroundings. A couple of water pumps located at strategic locations fill metal buckets with cool drinking water. Grab the long metal handle and pump up and down and before long you will have water flowing. Look at that boy with his hand and mouth cupped over the spout, slurping and pumping at the same rate of speed. Notice how he wipes his hands on his bib overalls when he's finished.

Some of the business establishments include the town barber, Orville Jarrell, who gave me my first haircut. Each time I climb up in the big barber chair located under an old black greasy overhead fan, Orville has to put a slat board across the arms of the chair so I will sit high enough for him to cut my hair. I don't mind Orville using scissors but I dread the hand-held metal clippers. For every hair that is clipped there are probably a dozen pulled out, or so it feels. There are always several active and retired miners sitting around spinning tales. I see "Old Tom" Foster is here today. I believe he has the scruffiest beard I have ever seen. Orville applies hot steamy towels to his beard and asks if the towels are too hot. "No, not at all," is the reply. It looks as the man's face is on fire. The shave sounds like someone scraping their fingernails across sandpaper.

Other business establishments are a shoe repair shop owned by George Harasohartis, a Greek immigrant, whose last name was shortened to Hartis. Adjacent to the shoe repair shop is a grocery store owned first by Carl Daniel and later by Johnny Price. That white bus also belongs to Mr. Price. It is used to pick up church goers from up and down the road to take them to his church located at Pettus. There is also a restaurant, pool hall and beer joint owned by another Greek immigrant, Mike Vergis. Mike's doesn't have a television but there are fist fights every Saturday night.

There are also two boarding houses one on the upper end of town run by Lottie Spencer, and one run by Nannie Jarrell, a small elderly lady. I occasionally help her by going out to the hen house to get her eggs. An earlier operator of the boarding house was Mrs. "Ma" Stewart, and the last will be Floda Mae Erwin.

Besides automobiles, other modes of transportation seen on the main street are horses, mules and horse drawn wagons. I once witnessed an individual riding by on a cow, saddle and all.

We must not forget the elementary school, a red brick four-room building with a rocky playground. Either by design or because of limited space, the third and fourth grades and the fifth and sixth are combined. My first grade teacher is a petite and understanding lady named Mrs. Jarrell. I can still picture myself standing in the doorway of the classroom bawling and crying as my Mother handed me over to her. Some of the other teachers are Vada Webb, Rosabelle Tabor and Inez Bone. At the front of each classroom is a picture of George Washington. I don't know why but the father of our country will disappear from his place of prominence. Every morning we line up in columns outside of the school and place our right hand over our hearts to recite the Pledge of Allegiance. A few years later when we would say, "to the flag," we would extend our hand toward the flag and complete the pledge. This was probably later changed to eliminate the motion because we wanted to get away from resembling Hitler's *Seig Heil* salute. Our principal, Clint Richmond, is a kind and wonderful man. One morning, he told me that I'd had eggs for breakfast, which amazed me. "How do you know?" I asked. He replied, "Because you still have some on your mouth." One day soon, Mr. Richmond will go off to "The Big One," World War II.

Today, April 12, 1945. The people of Edwight are somber. Most just walk around shaking their heads in disbelief. How will this tragedy affect America and the rest of the world? Just a few moments ago it was announced that Franklin Delano Roosevelt, our president, had passed away at his Warm Springs, Georgia spa, of a cerebral hemorrhage. Mike Vergis closed his restaurant, packed his family into his car, and just quietly drove around, still in disbelief of this day's momentous tragedy.

If President Roosevelt could have lived six months longer, he would have known why people are firing pistols and rifles into the air today. People everywhere are shouting, "At last, at last!" And so it is, the war is over! Later, some of our brave boys would come home, and some wouldn't, including my grade school principal and idol, Clint Richmond. I really liked and will never forget Mr. Richmond.

Going to the theater on Saturday nights is a big thrill, if not a dangerous thing to do. It isn't uncommon after the movie starts to get hit in the back of the head with a marble or some other object. One night some kid threw some .22 caliber bullets into the pot-belly Burnside stove. The western movie that night really came alive. The manager of the theater who is also the train station manager, is an elderly gentleman, Mr. Showen. He has grabbed many a kid by the ear and thrown him out of the theater—one in particular I remember. Most of the movies shown are westerns and in some ways they depict the brawling life of some of the miners. The stars of the day are Gene Autry, Roy Rogers, Wild Bill Eilliot, Sunset Carson, Charles Starrett, Hopalong Cassidy, Al "Lash" Larue, Tex Ritter and my favorite, Johnny Mack Brown.

We also entertain ourselves by playing baseball on various leagues or participating in the Boy Scouts. A special tribute should go to Bill Smith, our scoutmaster and friend, who in addition to securing proceeds from hot dog sales, must have gotten donations from other sources. As a result, we are well-equipped with army tents, backpacks cooking utensils, etc. and sometimes we are even able to go on camping trips and to a summer camp at Shanklin's Ferry. Because of Bill Smith, our lives have been much enriched. One of our scouts, Tommy Soulsby, even represented us at the Boy Scout Jamboree at Valley Forge, PA. The only mistake I ever knew Bill Smith to make was when he told me, "John, you were born here and will die here." Bill didn't know that Edwight would die first. Other sporting events include tackle football (without benefit of protective gear) and boxing. When someone shows up with a football, that's all it takes to get a mean game of football started. Participation in this gladiator sport must have had some benefit as Edwhuinjight will place three seniors, Bill Lamb, Tommy Soulsby, and Johnny Vergis on the Raleigh County Championship Football Team in 1951. This will be Marsh Fork's first championship with no county losses.

As for boxing, Harry Williams is best known for this sport. Harry and I go at it like two wild men. There must be a less painful way to work off steam. Man, that Harry can hit! As Harry is known as the boxer in town, King "Boy" Pettry is the muscleman of the town. With his well displayed physique, I suspect he sent off for the Charles Atlas muscle building course that appears on the back page of the comic books.

On Sundays, you can hear the church bell ringing. As a small child I was allowed, along with other children, to grab the rope and swing up and down on it to ring the bell, announcing time to go to Sunday school and church. Our place of worship was a pretty little wooden Presbyterian church in the shape of a rectangle with a pitched roof and a steeple on the front end. It is located behind and just to the right of the company store and you have to cross a small wooden bridge over Hazy Creek to get to it. To section off individual Sunday school classes they have to pull curtains hung on a wire. The system works well if the teacher next to you doesn't talk too loudly. One of our Sunday school teachers is Mr. Sharp, the company store butcher. The minister of the church is Davidena McNair, a wonderful lady. Funeral services are held in the church but the only one I can recall was for a German immigrant, Carl Biegan, who worked for Mike Vergis. He died with no known family, and is buried in an unmarked grave in Naoma.

As I look over the town I see some of the people that I know. That's Tommy Holley, one of the best baseball players on the Edwight team. Coming down the road on a horse is a black man with a big smile that you can see for a mile away. It can be no other than John Winbush. Little do

I know that these two people, along with numerous others, will become fatalities in the Edwight mine. I don't know how John Winbush will be killed but Tommy Holley will lose his life on a runaway motor car.

My earliest recollection of a fatality was that of a Mr. Kersey who was electrocuted when he touched a live trolley wire. I never met the man, but he was the father of my first playmates, Kenneth, Franklin and Scotty. This tragedy has left Mrs. Kersey with the responsibility of raising three young sons and a daughter. I am sure her oldest son serving in the Marines and two grown daughters will help with her financial obligations. Hats off to a gutsy woman!

Even if you don't become a mine fatality you can still suffer a very serious injury. Take the case of the Lee boys, the sons of the town doctor, John D. Lee. Both went into the mines, one came out minus a leg and the other became paralyzed from the waist down. See that man walking on the wooden sidewalk and stopping to get his breath? Being inquisitive, I learned for the first time what asthma is, and why Jim Adkins is always wheezing, coughing, and having difficulty getting his breath. Working in a coal mine is very hard and dangerous work. Edward Soulsby, the father of my closest childhood friend, Tommy, is so fatigued after coming in from work that he often lies on his back porch without taking his work clothes off. That fellow there coming in from the mine, stooped over and holding his metal dinner bucket with both hands in the small of his back is Bill Walker. Hard work has apparently taken its toll on him as well.

On a happier occasion, Mike Vergis is being presented with a copy of the United Mine Workers of America charter, which established local union No. 6815 at Edwight on December 22, 1933. The charter is showing Mike as he appeared in 1933 and 1947. The plaque reads, "Presented to Mike Vergis in appreciation of his great and unselfish service in the organization of local #6815 UMWA." It is signed by President Charles Williams, vice President Clarence Miller, Recorder-Secretary Monroe Johnson, financial Secretary James Blair and Treasurer, Benny Turner. Although it is not disclosed on the plaque, it is now known that Mike allowed the miners to secretly meet in the back room of his restaurant to organize and conduct business that would eventually lead to membership in the UMWA.

Looking down the street from inside Mike's restaurant, I see Jackie

Pettry riding by on his horse. As he trots by someone yells out, "Hi Yo Silver!" Jackie responds by saying, "You little hellion," and pursues the young lad on horseback. Today, this young culprit will be dressed down and learn respect for others, and he is going to especially learn that Mr. Pettry is very sensitive to being associated with The Lone Ranger. I personally don't yell out unless I am hidden behind a building.

Clink, clink! The sound of my scrip falling on the floor has just awakened me from my dream. For a fleeting moment, I thought I was back in the mountains of West Virginia, in the small town of Edwight, which is no longer on most maps. Gosh, those boyhood days were wonderful and I shall never forget them.

About the Author

Johnny M. Vergis was born in one of the front upper rooms of the Central Lunch Café, better known as "Mike's Place," in Edwight, West Virginia. He graduated Marsh Fork High School in the class of 1952. Upon graduation, John enlisted in The U.S. Air Force attaining the rank of Staff Sergeant. After his discharge he returned to Edwight for a few short months when friends beckoned him to Cleveland, Ohio.

John worked at The Republic Steel and Jones and Laughlin Steel Mills. He then returned to the Coal River area and daily commuted from Naoma to Beckley College. After receiving an Associate in Arts Degree, he returned to Cleveland for a short period of time and, upon a dare, headed for Tuscon, Arizona where he entered The University of Arizona. He received his Bachelor of Arts Degree, then entered and graduated from Officer's Training School at Lackland Air Force Base in San Antonio, Texas. John was then commissioned a Second Lieutenant and spent the next twenty-six years in the Air Force as an Administrative Officer, Special Agent and Commander in the Office of Special Investigations (OSI).

While assigned to OSI he was given the opportunity to attend graduate school and attain a Master of Education Degree from Louisiana State University, Baton Rouge. The highlight of John's career was when he was chosen to command all of the OSI units in Italy which occurred during the height of terrorism by the Red Brigades. He was personally held responsible for the protection of U.S. Air Force Generals assigned there. He retired from the military service as a Lieutenant Colonel in 1989, and now makes his home in Bossier City, Louisiana with his wife, JoElla Dormeyer, and three sons, Michael, Joseph, and Nick.

Chapter photo: Edwight Bridge, 1940's. Photo taken by Rick Bradford.

18

COALFIELD BASEBALL

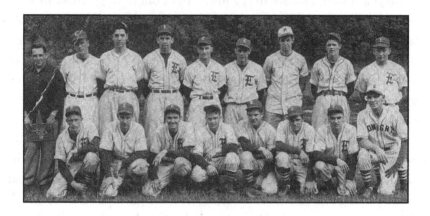

Most coal mining companies had their own company store, doctor's office, movie theater, barber and beauty shops, pool room, boarding house and beer joint. As stated previously, the Montcoal Mine community had the first YMCA in Raleigh County. Each "camp" was pretty much self-contained, with the unspoken philosophy that "if it wasn't there, you did not need it!" Coal camps could contain 100 or more "company houses" built by the company to rent to their workers.

Baseball is only one of many coal mine camp memories. During the 1930s, 1940s, and 1950s most coal mining companies fielded a baseball team. Mine superintendents were very competitive, they tried to attract the best players that they could to their team by offering good players a cushy job, overtime work, as well as other benefits if they would leave the "mine team" they were playing for. Nearly every mine in Raleigh county—as well as the surrounding counties—fielded a team, and the company paid for all team expenses including uniforms and equipment. Games were played on Sunday afternoons and residents of the coal camp—as well as the surrounding communities—turned out for the game. Much excitement centered around the games and attendance increased when the league developed all-star and playoff games. Other than high school games, this was the only sporting event in the area during the days before television.

My wife, Kay, has an uncle, Maynard Daniel, who was a right-handed pitcher. He had an assortment of pitches that included a very effective knuckle ball. While playing for Marsh Fork High School, he once pitched and won both games of a double header.

Maynard went to work in the mines right out of high school in 1950 and went to Seth to talk about joining a mine team there. He was told that he could pitch the following Sunday; if he won he would be paid $50. Maynard won that game and collected the $50 which amounted to a week's pay at his mining job. He played at Seth two years before leaving for Montcoal, the mine owned by Armco Steel. Maynard now regrets that he didn't take his game to a higher level.

Many players in the industrial leagues all over the country could have played major league baseball but they could not afford to take the pay cut. In those days, there was more money to be made by mining coal than in playing baseball. In 1980 when I became principal of Lake Worth High School I met Andy Hansen, a Lake Worth graduate who "went up" and pitched for the Phillies and Giants in the 1940s. He had to work in the Lake Worth Post Office during the off season in order to make ends meet. Harry Perkowski, who pitched for the Eccles mine, played for the Cincinnati Reds but—like Andy—also had to work during the off season. In those days professional baseball players were paid only a pittance compared to the millions of dollars that players earn today.

Larry Cassell, a Marsh Fork High School grad from the class of 1955, was an outstanding athlete and was a star at every sport he played. As a young boy, he recalls being the bat boy for the Edwight team that won the Southern Regional Championship at Oak Hill in 1949. The regular team members were: Don Lamb (catcher), Glen Rutledge (first base), Bill Smith (second base), Dean Jarrell (third base), Ed Soulsby (shortstop), Johnny Cassell (left field), Tommy Holly (center field), and Kenny Larabee (right field). Larry told me that Lamb and Rutledge also pitched, but he couldn't recall the other pitchers' names. Larry remembers the team picking up

Carly Dominion from the Dorothy team at shortstop and Ralph Pauley, their main pitcher for the playoffs. Pauley had pitched for the Prenter Mine team during the regular season. Larry also spoke of future Marsh Fork High School coaches, Virgil Carr and Dewey Romine playing for Montcoal in later years.

On one of the visits with Jeter Barker and Jim White to Big Stone Gap, Virginia for a reunion with some of Jeter's football players, I overheard a conversation among some people saying they'd gone to Emory and Henry. I told them that I'd attended Morris Harvey College, someone in the group said, "We played Morris Harvey in The Tangerine Bowl in 1950." I told them that my high school coach, Dewey Romine, had played for Morris Harvey in that game. Immediately, one of the group blurted out, "We hate him, we hate him!" Needless to say, Morris Harvey had been victorious and Dewey must have had a very good game.

I remember—as a skinny kid of about 15—hitchhiking rides to Edwight so I could watch baseball games. As I recall, both Edwight and Montcoal played on the Edwight field as there wasn't exactly an abundance of level land available to be used for a baseball field on Coal River.. One player who still stands out in my mind is Glenn Rutledge. To me, he looked like a giant who had utility poles for arms. One day I heard Jim Salters—the manger-catcher of the Montcoal team—say, "Rutledge hit one plumb out of Whitesville last Sunday." Montcoal must have played some games at Whitesville Junior High School.

Sadly, coalfield baseball was on its way out when mining declined during the 1950s. In a story that appeared in *The Huntington Herald Dispatch,* Maynard was quoted as saying that technology caused layoffs in the mining industry. He said a mine that had previously employed 350-400 workers could—with new technology—mine the same amount of coal with only 60-70 men.

The coal camps have disappeared. If you want to see what one looked like, you can get a glimpse by visiting the Beckley Exhibition Mine in Beckley, West Virginia. Take a tour of a mine as it looked in the 1920s-1930s, and then walk through a miner's house with "four rooms and a path". That exhibition mine is about all we have left.

David Dee Cantley

Chapter photo: Edwight Baseball Team of Raleigh County, circa 1949. **Front row, left to right:** Bobby Woody, Bill Smith, Dean Jarrell, Azel Farley, Jr., Teddy Lacy, Bill Radar, Tommy Hawley, and unknown. **Back row, left to right:** Eugene Griffith, Glen Rutledge, James Anderson, Kenneth Larabee, Don Lamb, Bob Griner, Tommy Jarrell. Dicky Darby, and Jack Kyle. Photo courtesy of Teddy Lacy. Included with permission from The Register-Herald.

DEDICATION OF MARSH
FORK ELEMENTARY SCHOOL

Marsh Fork Elementary School was built on the site of the farm that was
pioneered by my great, great grandfather, Alexander James Cantley, and
expanded by James Adam "Big Jim" Cantley, my grandfather. My cousin,
Barry Cantley, inherited the farm from his father, Ovet, and sold it to The
Raleigh County Board of Education for the purpose of building the school.

Jim Brown, Superintendent of the Raleigh County School Board,
invited me to speak at the dedication of the school on January 18, 2013.
I felt honored to be invited and I was anxious to speak to the students,
faculty, school board members, and the community at large about the
history of the land on which the school was built. My wife, Kay, and I

drove to West Virginia for the event and missed a paralyzing snow storm in Virginia by only three hours as we drove into Beckley ahead of the storm. It was an honor to meet Senator Joe Manchin who, as governor, had provided partial funding for the school.

Wendy Holdren of *The Register-Herald* covered the event and wrote the following story which appeared in the paper on January 19, 2013:

"Success is not a path you follow, but a trail you blaze," Raleigh County Schools Superintendent Jim Brown said Friday during the dedication ceremony of Marsh Fork Elementary School, the brand new home of the Bulldogs.

Before the ceremony started several students offered tours to visitors showcasing not only the state-of-the-art building, but also the leadership skills already being crafted there.

"The opening of the new Marsh Fork Elementary School is not only a milestone, but is also a journey that has taken many decades," Brown said. "On many levels this new school will set the standard for education in Raleigh County and throughout the entire state of West Virginia."

The school features a smart board in every classroom, a recessed floor in the cafeteria, a beautiful gymnasium and security code locks on every classroom door.

Rick Snuffer, president of the Raleigh County Board of Education, said this is the completion of a five-year journey. "When political differences are put aside, and students are put in mind, great things can be accomplished."

Dave Cantley shared the history of the land with the officials, state leaders, teachers, parents and students who gathered at the dedication ceremony.

Kimberly Gross spoke on behalf of Gov. Earl Ray Tomblin, who said the school has his complete support. "Congratulations for a job well done."

Phil Lewis spoke on behalf of U.S. Sen. Jay Rockefeller, D-W.Va.

"This day has been a long time coming, and I congratulate the entire community for making it a reality."

Lewis also pulled his fourth-grade tour guide, Emma, from the bleachers and asked her to lead everyone in a loud "Let's Go, Bulldogs" chant.

U.S. Sen. Joe Manchin, D-W.Va., said he felt a wave of emotions and memories from being at the previous school while everyone was hoping the Upper Big Branch miners would return safely.

"Our lives and communities are changed forever, but it reinforced my belief in the strength of human beings, especially West Virginians."

He quoted Benjamin Franklin, "Investment in knowledge always pays the best interest."

He asked that all the students realize how lucky they are to be able to attend a state-of-the-art school. "This school has one of the best designs in the country today."

Manchin said the school provides excellent safety features, starting from the front doors, but he promised he will do everything he can to prevent future violence. "We have a responsibility to change that culture. It's been glorified."

He said he believes "preventative resource officers" will be placed at every school in the future. "It just seems to be the most logical thing to do."

Charlotte Hutchens, former superintendent of Raleigh County Schools, said the leaders of the project laughed together, cried together and didn't always see eye to eye, but the dedication ceremony was a bittersweet moment for her. "Everyone always had the students' best interests at heart."

She said she loves the entrance and the security features at the school, but her favorite part is the gym which shows great Bulldog pride.

While many involved in the project say the opening of the school is the completion of a five-year journey the history behind the land on which the school now sits is much richer.

Dave Cantley traveled from Florida to share the history of the land. "My great-great-Grandfather, Alexander Cantley, was given this land by the U.S. government for his services in the War of 1812."

Alexander, or "Eleck," built his cabin near the creek that ran out of the mountain behind us and now runs underground in a huge culvert.

He passed the farm to his son, James Alexander, who was wounded while fighting for his country in the Civil War at the Battle of Cross Keys, Va. He died while traveling homeward with his brother-in-law, Jim Clay, and was buried in an unmarked grave.

While James Alexander was at war his wife, Rebecca Jane Clay, operated the farm along with her kids. Dave said the soldiers would often "steal anything not nailed down."

A rebel officer in charge of a "visiting" group asked Rebecca where her husband was one day, when she told him he said if she would cook a meal for him and his men he would see to it that nothing was touched on the farm.

While she was cooking one of the officers looked at Dave's grandfather, James Adam Cantley, while he was lying in his cradle. The officer asked Rebecca what his name was and she replied, "James." The officer asked what his middle name was and she said James had no middle name.

"Give him my name, Adam," he said.

"That's how my Grandpa became James Adam," Dave said. "My Dad always said, 'If you wanted to make Pa mad, all you had to do was call him Adam.' He would let you know that he didn't appreciate 'being named after no dad-blamed rebel Democrat.'"

Dave's grandpa, James Adam, could not attend school as a young boy. He had to stay home and learn to farm from his grandfather, Alexander.

At his death, he had expanded his 60 acres to more than 200 acres. He grew every fruit and vegetable that would grow in this area. His farm had cattle, sheep, chickens and horses. He built a grist mill down by the river where a large wheel was driven by water to turn the mill stones that ground corn into cornmeal.

One of those mill stones now sets outside Marsh Fork Elementary. It was donated by Dave's brother, Ronald B. Cantley Sr., a former superintendent of Raleigh County Schools.

"Most people in the 1800s heated their homes and cooked with wood fires, but my grandpa discovered a seam of coal near the top of the mountain behind this school."

After the crops were gathered he and his sons would dig enough coal from the mine to last all winter long. He also had an ice house near the river because there were no freezers or electricity back then.

"My grandpa did not go to school, so he could not read or write. However, this did not stop him from being a strong supporter of education. He saw to it that all his children received the education that was available to them at the time."

He was elected chairman of the Marsh Fork School District for twelve years.

"My dad said when you saw Pa wearing his good hat and his little black mare was hitched to the buggy, you knew he was on school board business."

Dave worked 37 years in public education, three years at Marsh Fork High School and 34 years in Palm Beach County, Fla.

"I learned that you don't have to know how to read and write to be a school board member," Dave joked.

After his grandpa's death, the farm was passed to his youngest son, Ovet, and from Ovet to Dave's cousin, Barry.

Barry sold the farm to the school board so Marsh Fork Elementary could be built.

"Grandpa Jim would be happy to know that his farm has become the site of a school."

The Cantley Clan turned out for the dedication of Marsh Fork Elementaty School on January 18, 2013. Here they are pictured around Grandpa Jim's mill stone. **Pictured standing (L-R):** Nelson Lee Cantley, Dr. Michael Lewis, Jerry Cantley, Stephan Cantley, Randy Cantley, Alan Dale Cantley, Kay Cantley. **Seated (L-R):** David Cantley, Susie Cantley Sayre, Danielle Meltz, and Kin Sayre

Aerial view of Marsh Fork Elementary, July 2020. Photo courtesy of Craig Smith.

Chapter photo: Mt. View School circa 1926. The new Marsh Fork Elementary is on the site of the "Big Jim" Cantley farm. Dedicated January 18, 2013.

THE MASSACRE AT
CLOVER BOTTOM

When reading of the struggles between Native Americans and the settlers, one has to ask if there could have been a way they could have lived in harmony. But as the reader will discover later in this essay, the Indians couldn't even live in harmony among themselves. Rival tribes were constantly at war with each other—as if they were honor bound to do so.

May 26, 1637 several Pequot Indians, mostly women and children, were slaughtered. Nearly one hundred Puritans (Englishmen), 90 Mohegan Indians, and 500 Narragansett Indians attacked the village on Mystic River in Connecticut. Wigwams where women and children were holed up were set afire and those who were in them were killed.

Major John Mason said the act against the Indians pleased the English God in Puritan form. This was to be the first of countless battles between the Indians and settlers.

Before the advent of the white man into what is now West Virginia, the Indians found "adventure and excitement" with wars between the Indians of the North (like the Iroquois and the Cherokees) and other Indians of the South. Prior to that time, there were numerous Indian camps and Indian villages along the New River; the main Indian camp was at Crump's Bottom. This spot is now in the Pipestem District of Summers County-- between 1827 and 1871 the area was known as Mercer County.

During the Indian Civil Wars, raids were often made by the Iroquois into southern territory as far south as Alabama and Tennessee. By 1700, all Indian towns and villages along New River were wiped out; New River became a sort of Indian Mason-Dixon Line. By that time, the Indians who had inhabited this area had either moved south or west into Ohio. It appears that if the Indians could not even live in peace among themselves, then the white settlers were doomed.

In 1760, Mitchell Clay was married to Phoebe Belcher in Bedford County, Virginia. My great-grandmother, Rebecca Jane Clay Cantley, was a descendant of Mitchell Clay. Mitchell and Phoebe were to have 14 children—seven boys and seven girls. The sons were Mitchell III, Henry, Charles (the father of Rebecca, my great-grandmother), William, Bartley (who was killed by Indians in 1783), David and Ezekiel (who were captured by Indians). The daughters were Rebecca, (who married Col. George Pearis), Patience (who married George Chapman), Obedience (who married John French—a soldier of the American Revolution), Polly (who married William Stewart), Tabitha (who was killed by the Indians in 1783), Sally Peters and Nannie (who married Joseph Hare).

In April 23, 1774, Lord Dunmore—The Royal Governor of Virginia— granted to Mitchell Clay (assignee of Lt. John Draper) 803 acres of land described as being situated, "On both sides of Bluestone Creek, a branch of New River and called Clover Bottom." It's now in Mercer County, West Virginia. By terms of the grant, Clay was required to take possession of this land within three years, clear a certain amount per year, and then render an amount of ground rent to the British King.

A copy of this grant is on file in the clerk's office of the Mercer County

Courthouse. In payment for this tract of land, Mitchell Clay gave Draper a female slave and her children, as a bill of sale executed to him. Many years later, after the death of Mitchell Clay in 1811, this trade gave rise to two interesting lawsuits. One was by the Negro woman and her children who sued Draper for their freedom which they succeeded in establishing. Then the representatives of Draper sued the executors of Clay and their sureties, recovering a large decree against them. This resulted in the bankruptcy of Captain William Smith and the estate of Mitchell Clay's son-in-law, Colonel George N. Pearis, sureties of Clay's executors.

Mitchell Clay served as a private in the Virginia Militia at the Battle of Point Pleasant in 1774. The battle was between Virginia Militia and the Shawnee and Mingo Indians. Because many people at the time felt that Lord Dunmore, Governor of Virginia, was working with the Indians after the battle to attack the American Militia the Battle of Point Pleasant is considered to be the first battle of the American Revolutionary War. The battle was fought six months before the Battle of Concord and Lexington. Soon after the Battle of Point Pleasant, Lord Dunmore was driven out of Virginia and forced to return to England.

In 1775, Mitchell Clay built his home—a long log cabin with a partition on a high knoll—and moved his family there, becoming the first white settler in Mercer County. For the next eight years, Mitchell Clay occupied himself with living in peace and the tasks of clearing his land, planting crops, and raising livestock.

The Shawnee Indians were reputed to be especially vicious, as there had been several skirmishes between the settlers and them. The Shawnee chief Cornstalk was murdered by the American Militia while on a diplomatic visit at Fort Randolph in 1774. This act was condemned by the settlers, but resulted in the Shawnees going on the warpath. The Shawnees knew that Mitchell Clay had participated in the Battle of Point Pleasant.

In August of 1783, Mitchell had harvested his crops and was on a hunting expedition to get meat to feed his family. He left his sons, Bartley and Ezekiel, behind to build barricades around hay stacks. His two daughters, Tabitha and Rebecca, as well as his wife were at the creek washing clothes when suddenly eleven Indians appeared and shot Bartley, killing him instantly. After they killed Bartley, they started to scalp him and Tabitha ran to his defense. She called to her sister, "Run, Becky, run!"

The Indians killed Tabitha along with Bartley. I found two sources that said Tabitha was cut to pieces. A younger son, 16-year-old Ezekiel, was kidnapped. The family's horses were also stolen.

A man on horseback named Blankenship was present while this attack was taking place. I found two different accounts of Blankenship's role on that fateful day. One reported that Mrs. Clay begged Blankenship to shoot the Indians with a rifle he carried on his saddle, but instead he fled to Giles County (in present-day Virginia) where he told settlers there that Mitchell Clay's family had been slaughtered. The other version was much kinder to Mr. Blankenship; it stated that he actually created a diversion for Mrs. Clay and her children by continually riding ahead of the Indians which gave the mother and her children sufficient time to carry Tabitha and Bartley's bodies into the cabin, place them on a bed, and then retreat to the house of a neighbor—James Bailey—near New Hope to seek protection.

Upon returning from his hunting trip, Mitchell Clay assumed that his entire family had been either killed or kidnapped. He then went to the mouth of East River where he organized a pursuit party. The party consisted of Captain Matthew Farley, Son of Mitchell, Charles Clay, (my great-great-grandfather--father of Rebecca Jane Clay Cantley), Mitchell Clay Jr., James Bailey, William Wiley, Edward Hale, Isaac Cole, Joseph Hare, John French and John Moore. The party buried Tabitha and Bartley, then pursued the Indians. The Indians had originally joined another raiding party but had then split and gone separate ways on Pond Fork in Boone County. The pursuit party killed a number of Indians and recovered horses they had stolen from Mitchell Clay. One Indian, a very large man, pleaded for his life in broken English. But Charles, remembering his slain brother and sister, shot him without hesitation. Edward Hale and William Wiley cut two sections of flesh from the Indian's back to be used for razor straps. One was given as a tribute to young Charles because he had enjoyed the honor of slaying the savage. I remember as a young boy hearing that that razor strap was still in the Clay family.

Mitchell Clay's pursuit party could not retrieve Ezekiel; the Indians had taken him to their camp in Chillicothe, Ohio. When Mitchell announced plans to go in search of Ezekiel, Phoebe refused to let her sons go with him. James Bailey, her nephew, and James Moore accompanied Mitchell to the Indian camp. When they came near the camp, Mitchell told his companions to wait outside the camp for him. As he walked into the camp, smoke was still rising from the fire where his son had been burned at the stake; Mitchell walked into the smoldering ashes, kicked the remaining hot embers away, and removed Ezekiel's charred body from the stake. Surprisingly, he was never challenged, and he even borrowed a horse from the chief in order to transport Ezekiel's body back to the farm at Clover Bottom. He buried his son's remains on a hill above the cabin. Then he relocated Tabitha's and Bartley's bodies to the same spot. Our schools do not tell the truth about the savagery of the Indians. They were extremely cruel to their captured enemies, torturing them before killing them outright or burning them at the stake. Popular belief is that Indians learned scalping from the white man but there is evidence that they were scalping rival tribe members before the white man came to America. Plains pioneers were told to "save the last bullet for yourself," rather than be captured and tortured.

I remember from childhood the story of the Indian Massacre at Franklin, in Pendelton County. In the days of the early Virginia settlers, about eight miles outside of Franklin was the scene of a massacre by Indians in the area. It happened in 1758 at Fort Seybert. Though I could not find a death count, the incident was called "one of the most atrocious and bloody Indian crimes ever committed in present day West Virginia." The Indians first killed the older people with tomahawks and then took the others captive, probably torturing them before burning them at the stake. At one point, one account said that an Indian took a baby from its mother's arms, cut its head off and dashed the head against a tree until the brains came out. No wonder they were known as "savages."

Phoebe never returned to the farm; she opted instead to live near Pearisburg where a fort was being built to provide a safe haven for the settlers, but Mitchell Clay returned to his land on a daily basis to tend to chores. One day he went to the farm and found that the horse he had borrowed from the Shawnees was gone. The Indians had come for it, but they were careful to secure the gate to prevent Mitchell's livestock from escaping the pasture.

After the murder of his children Mitchell Clay moved his family to a farm near Pearisburg, Virginia on the New River where they would enjoy a more secure life. He died in 1811 at the age of 76. The statue of Mitchell and Phoebe Clay previously placed on the Mercer County Courthouse lawn in Princeton, West Virginia has been moved to the Clay Cemetery at Lake Shawnee.

Kay and I visited our friends, Jim and Ellie White, at their bed and breakfast, Nostalgia Inn, in Pipestem West Virginia during the summer of 2016. Jim and I went "cemetery hopping" in hopes of locating the graves of the Clay family. We first visited Lake Shawnee, the land that Mitchell and his family homesteaded, in hopes of finding the graves of Tabitha, Bartley and Ezekiel. We did not find any marked graves, only monuments placed by the Clay Memorial Park Foundation, Inc. on a high point overlooking the bottom land farmed by Mitchell Clay. I assumed this to be the spot where the Clay children were buried.

The monuments are granite and beautifully done. One monument tells the story of the Clay family and the Indian massacre. Another lists the names of people buried there, but there are no gravestones to be seen. Tabitha and Bartley are the first names on the stone (1783) and Luther Sherman Brown (1915-1917) is the last.

While doing research on the Clays, I found a picture of a large granite or marble stone with Tabitha's and Bartley's names on it, but it was not in the Clay Memorial Park and Cemetery. Jim and I checked with a man living in a large home on the property about the location of that monument. He assured us that he had been all over the property, and that there was no such monument. With the limited time the man allowed us, we came to the conclusion that he or a previous owner had donated one quarter of an acre for the Clay Memorial Park and Cemetery.

Our next stop was the Pearisburg Courthouse where we met the Clerk of the Court. I told him that Mitchell and Phoebe were buried in a cemetery across from the railroad station in Pearisburg. He grinned and said there had not been a railroad station in the town for the past 40 years but he told us where the station had been located. We went to the spot but could not find a cemetery. We then backtracked to the main road and stopped at a farm supply store and asked for directions. The young lady at the counter gave Jim the information we needed to find the cemetery while I searched for the perfect gift for my grandson, Jackson. I thought he could use a cowbell to take to football games if he would keep it at his home.

The directions included hiking the Appalachian Trail, which gives me the right to tell people that I have hiked the Appalachian Trail; I don't have to say it was only a two thousand foot hike up the mountain. The cemetery was a big disappointment; I expected to find Mitchell's and Phoebe's graves marked by headstones. Many graves were marked only by stones, some by large river rocks that had been hauled up the mountain. We could find no sign of the Clays having been buried there. The cemetery was old with grave markers dating from the 1700s and 1800s. Large trees had grown throughout the cemetery covering the graves and stones. The cemetery was not well kept; grave markers were turned over and covered with dirt and leaves. Large dead trees had fallen onto the graves, breaking the stones.

Not being fully satisfied that the old Pearis Cemetery was the final resting place of Mitchell and Phoebe, I did further research on the subject when I returned home. I knew there had to be a grave marker somewhere; the Clays were of above average means for their time and place. I found that Mitchell had bought a farm near Pearisburg on the New River after their children had been massacred and that he and Phoebe were buried there. When the farm was purchased by an industrial company (Celanese) in 1985 the bodies were disinterred and moved to Birchlawn Cemetery in the Pearisburg area. Pictures on the internet appear to show Birchlawn to be a very attractive and well-maintained cemetery. My thanks to Jim and his grand-daughter, Angela, for going to Pearisburg, looking up Birchlawn Cemetery and taking a photo of Mitchell's grave *Rest in Peace*, Mitchell and Phoebe Clay--my great, great, great grandparents.

Information on the Indian Massacre was obtained from a variety of sources. I wasn't there when it happened, so I relied on hand-written information from Uncle Okey, a column by Rev. Shirley Donnely in the Raleigh Register, and pages provided by an unknown author that I obtained from Uncle Okey. There was nothing on those pages I could use to gain the author's permission to reprint his/ her work. I wrote this essay in the spirit of perpetuating the legacy of the Mitchell Clay family and of providing my family with a record of their ancestry.

THE WILL OF MITCHELL CLAY, JR.
GILES COUNTY, VIRGINIA, 1810

In the name of God Amen, I, Mitchell Clay, Jr. of the County of Giles and State of Virginia being very sick in body, but of perfect mind and memory, thanks be given to God, calling into mind the mortality of my body and knowing that it is appointed for all men once to die, make and ordain this my last will and testament. That is to say, principally, and first of all, I give and recommend my soul into the hands of almighty God that gave it and my body I recommend to the earth to be buried in decent Christian burial at the discretion of my executors nothing doubting but at the general resurrection I shall receive the same again by the mighty power of God as touching such worldly estate where it has pleased God to bless me within this life. I give demise and dispose of the same in the following manner and, firstly, all I give and bequeath to my dearly beloved daughter, Patience Chapman, one dollar to be raised and levied out of my estate. Secondly, I give and bequeath to my dearly beloved daughter, Rebecca Pearis, one dollar to be raised and levied out of my estate. Thirdly, I give and bequeath to my dearly beloved daughter, Obedience French, one dollar to be raised and levied out of my estate. Fourthly, I give and bequeath to my dearly beloved daughter, Polly Stuart, one dollar to be raised and levied out of my estate. Fifthly, I give and bequeath to my beloved daughter, Sally Peters, one dollar to be raised and levied out of my estate. Sixthly, I give and bequeath to each of the children of David Clay, deceased, one dollar to be raised and levied out of my estate.

Seventhly, I give and bequeath to my dearly beloved son, Mitchell Clay, the younger, one Negro girl named Lidy to him and his heirs forever. Eighthly, I will give and bequeath to my beloved son, Charles Clay, one Negro boy, May, to him and his heirs forever. Tenthly, I will and bequeath to my beloved son, Henry Clay, one Negro girl named Rachel, together with all and the singular tract of land whereon I now live on the northeast side of New River adjoining and below the lands of Mitchell Clay the younger with all its appivelenances [?] Missuges [?] tenements, dwelling houses and out houses. Also, all my stock of horses, cattle, hogs, and stock of every kind, household and kitchen furniture unto him and his heirs forever, excepting three cows of average value, which I give and bequeath unto my son, Charles Clay. Also, I give and bequeath to my sons, Mitchell Clay the younger and Henry Clay, the tract of land I bought from Reuben Roberts and was by the heirs of Reuben Roberts to (be?) me to them and their heirs forever to be equally divided between them.

Provided the said Mitchell Clay the younger and Henry Clay do not pay unto Reuben Roberts the sum of one hundred sixteen dollars or thereabouts with the interest on the same, which sum I am owing to the said estate of Roberts, and in case they and said Mitchell and Henry Clay fail to make the payment aforesaid then it is my will and desire that the said tract of land be sold and the money arising therefrom to be appropriated to the payment of debt aforesaid. Also, it is my will and desire that a tract of land I own on the five-mile fork of East River of about one hundred acres shall be sold to pay my debts. I also give and bequeath unto my four sons, Mitchell Clay the younger, Charles Clay, William Clay and Henry Clay, one Negro woman named Phoebe and her boy, Jack, to be equally divided between them, that is to say that either two of my sons may keep the said two Negroes and pay the other two of my sons their share of their value, and in case they cannot agree then said two Negroes to be sold and the money divided between my four sons, Mitchell Clay the younger, Charles Clay, William Clay and Henry Clay do pay all my debts that may remain after the payments are made heretofore provided for and in case they fail to pay the remaining debts aforesaid then the Negro woman and her child, Jack, to be sold and the remaining debt paid and the residue of the money, if any, equally divided among my four sons aforesaid. Also, it is my will and desire that my executor collect all the debts that are coming to me and appropriate them in the payments of my debts and I do hereby utterly disallow, revoke and disannul all and every other former testament, wills, legacies and bequests ratifying and confirming this and no other to be my last will and testament, and I do hereby ordain, constitute and appoint my four sons, Mitchell Clay the younger, Charles Clay, William Clay and Henry Clay my executors of this, my last will and testament in witness whereof I have here unto set my hand and seal this twenty-sixth day of July 1810.

Signed, sealed and Mitchell (his mark) Clay Seal
Delivered in presence of
A Johnston
John Brown
Joseph St
Henry (his mark) Dillan

Phoebe had passed away in 1809, Mitchell wrote his will in 1810, and he died in 1811. He made some changes in his will through a document known as a Codicil, which is a change to a previous document. Here is his Codicil:

I, Mitchell Clay, Jr. of the County of Giles and State of Virginia being in perfect health of body and of sound mind and memory do make, ordain and constitute the following Codicil as part of my will made and acknowledged the twenty-sixth of July, 1810. That is to say that so much of the said will and desires as bequeath one Negro girl named Lidy to my son, Mitchell Clay the younger. I do hereby revoke and disannul and in lieu thereof give and bequeath to my son Mitchell Clay my black woman named Phoebe and her boy child, Jack, to him and his heirs forever revoking and disannulling that part of said will here referred to as gives the said Phoebe and her child, Jack, to my four sons Mitchell Clay, Charles Clay, William Clay and Henry Clay. Secondly, I give and bequeath to my son, William, one Negro girl named Liddy to him and his heirs forever in lieu of a Negro boy named Ned as mentioned in my former will to which this is a supplement revoking that part of said will as said bequeaths said Ned to my son William Clay.

Thirdly, I give and bequeath to my son Charles Clay three cows of an average value and since the making the said devise I have given him two of the cows therein mentioned, therefore I give and bequeath to Charles only one cow agreeable to the terms in the said will mentioned.

Fourthly, it is my will and desire that my Negro boy named Ned shall be sold, and the money applying to the payment of my just debts. In case the provisions made in my former will, to which this is a supplement, proves insufficient to the payment of my debts but in case the provisions therein mentioned be found equal to meet my debts or in case there should be a surplus of the price of the Negro boy after paying the debts in either case, my will is that the money be equally divided between my four sons, Mitchell Clay, William Clay, Charles Clay and Henry Clay and I hereby disanull all and every part of my former will to which this is a supplement so much thereof as is not altered or changed by the Codicil to my last will and testament in which whereof I have here unto set my hand and seal this thirtieth day of March in year of our Lord 1811.

Signed, sealed and acknowledged Mitc
hell (his mark) Clay Seal at Giles April Court signed 1811 this last testament of Mitchell Clay, Dcd.
Sam Brown was proven in Court oaths of:
Wm Chapman
Andrew Johnson
John Brown
D Johnston Henry Dillon

It would appear that my great, great grandfather, Charles Clay—an Indian fighter at a very young age on the Clay family side was nearly disinherited by his father. Only one cow of average value? One has to wonder what caused him to fall out of favor with his dad.

Chapter photo: The statue was originally located on the lawn of the Court House in Princeton, Mercer County West Virginia. It now resides in the Clay Family cemetery. It is the depiction of two parents, Mitchell and Phoebe Belcher Clay and recalls the pain, agony and loss their family experienced in 1783. The sculpture is titled: Torment in Stone.

BATTLE OF POINT PLEASANT

ANDREW & CHARLES LEWIS
MARCH
The nearby highway is part of route
traversing W. Va. from Lewisburg to
Point Pleasant memorialized by the
state to commemorate the march of
the American Colonial army of 1,200
men led by Andrew & Charles Lewis.
After a month's march this army
defeated a Shawnee Indian force led
by Cornstalk at the Battle of Point
Pleasant on the banks of the Ohio &
Kanawha rivers, October 10, 1774.

My uncle, Okey R. Cantley, a veteran of WW I, was the historian of the family. He was an avid reader and had excellent recall of everything he read. He especially liked military history and left us with a handwritten account of books he had read. He had an astounding memory (except for the fact that he had told you the same story a dozen times.) He also left us stories that had been handed down through the family for several generations. I was spellbound by his Battle of Point Pleasant writing. To write The Battle of Point Pleasant I also called on my college professor, John B. Van Dyke, a student and teacher of American history, especially as it relates to West Virginia.

We were taught in school that the first battle of the Revolutionary War was the Battle of Concord, Massachusetts. Not true! I have learned that, according to many historians, the first battle of that war was not at the

Concord Bridge but it was at Point Pleasant, Virginia now West Virginia. Albeit a bit of a stretch, I will claim that my great grandfather four times removed on the Clay side of the family was the first casualty of our war for independence. Indulge me!

The Battle of Point Pleasant was fought on October 10, 1774 between Lord Dunmore's Virginia Militia and the Shawnee Indians. Dunmore was appointed Royal Governor of Virginia by King George III, the king of England and Ireland. To prevent colonial advancement into Indian territory Chief Cornstalk led the Shawnee Indians in an attack on the Virginia Militia. Approximately 85 Virginians were killed and 150 were wounded. The Shawnee's losses were considerably higher but could not be determined because they threw their dead into the Ohio River and hastily buried some in shallow graves before retreating. Cornstalk was forced to sign a peace treaty which also required him to return all captives.

The Shawnees knew that Mitchell Clay Jr., my great grandfather three times removed and his brothers had fought in the Battle of Point Pleasant. This was their way of getting revenge when they shot, killed, scalped and burned at the stake Mitchell Jr.'s children Tabitha, Bartley and Ezekiel.

While serving in the Virginia Militia at Point Pleasant, Mitchell Jr.'s father, William Mitchell Clay, Sr. (1708-1774) was sent out with another militiaman to hunt deer to feed the troops. Clay Sr. shot a deer but as he was approaching his prey he was shot and killed by an Indian. While the savage was preparing to scalp Clay he was killed by Clay's partner which prompted his companion to report to his chief that militiamen were in the area. I believe this to be the first shots fired in the Revolutionary War.

As stated earlier, many historians consider the Battle of Point Pleasant to be the first battle of the Revolutionary war. In fact, a bill was introduced in Congress in 1908 that declared the Battle of Point Pleasant to be a battle of the Revolutionary War. The bill was passed by the House of Representatives but was defeated in the Senate.

So, if you accept the afore told to be fact, as I do, my great grandfather four times removed, William Mitchell Clay, Sr. holds the dubious distinction of being the first casualty of the Revolutionary war.

Chapter photo: Historical marker for the Battle of Pt. Pleasant.

WHO DO YOU THINK YOU ARE? A GENEALOGY

My family has always thought that we were of either English or Scottish descent. My research has traced our roots to Scotland and Ireland. The people of Scotland prefer to be called "Scotts" and only use the term Scotch when referring to whiskey.

America's Scots-Irish came from the harsh mountainous land of Scotland to America. The farmers of Ireland who were constantly fighting with both the church and the King of Ireland; they were hard-scrabble individuals. This group migrated to Scotland where they could be independent and free from the aristocracy of the church and the king. Their religion was a harsh and demanding Calvinism that sowed the seeds of America's Bible Belt. On occasion they sold themselves as indentured servants to earn their passage on a ship to America to escape the hard life in

Ulster (Northern Ireland) and they quickly became known as disagreeable with an in-your-face attitude.

During the 18ᵗʰ century, 250 to 400 thousand Scots-Irish migrated to America—some were rebels, outcasts, and undesirables. (The term "redneck" had not been coined at that time.) There were also skilled frontiersmen and guerilla fighters among them. They were rugged individualists who had escaped aristocracy, mistrusted central authority, and possessed an odd indifference to wealth. Upon migrating to America, the Scots-Irish chose not to settle in colonial communities. Instead, they took their axes, farming tools, seed potatoes, and the newly invented rifle and headed westward into the Appalachian Mountains. That is where their families cleared farmland and fought off raiding Indians.

Over time, the Scots-Irish defined the attitudes and values of the military and working-class America. They fought the Indians as well as the British; they comprised 40% of the Revolutionary War Army. Those were the pioneers (including Daniel Boone, Lewis and Clark, and Davy Crockett among others) who blazed trails westward into Kentucky, Ohio, Tennessee and beyond. The Scots-Irish reshaped American politics by moving away from the aristocratic English-Americans. This gave us at least a dozen presidents beginning with Andrew Jackson, Chester Arthur, Ulysses Grant, Theodore Roosevelt (through his mother), Woodrow Wilson, Ronald Reagan (again, through his mother) and Bill Clinton.

The Scots-Irish formed the bulk of the Confederate Army and a good part of the Union Army. Military leaders include Stonewall Jackson, Sam Houston, Nathan Bedford Forrest, Ulysses S. Grant, George S. Patton and many chiefs of staff and commandants. Not to be forgotten are Sgt. Alvin York in WWI, Audie Murphy (the most decorated soldier of WWII), and David Hackworth (the most decorated soldier of the Korean and Vietnam Wars).

The Scots-Irish have fed dedicated soldiers to this nation far beyond their numbers in every war—for instance, the heavily Scots-Irish people of West Virginia ranked first, second or third in military casualty rates in every U.S. war of the twentieth century. West Virginia's casualty rate was twice that of New York's and Connecticut's in Vietnam and more than two and a half times the rate experienced by those two states in Korea.

The roots of NASCAR racing can be traced to the Scots-Irish and moonshine runners during the days of prohibition. They created and still dominate country music which, along with jazz and soul, is a truly American musical form. Country music is at the heart of the Scots-Irish culture. It percolated for more than a century in the remote mountains until WSM Radio in Nashville took it national in the 1930s through the Grand Ole Opry. In the hollows through those isolated earlier years, the dulcimer (Aunt Lou owned Grandpa Jim's "dulcimore") found its plaintive notes, the traditionally exquisite violin turned into such a hot fiddle that some warned had come from the devil, and the "banjar," a native African instrument made with a gourd, evolved into the bluegrass banjo.

Many writers have Scots-Irish background such as Mark Twain, Horace Greely, Edgar Allan Poe and Margaret Mitchell. Accomplished thespians with a Scots-Irish background including Tallulah Bankhead, Ava Gardener, Jimmy Stewart, John Wayne, Robert Redford and George C. Scott from Wise County, Virginia--home of Jeter Barker and Senator Jim Webb.

Over 27 million Americans can trace their roots to the Scots-Irish, most of whom would have no idea about their heritage. I am now sure of mine.

The Cantley Family (also spelled Cantlie) originally came from County Norfolk. Evidently, the name comes from the Yorkshire place of the same name. William Cantully was admitted burgess of Aberdeen, 1452 and William Cantuly or Cantuli held land there before 1497. Andrew Cantly was admitted burgess in 1508. Master John Cantly or Cantely appears as Archdeacon of St. Andres, 1524 and 1541. Gilbert Cantlie, witness in Shetland, 1626.

It is possible that some Cantley ancestor went to Northern Ireland at the request of the English government (as did many during the reign of James I) following the conquest of that land by Queen Elizabeth I. If so, they probably came to the United States during the large Scots-Irish emigration that began about 1717 and lasted until about 1775. As was common for those Scots-Irish families who settled in the Shenandoah Valley of Virginia, they probably settled first around Lancaster, Pennsylvania before coming to Virginia. This particular Cantley Family might have been part of the Cantley Family that had settled in the mid-18th century in South Carolina. Migration from South Carolina westward through Virginia was quite common following the Revolutionary War and the opening of the lands of Western Reserve, Indiana and Illinois. The two John Cantleys who appear in the 1790 census of South Carolina could have had children who migrated to Virginia. Judge Lyman Chalkley included legal records of John Cantley of Virginia in his Chronicles of Scots-Irish of the Shenandoah Valley. Angus Cantley, a great grandson of John Sr., who lived in Franklin County, Missouri, stated in a short sketch of the family that they were of Irish descent. This probably meant that the family came from Northern Ireland as the religious affiliation of the majority of the family members appears to have been of the Protestant persuasion.

Some descendants of John Cantley, Sr. pushed westward with the opening of the western lands, settling in Indiana, Missouri, Arkansas, Kansas, Texas, Oklahoma, Iowa, and Wisconsin while the remainder stayed in western Virginia, now West Virginia.

Members of the family have served in the military forces of the United States with three members in the War of 1812 and two in the Mexican War. During the tragic period of the Civil War, four members served in the Union forces with one of these dying of wounds received in battle; while twelve members served in the Confederate forces with two known dying.

The family information included herein has come from records in the National Archives, the Library of Congress, and the Library of the Daughters of the American Revolution. For a thorough study of the Scots-Irish in America, I recommend Senator Jim Webb's *Born Fighting.*

THE CANTLEY FAMILY

The first record of any of this family is mentioned as early as September, 1758 when John Cantley is recorded as serving in the militia of Augusta County, Virginia. That same year the Virginia legislature passed the following, "John Cantley, James Brinton, and Samuel Edemston, one pound, 14 shillings each, September, 1758 under the Act, passed the thirty-second year of the reign of George II to pay for the militia of the County of Augusta and for the provisions supplied by sundry inhabitants." Whether this money was in payment for the military service or for payment for provisions is not known, but the former is probably correct. John Cantley served with Captain Christian's Company of Rangers in 1760. In 1767, he was listed as delinquent in payment of taxes in Augusta County. It is probably because he had moved since he was among those serving on jury duty in Botetourt County, Virginia on May 16, 1771, and was among those taxed in that county when Benz Hawkins took the taxes of all residents on August 12, 1771.

On September 10, 1772, the Botetourt County Court directed "John Cantley, John Hamilton, Archibald Handley, and Isaac Tyler or any three of these, being sworn to view the nighest and best way from Sweet Springs to John Handley's on Indian Creek and make a report thereof to the next court." (Indian Creek is in present-day Summers and Monroe Counties, West Virginia). The Botetourt County Land Surveys of Samuel Lewis for the Loyal Company granted John Cantley 500 acres on March 21, 1774. He did not, however, appear to have received this land. On December 10, 1779, the Botetourt County Court certified John Cantley's claim for service under Captain Christian in 1760. In December 1780, the Commissioners sat to consider the title claims in Greenbrier County, Virginia. John Cantley was listed as one having claims. He must have been granted title or expected to receive title to 400 acres of land on Indian Creek as it was surveyed by Thomas Edgar on March 30, 1781. At a hearing held in Greenbrier County on Wednesday, June 18, 1782, with Samuel Brown, William Ward, Michael Woods, John Henderson, and John Anderson presiding, the following claims were allowed and ordered to be certified: John Cantley for two blankets…1 pound 17 shillings. Blankets supplied to the state.

In 1782, John Cantley was taxed $5.96 for his possessions—10 horses and 23 cattle. On October 5, 1783, the following deed was recorded: John Cantley and Elinor, his wife, of Greenbrier County to Walter Lindsay. Consideration 50 pounds, tract on south side of James. Acreage not given. Witnesses: William Anderson, Malcolm Allen, and Isaac Robinson. (Walter Lindsay was John, Sr.'s brother-in-law).

In 1786, John Cantley, Sr. is listed as acquiring 400 acres of land on Indian Creek, Greenbrier County, Virginia. This land was acquired from James Ellison, also of Indian Creek. In 1799, John Cantley, Sr. and John Cantley, Jr. are listed as residents of newly formed Monroe County, Virginia. John Cantley, Sr. sold 326 acres of land for $1.00 to John Cantley, Jr. as part of a grant of 400 acres adjoining land of John Byrnside on Indian Creek. This was confirmed in the September, 1802 Court. John

Cantley, Sr. voted in the election of 1800. He apparently died sometime after April 22, 1802 when he is recorded as paying his taxes in Monroe County, Virginia and selling most of his land to his oldest son as was the custom of the day. **John, Sr. married Elinor Lindsay** (born circa 1740's; died before 1804), daughter of Samuel Lindsay (died 1783 in Botetourt County, Virginia) and Margaret Lindsey (died 1804 in Botetourt County, Virginia). My great, great, great, great. **John Cantley and Elinor Lindsay Cantley, had two children—John Jr. and Samuel.**

John Cantley, Jr., was born circa 1765 and died between 1830-40 in Franklin County, Missouri. He married Jane Kincaid on June 5, 1787 with John McCue officiating. John acquired 88 acres of land on Stewarts Knob, Greenbrier County, Virginia in 1790. He acquired a like amount on Lick Run in Greenbrier County in 1792. (This appears to be a duplicate of the previous record). In 1800 he was living on the north side of Swope's Knob, Monroe County, Virginia. In 1802, he purchased the place of John Cantley, Sr. On September 15, 1807, John Cantley, Jr. sold one moiety (one half of a tract of land) containing 163 acres (which was part of the land he received from John Cantley, Sr.) to James Ralston and Matthew Ralston. He then moved with his family to Franklin County, Missouri; he appears in the 1830 census of Franklin County as living in St. John's Township. He does not appear in the 1840 census. Descendants of John Jr. moved westward to Missouri, Colorado, Tennessee, Kansas and Oklahoma.

At this point we will concentrate on the author's direct lineage.

SAMUEL CANTLEY: (great, great, great grandfather) (born circa 1760's in Augusta County, Virginia; died in 1810 in Monroe County, Virginia—now West Virginia). He married Rebecca Clark (born circa 1769 in Augusta County, Virginia; died about 1841 in Monroe Co., Virginia) on February 3, 1789 in Greenbrier County, Virginia with Rev. John Alderson officiating. She was the daughter of Alexander Clark and Sarah Lafferty, and the granddaughter of Ralph Lafferty—a prominent man of the Cowpasture River area in Virginia. (Sarah Lafferty Clark's will was proved on May 26, 1812 and her estate was appraised at $1,389.13). Alexander Clark's grandfather, John Clark, was a brother of Jonathan Clark, grandfather of General George Rogers Clark and William Clark of the Lewis and Clark Expedition. In 1840, Rebecca Clark Cantley was living with her son, William.

On June 17, 1800, Samuel purchased from James Ellison for 5 shillings, lawful money of Virginia, 236 acres of land on Indian Creek—part of a grant of 600 acres of James Ellison, Sr., made to James Ellison on June 18, 1790. This land was bounded by land of Lewis Booten, David Koho, and Joseph Seirs. Samuel died intestate (without a will); his estate was appraised on May 28, 1810 at a value of $322.98. Included in the estate was 44 acres of land on Indian Creek, which he had purchased from James Ellison in 1800. This land bounded that of Alexander Clark. Descendants of Samuel Cantley now outnumbered the descendants of the other children of John Cantley, Sr. The children of Samuel Cantley and Rebecca Clark Cantley were—Eleanor, **Alexander James**, John, Sarah, James Alexander, Polly, William, and Rebecca.

ALEXANDER JAMES CANTLEY: My great, great grandfather (born February 23, 1794 in Giles County, Virginia; died March 2, 1884 in Raleigh County, West Virginia.) In Towerhill, Monroe County, Virginia, during April, 1817 he married Mary (Mollie) Scott (born 1797; died November 20, 1875) by whom he had all of his children. On August 21, 1876 at Dry Creek, Raleigh County, West Virginia, (with the Reverend Joseph N. Estep, Baptist Minister, officiating), he wed Mrs. Tempay (Ball) Hopkins (born Oct. 14, 1827; died Dec. 8, 1903 at Lewiston, Kanawha County, West Virginia). She was the widow of Jonathan Hopkins, and daughter of Albert Ball and Hattie M. Ball.

Alexander served as a private in Captain William McDaniel's Virginia Militia during the War of 1812. His two terms of service were from Sept. 13, 1813 to October 9, 1813, and from October 10, 1813 to March 10, 1814. He was discharged at Norfolk, Virginia. Alexander received 160 acres of bounty land in Michigan, which he sold forthwith. He then acquired 60 acres of bounty land at present day Rock Creek. This became the Cantley homestead and is the site of Marsh Fork Elementary School. The children of Alexander James Cantley and Mary Scott Cantley were—Elizabeth, Samuel, John, **James Alexander**, Jorden, George, Richard, Caroline, Lodocie, and Alice.

JAMES ALEXANDER CANTLEY: My great grandfather (Born 1827; died June 26, 1862 of Valvus Sclopseticum at the General Hospital at Claysville, near Cumberland, Maryland). He married Rebecca Jane Clay (born June 1828; died May 10, 1910) at Masseyville or Rock Creek,

Raleigh County, West Virginia) on August 1, 1852 at her father's house with the Reverend Felix Ellison officiating. James enlisted in the Union Army on November 2, 1861 at Charleston, Virginia (now West Virginia) in the 8th Virginia Volunteers commanded by William H. Parker. He was wounded in the breast on June 8, 1862 at Cross Keys, Virginia and taken to the hospital where he died. The children of James Alexander Cantley and Rebecca J. Clay Cantley were Janetta Cantley, Nancy Jane, Ellen, and **James Adam Cantley.**

JAMES ADAM CANTLEY: My grandfather (born August 12, 1861; died January 1934). He married Celia B Hunter (born November 3, 1857; died January 2, 1932) on August 18, 1882. James was a blacksmith, farmer, and served as president of the Marsh Fork District School Board for twelve years. His will was probated January 30, 1934. The eight children of James Cantley and Celia Hunter Cantley were May, Hubert, Ellen, Louisa, James, Okey Ray, Scholle and Ovet.

May Cantley: (Born February 23, 1886; died before 1929) She married Charles Rumberg (born 1884; died?). They had two children: Myrtle and Guy.

Hubert Cantley: (Born February 23, 1888; died September 26, 1969). He married on July 4, 1915 to Grace Lee Price, (born March 18, 1898; died January 3, 1979), daughter of Lightburn H. Price and Viola Workman Price. They lived in Rock Creek, West Virginia. His will was written on October 3, 1968; proved on May 16, 1970. Her obituary states that she had 26 grandchildren and 11 great grandchildren. They lived in Rock Creek, West Virginia. Children (11) of Hubert Cantley and Grace Price Cantley were Baby James, Eustace Glen, Eugene Keith, Hubert, Jr., Doris Lee, Betty Lou, Barbara Ellen, Noel Dean, Ronald Bee, David Dee, and Thelma May.

(1) James Cantley: (Died in infancy)

(2) Eustace Glen Cantley: (Born March 6, 1917; died August 31, 1995). He married in January 1940 to Thelma Grace Cavendish (born March 28,1918; died 2004). She was the daughter of Wyatt Sheldon Cavendish and Grace Cummings Cavendish. They lived in Rock Creek and Flat Top Lake, West Virginia, Louisville Kentucky and Lake Worth, Florida. The children of Eustace Cantley and Thelma Cavendish Cantley were Glenn Sheldon, Mary Jo Anne, Byron Ross, Cynthia Susan, and Stephen Jay.

Glenn Sheldon Cantley: (Born April 3, 1942). He married Patricia M. Skaggs on December 23, 1962; they divorced in the 1980s. He married Donna Cantley (born September 27, 1938) on November 21, 2007. They live in Lake Worth, Florida.

Mary-Jo Anne Cantley Broyles: (Born August 27, 1946). She married on June 22, 1968 to Kyle Joseph "Joe" Broyles, II (born June 16, 1947) son of Kyle Joseph Broyles, Sr. and Mary Margaret Broyles. They live in Louisville, Kentucky. Children of Mary-Jo Broyles and Kyle Joseph Broyles are Kyle Joseph, III and Stephanie Ann. (1) Kyle Joseph Broyles, III (born July 5, 1970). His partner is David Maurice Hardesty (born November 2, 1978). (2) Stephanie Anne Broyles (born March 7, 1972). She married on October 5, 2005 Daniel Lee Woerner (born August 24, 1969). Stephanie and Daniel Woerner have two children: Megan Grace Woerner (born June 10, 2006) and Katelyn Anne Woerner (born September 1, 2011).

Byron Ross Cantley: (Born November 26, 1947) Byron (Ron) is retired from the Broward County Sheriff's Department. He lives in Lake Worth, Florida and Melbourne Beach, Florida.

Cynthia Susan Cantley: (Born May 30, 1954) in Beckley, West Virginia. She married on October 14, 1978 to Marion Lee Goodman, Jr. (born March 2, 1956) son of Marion Lee Goodman, Sr. and Virgie Harvey. They had two children: Grace Leigh (born December 8, 1981) and Thomas Wyatt (born March 13, 1983). They divorced. She married on April 23, 1988 at Shady Spring, West Virginia to Floyd McKinley "Kin" Sayre, III (born June 10, 1962) son of Floyd M. Sayre, Jr. and Ruth Thomas. Susie and Kin live in Martinsburg and Flat Top Lake, West Virginia. They had one child, Floyd McKinley Sayre IV (born December 29, 1988). Children are (1) Grace Leigh, married on June 15, 1981 to Jennifer Lynn Vanmatter (born March 31, 1982). They have one child:

Alexander Edward Sayre (born June 13, 2015). (2) Thomas Wyatt Goodman married on April 5, 2013 Courtney Rose Gleason (born March 19, 1993). They have three children, Myles William born May 7, 2015, James Thomas born June 10, 2016, and Carson Elliot born October 4, 2019. (3) Floyd McKinley Sayre, IV.

Steven Jay Cantley: (Born April 22, 1958 in Beckley, West Virginia). He married on November 20, 2015 in Key West, Florida to Scarlet Lea Tyree (born August 25, 1967 in Portsmouth, Virginia). Step-daughter of Steve: Jessica Lynne Bodnmer (born March 16, 1993). They live in Lake Worth, Florida

(3) Eugene Keith Cantley: (Born August 5, 1918; died February 4, 2006). He married Audrey Jarvis (born October 7, 1920; died May 1, 2012) daughter of Howard Jarvis. They lived in Glen Daniel, West Virginia. Children of Eugene Cantley and Audrey Jarvis Cantley: Larry Gene and Jerry Wayne.

Larry Gene Cantley: (Born February 13, 1943; died November 24, 1961). Larry died following an automobile accident. At the time of his death, he was a student at Morris Harvey College in Charleston, West Virginia.

Jerry Wayne Cantley: (Born October 9, 1947) He married Inez Lutecia (Tish) Brooks (born July 30, 1946) on November 14, 1964. They live in Glen Daniel, West Virginia. They had four children: Jerry Wayne, Jr., Lesba Gail, Travis Bret and Lindsey Beth. (1) Jerry (Jay) Wayne Cantley, Jr (born June 21, 1965 in Manassass, Virginia). He married on June 8, 1988 in Beckley, West Virginia to Kimberley D. Parent (born March 3, 1966) in Beckley, West Virginia. They have two children: Brittany and Kaitlyn. (a) Brittany E. (Cantley) Paitsel (born February 19, 1990 in Palm Beach Gardens, Florida). On May 2, 2013 she married Justin M Paitsel (born December 28, 1989). They have one child—Jura Maeve Paitsel (born December 30, 2013 in Lakenheath AFB, Great Brittain. (b) Kaitlyn Nicole (born August 17, 1995. (2) Lesba Gale

Cantley (born August 8, 1967). She married on September 25, 1983 at Sophia, Raleigh County, West Virginia to Arnold Bret Acord (born May 5, 1964) son of Arnold Acord and Gladys McKinney. Children of Lesba Gale and Arnold Acord are: Zachary Seth, Zane Colten and Zeke Daniel. (a) Zachary Seth Acord (born August 11, 1990) on August 15, 2015 married Kelsey Marie Allen (born June 15, 1991). (b) Zane Colton Acord, (c) Zeke Daniel Acord. (3) Travis Bret Cantley (born July 26, 1971 in Beckley West Virginia) married Heather Dawn Hughes (born March 15, 1978) on June 8, 1996. Travis and Heather Cantley have four children. They are: Tanner Bret Cantley (born September 15, 1997), Kylee Breann Cantley (born September 21, 2000), Allyson Brook Cantley, (born January 22, 2003, and Conner Blake Cantley (born January 31, 2005). (4) Lindsey Beth Cantley (born January 18, 1980) married Jerome Keith Stone (born January 12, 1977) on March 14, 1998. Lindsey and Keith Stone have four children: Madison Paige Stone (born October 5, 1998), Erin Makenna Stone (born October 26, 2000), Josie Kailyn Stone (born September 25, 2003, and Colt Elliott Stone (born April 2, 2010). All of the children of Jerry and Tish Cantley live in Southern West Virginia.

(4) Hubert Cantley, Jr.: (born May 31, 1921; died December 24, 2005) He married Lucille Lydia Fields (born September 30, 1923; died July 10, 2009) daughter of Thomas Fields and Ida Jane Kiser Fields. They lived in Comfort, WV. Children of Hubert Cantley, Jr. and Lucille Fields Cantley: Paula, Debbie, Sherrie, Brenda, and Kevin.

Paula Kay Cantley: (born September 5, 1945; died December 22, 2004).

Debra Lynn Cantley: (born August 16, 1951) on July 29, 1980 she married Johnny Joe Mitchell (born December 20, 1944--died June 29, 2004). They have two children: Nicholas and Amanda. (1) Nicholas Mitchell (born July 3, 1981) married to Angeleigh Maddon (born January 13, 1980). They have one son, Corban (born March 13, 2008). (2) Amanda Grace Mitchell (born June

20, 1984) married to Jan Paul Mitra-Cenzon (born May 23, 1978). They have two sons: William Cenzon (born April 12, 2006) and Xavier Cenzon (born December 9, 2011). The family of Debbie Cantley Mitchell live in Virginia Beach, Virginia.

Sharon (Sherrie) Lee Cantley: (born January 20, 1953) married Ricky Joe Foster (born October 4, 1952) on July 6, 1974. They live in Comfort, West Virginia. Ricky and Sherrie (Cantley) Foster have two children: Adam Joseph Foster and Melissa Jane Foster. (a) Adam Joseph Foster (born August 21, 1975) on February 26, 2005 married Patricia Suzette Blount (born June 10, 1975. They have four sons, Devynn Seastien Foster (February 4, 1997), Adam Joseph Foster, II (born January 9, 1998), Tyler Andrew Foster (born March 15, 1999) and Jackson Cole Foster (born September 26, 2006). (b) Melissa Jane Foster (born July 23, 1984) married Frederick Joel Blackwell (born November 19, 1983) on October 22, 2005. Melissa and Frederick Blackwell have two daughters: Maizie Jane Foster (born June 27, 2008) and Addison Brooke Foster (born September 29, 2010).

Brenda Joan Cantley: (born April 6, 1957). Son, Jeffrey Wayne Monhollen (born April, 28, 1976) married on August 8, 2008 to Anna Pamela Mitra Cenzon (born April 27, 1978). They have two daughters: Abigail Hope Monhollen (born May 20, 2002) and Ariana Faith Monhollen (born March 11, 2009).

Kevin Wayne Cantley: (born September 30, 1963). He married Lori Ann Casino (born December 13, 1964). Kevin and Lori had one child, Kevin Ryan Cantley (born September 1, 1993). They divorced and Kevin married Tresa McDermot.

(5) Doris Lee Cantley: (born December 21, 1924; died 2002) She married on March 12, 1949, Ralph Kinley Dickens (born March 7, 1918; died November 22, 1991), son of Otis Dickens and Eve Brown. She lived in Rock Creek, West Virginia and Roanoke, Virginia. Children of Ralph and Doris Cantley Dickens: Nancy Lou and Peggy Lee.

Nancy Lou Dickens: (born February 23, 1950) married Robert Steven Kellis. They had one son, Robert Steven Kellis, II (born September 12, 1972).

Peggy Lee Dickens: (born June 23, 1956) married to Larry Dean Weidensall (born March 7, 1957) Peggy Lee Dickens Weidensall has one son, Matthew Phillip Weaver, (born May 5, 1979). He married Jaya West (born September 14, 1972) and they have one child: Matthew Zebediah (Zeb) Weaver born June 20, 2006.

(6) **Betty Lou Cantley:** (born November 26, 1926; died January 5, 2009) She married on September 4, 1951 to Billy Richards Billings (born August 16, 1929; died December, 2010 son of Fred Billings and Roxie Billings. They had no children. They lived in Orlando, Florida.

(7) **Barbara Ellen Cantley** (born January 8, 1929; died October 8, 2017) She married on August 2, 1947 to Bill Ross Asbury (born May 22, 1927; died 2012) son of Mont Asbury and Anna Asbury. Children of Bill and Barbara Cantley Asbury: Betty Jane, Kathy Ann, and Billy Ross II. They lived in Cleveland, Ohio.

(8) **Noel Dean Cantley:** (born February 27, l931; died April 9, 2012). He married on December 26, 1951 to Mary Lou Mynes (born August 3, 1933; died December 2011) daughter of Roy Mynes and Lizzie Mynes. They lived in Perrysburg, OH. Children of Noel Dean and Mary Lou Mynes Cantley: Noel Dean, II, Randal David and Alan Dale.

Noel Dean Cantley, II: (born December 13, 1954; died December 2, 2001). On September 13, 1975, he married Pamela Lynn Coon (born June 11, 1956). They had two children: Sarah Cantley and Jessica Cantley. (1) Sarah Cantley (born October 14, 1981) married on March 3, 2007 to Christopher Foster (born February 5, 1977) Sarah and Christopher have four children: Phineas David (born August 22, 2011), Jonas Andrew (born April 14, 2013) Gideon Lucas (born October 24, 2016) and Vivian Joy (born March 2019) They live in Tulsa, OK. (2), Jessica Rose Cantley (born July 25, 1983) married on December 30, 2010 Richard Allen Rehkemper (born March 15, 1985) Jessica Rose and Richard Allen Rehkemper have one child: Richard Dean Rehkemper (born September 10, 2011).

Randal David Cantley: (born July 5, 1957) married on August 31, 1980 to Linda Jane. They live in Tiffin. OH.

Alan Dale Cantley: (born February 4, 1964). Dale works and lives in Perrysburg, Ohio.

(9) Ronald Bee Cantley: (born November 3, 1932; died January 17, 2005). He married Donna R. Allamon (born September 27, 1938). They lived in Shady Spring, WV Children of Ronald Bee and Donna R. Allamon Cantley: Ronald B. Cantley, II, Mildred Jane, Rebeccah Rae and Adam David.

Ronald Bee Cantley, II: (born August 13, 1960) married on July 3, 1982 to Deborah Gale Fields (born February 18, 1961). They have two children: Geoffrey Adam and Stephan Robert. (1) Geoffrey Adam Cantley (born March 21, 1987) he is married to Sarah Marie McGrath (born August 1, 1983). Geoffrey Adam and Sarah Marie Cantley have two adopted children: Miles Adam Cantley (birth name; Myles Anthony Canterbury born November 14, 2011) and Paisley Anne Cantley (birth name: Paisley Anne Cook born January 16, 2015.

Mildred Jane (Millie) Cantley: (Born August 16, 1963) married Wesley E. Mason, Sr. (born November 19, 1963) on August 17, 1981. They have two children: Nichole Chareene Mason and Wesley E. Mason, II. (1) Nichole Chareene Mason (born March 12, 1982) married Thomas DeWayne Hazewood, Sr. (born October 15, 1978) on April 14, 2001. They have four sons: Thomas DeWayne Hazelwood, II (born September 15, 2002), Christian Riley Hazelwood (born December 12, 2004), Cayden Reece Hazelwood (born March 14, 2012), and Braylon Cole Hazelwood (born September 18, 2015). (2) Wesley E. Mason, II (born February 13, 1984) on October 2, 2009 he married Nichole

Lareigh Lynch (born December 2, 1986). Wesley II and Nichole (Nicci) Mason have two children, Falyn Rochelle Mason (born April 17, 2011) and Gemma Mason (born January 7, 2019).

Rebeccah Rae Cantley: (born June 15, 1978) Married Matthew Lutz (born January 30, 1979) on April 14, 2012. They live in Tallahassee, FL. They have one child, Richard Lafayette (Richie) Lutz (born May 13, 2015).

Adam David Cantley: (born August 6, 1980). Married Joe Panzer (born June 4, 1985) on October 22, 2016. They live in Delaware.

(10) **David Dee Cantley:** (born September 30, 1938). He married Gweneth Kay Jones (born June 16, 1938) daughter of Damon Jones and Mary Elizabeth Daniel Jones on December 27, 1964. This was a second marriage for Kay and our daughter, Elizabeth, was born of the first marriage and adopted by me. We live in Lake Worth, FL. Children of David Dee and Kay Jones Cantley: Elizabeth Louise and DeeAnne.

Elizabeth Louise Cantley (Beth): (born November 28, 1960). Married on April 28, 1984 to Walter John Kaczmarek, III (born July 3, 1959). They live in Longboat Key, FL. They have three children: (1) Christopher Blaine Kaczmarek (born September 25, 1989) on November 24, 2017, he married Maegan Reese (born September 13, 1992). They have one child, Elise Jean Kaczmarek, born January 14, 2020. (2). Tyler Michael Kaczmarek (born March 5, 1991) on June 25, 2017 he married Tara Martinez (born May 7, 1991). Tyler and Tara have one child, Oliver Tzeentch Kaczmarek, (born April 10, 2019). (3) Logan Daniel Kaczmarek (born August 12, 1994), he married Jessica Cannata on November 9, 2019.

DeeAnne Cantley: (born August 13, 1965). Married on April 7, 1990 to Jeffrey Lewis Feulner (born March 16, 1963). They live in Atlantis, Florida. They have two children: Taylor Grace Feulner (born August 8, 1994) and Jackson David Feulner (born April 22, 2001). (Taylor Grace Feulner graduated from University of South Florida in May 2019; she lives in Japan and teaches English. (2)

Jackson graduated May, 2020 from Park Vista High School in Lake Worth, Florida.

(11) **Thelma May Cantley:** (born February 20, 1940; died August, 1997). She married (1) on August 31, 1957 to Leo Boggs (born January 13, 1936) son of Raymond and Emma Boggs; (2) to Joe Briguglio. She lived in Orlando, FL. Children of Thelma: Karen Elaine Boggs and Angela Grace Briguglio.

Karen Elaine Boggs: Karen lives in Bluefield, VA. and she has two daughters: Sarah and Holly

Angela Grace Briguglio: (born October 6, 1964). Married on May 26, 1984 to David Spencer (born June 20, 1962). They live in Virginia. They have two children: Danielle Marie and Jessica Anne. (1) Danielle Marie (born February 18, 1985) married Andrew David Metz (born March 6, 1986) on October 22, 2011. They have one daughter, Ava Danielle Metz (born January 11, 2015). (2) Jessica Anne (born August 15, 1987). Partner and father of Jessica's children, Zachary Thornhill (born December 21, 1988). They have two children: Gabriel Owen Spencer (born March 1, 2008 and Alyana Rayne Thronhill (born April 17, 2015).

Ellen Cantley: (born July 6, 1891; died July 25, 1978). She married (1) Arden King Wiley and (2) William Lacy Pettry. She lived in Rock Creek, West Virginia.

Louisa Cantley (Lou): (born August, 1893; died March, 1986) She married on September 17, 1913 to Nelson Cooper (born 1887; died 1966). They had no children. They lived in Rock Creek, WV.

James W. Cantley: (born October 15, 1895; died November, 1975) On September 4, 1922 he married Pearl Bailey (born January 27, 1905; died September 12, 1971) They lived in Rock Creek, WV. They had three children: Irene Christina, Rita Marie and George Curtis.

<u>**Okey Ray Cantley**</u>: (born September 25, 1898; died July 18, 1982). He married, on June 16, 1923, Winnie May Burnside (born May 5, 1907; died May 22, 1972). They lived in Rock Creek, WV. They had seven children: Okey Ray, Charles Phillip, Lloyd Gordon, Willa Mae, Nelson Lee, Margaret and June.

Okey Ray Cantley, Jr.: (born March 4, 1928; died October 14, 1932)

June Cantley: was the mother of Michael Lewis and lived in Alaska.

Charles Phillip Cantley: (born August 29,1930; died). On May 19, 1953, he married Pearl Lucas (born May 13, 1936). They lived in Rock Creek, WV. Children of Charles Phillip and Pearl Cantley: Charles Ray, Carlos Roger, Lewis Lee, Rhonda Lynn and Jody Earl.

Nelson Lee Cantley: (born 1934) Lives in Columbus, Ohio.

Margaret Louise Cantley: (born August 30, 1936). She married Willard Holt. Margaret lives in White Pine, Tennessee. Willard and Margaret Holt had five children: (1) Donald Ray (2) Debra Louise, (3) Thomas Leonard, (4) Janie and (5) Robert Lewis. In addition to her five biological children, Margaret raised three stepchildren: Willard Clinton Holt, Jerry Wayne Holt and Gary Lynn Holt.

Donald Ray Holt: (born February 16, 1956). Children: Chairssa Joyce and Donald Nathan.

Debra Louise Holt: (born July 24, 1957) Children: Anthony, Heather and Candice.

Thomas Leonard Holt: (born August 25, 1959). Children: Thomas Jason, James Alexander and Christopher Isaac.

Jane Holt Valentine: (born March 30, 1962). Children: Breanne and Bryson.

Robert Lewis Holt: (born February 10, 1964). Robert married April Wise (born July 24, 1972). Robert and April Wise Holt have one child, Mason Robert Holt (born December 7, 2012). They live Knoxville, Tennessee.

Willard Clinton Holt: (born April 5, 1950). Children: Natalie, Elizabeth, Christian and Willard Clinton, II.

Jerry Wayne Holt: (born December 23, 1951). Children: Holley, Ashley, Brittany and Taylor.

Gary Lynn Holt: (born October 1, 1955). Children: Gary Lynn, Jr., Michelle and Bradley Jay.

Ovet Cantley: (born February 12, 1903; died August 16, 1973). May 7, 1930, he married Ora Minnie Bradford (born February 25, 1910; died May 9, 1994). They lived in Rock Creek, WV. Ovet and Ora had three children: Peggy, Thomas Leland, and Barry Ned.

Scholle Cantley: (born February 12, 1903: no death record found) I have found in my research that Scholle was "probably a twin to Ovet." This was never discussed by family.

Great effort was exerted to include everyone in my family. Several did not wish to have their names included; I respect their wishes, and I apologize to anyone I might have inadvertently overlooked. It is my hope that present and future generations will find this information to be of interest, useful, and worthy of continuing to update.

Chapter photo: Uncle Nelson Cooper, back row, second from right; Aunt Ellen Cantley Pettry, front middle; Aunt Lou Cantley Cooper, front row, right. Others unknown.

PART II

PART II

23

GRADES 1-12 EDUCATION

The first centers of learning in my community were one-room schools. They could be found in practically every holler and wide place in the road as no public or school transportation was available. In Rock Creek, our "up-the-holler" school was named The Buffalo School. Dry Creek had two schools, Muddy Lyn and Dry Creek. The Dry Creek School was located across the road from what used to be Wood Jarrell's store, and it was situated near the river. Muddy Lyn was located at the forks of Dry Creek and Sturgeon under a lyn tree and near a muddy spring.

At one time my Uncle Okey was the teacher at the Dry Creek School. Years later my good friend, Quentin Barrett, a local educator, told me that his dad, Robert (who operated the Dry Creek store, the oldest continually operating business in Raleigh County), had told Okey—his teacher at the time—that if he would triple promote Quentin, he would give him a new suit. Quentin said, "That really messed me up because I was always the smallest boy in the class, and it kept me from playing sports."

The Montcoal and Mt. View High Schools were both built in the early 1920s. Quentin told me that students who lived "up the way" from Mt. View would ride horses to school, and their fathers built a shed for the horses to stay in while the students were in class. He also told me that Carl Jarrell's uncle bought him (Carl) a horse to ride to Mt. View. Unfortunately, it took the horse longer to navigate the holes and ruts in the road than it took Carl to walk the two miles to Mt. View. In those days, poor roads as well as the lack of bridges had a negative effect on the entire community. Route 3 was paved around 1930 which gave many people their first opportunity to travel. By then cars were becoming fairly common and the new "hard road," as it was called, allowed cars to travel without stopping every few miles to fix flat tires. Uncle Ovet, being a fully certified Cantley storyteller, told us about three brothers from the area who were taking their dad to Beckley when the new road was completed. Clearly, this was a momentous occasion and a very exciting event for all of them; the brothers and their dad left early and arrived in Beckley in time to have breakfast. When the waitress asked the elderly gentleman how he wanted his eggs fried, he replied, "What?" Again, she asked him how he wanted his eggs fried, "Why, in a hell-fired skillet of course. How else would you fry an egg?" The old man then turned to his sons and said, "That's the trouble with city people; they ain't got a lick of sense."

The new road also affected what the local school system would look like. Along with the new road came better transportation options for everyone including school buses. In 1932 Mt. View High (1926) students were sent to Montcoal High (1925) which would later become Marsh Fork High). Mt. View then became a grade one through nine school. So much of the area's local history has been lost—Why didn't I take a tape recorder and turn it on for my Dad, aunts, uncles and Quentin Barrett?

As previously stated, I refused to start first grade at Mt. View School because I wanted to "stay home with Daddy." But the next year, when Dad got the janitor's job at the school, I agreed to go to school. I would go to the boiler room each day to have lunch with him; we would have tomato soup with saltine crackers, peanut butter sandwiches, and graham crackers dipped in milk for dessert. The tomato soup was a real treat for me because we never had it at home. The only soups I remember were the delicious vegetable soups prepared by my mother. Unfortunately, Dad's job only lasted two or three years because he was physically unable to do the work.

My favorite elementary teacher was Quentin's brother, Lawson Barrett, my sixth grade teacher. He read aloud to the class every day after lunch. He'd read about Lewis Wetzel, a West Virginia Indian fighter, and we would beg him to please keep reading. One day he walked around the room looking at all the students' desks and found out which kids had been defacing school property. I was one of five or six guilty students who had written on their desks. Mr. Barrett never said a word to us. Instead, he went to the chalkboard, wrote our names in the upper right corner, and drew a box around our names. That was all that was necessary. We washed and erased our names off the desks--nothing else was ever said about our sixth grade crime spree. Most teachers would have made a big deal out of it.

Another day, Mr. Barrett walked around the class looking at what we had in our lunches and discovered that I was only eating apple butter sandwiches. Apple butter was one of the main things my mother canned. He was well aware of the fact that Daddy was disabled and had been forced to resign his janitorial job. Mr. Barrett called me outside the classroom and explained that he had a job he needed me to do for him; he said that he could not pay me in money but he would "compensate" me with a meal in the lunchroom each day. He told me to go into the new janitor's (Mr. Combs) area down in the basement where I would find a wastebasket. My "job" would be to empty that wastebasket into the barrel that stood next to it. That was his kind way of giving me a healthy lunch while saving my pride. Today, I regret that I never took the opportunity to thank him later in life for his caring generosity.

Apparently, Mr. Barrett was onto Mr. Combs' case often. One cold winter day our classroom was getting quite chilly and our teacher said to me, "Dee, go down and tell Mr. Combs that I said to shovel a little more coal into the furnace." When I got back to the classroom, Mr. Barrett must have suspected that Mr. Combs didn't take that request very well. When he asked me, "What did Mr. Combs say?" I told him exactly what the janitor had said. "He said for me to tell you that he hopes when you die that you go to a warmer place." Without saying anything, Mr. Barrett just smiled. I graduated from Mt. View as a ninth grader in the spring of 1955 and Mr. Barrett became principal of Mt. View in the fall of 1955.

My classes in grades seven through nine at Mt. View were uneventful until I got into Coach McGinnis' civics class and was able to play on his basketball team. Our ninth grade team was made up of Tom Bryant, Tommy Scarbro, Edsel Simmons, Jack Price, Dean Bradford and me. Our record that year was 14-2. It would be an understatement to say that Coach McGinnis was a big influence in my life. He even allowed me to carry the keys to the gym--I would take my friends to the gym and play basketball during weekends. As a principal I used his line, "Two wrongs don't make a right." When a basketball player kept missing shots he would yell, "You couldn't hit a bull in the rear end with a bass fiddle." He was one of the very few coaches that I never heard utter a curse word.

During those days, West Virginia's teacher's pay was probably the lowest in the nation. One day Coach got on a roll during civics class about how poorly he was paid. He wrote his salary on the chalkboard, added his coaching supplement, then deducted taxes, retirement, expenses for travel to games, etc. When all was said and done, he was making about $1.50 per hour. That's when Richard Dilly raised his hand and asked, "Coach, do teachers have to pay income tax?" This really set Coach off. After the 1954-1955 school year, Coach McGinnis left for California. I never tried to contact him until sometime in the 1980s, I learned that I had waited too long; he had passed away. Another big regret!

Every year Mt. View had a carnival to raise funds for the school. That little gym was packed and people would elbow their way through the crowd to get to the various games. "Quincy the Talking Duck" was the main attraction. Quincy was a big ugly Muscovy duck owned by Uncle Okey's family; his handler (usually, one of Uncle Okey's children) would set him up on a table and people would pay something like a dime to try and get two aluminum rings to throw around Quincy's head. If they were successful, they would win a prize. The duck, of course, had been to the carnival before and he seemed to remember what was expected of him. Every time he would see a ring coming his way, he would duck his head which would rob the player of a prize. Once Gordon (one of Uncle Okey's kids) put up a strong argument that he should get a cut of whatever money Quincy made for the school. Coach McGinnis asked, "Gordon, where do you think we get the money to buy the equipment: bats, balls and other equipment you play with in physical education class?" It was a good point, but I don't think he ever won Gordon over.

When school started in the fall of 1955, I was in class at Marsh Fork High School only a few days before I was summoned to the courthouse in Beckley to testify in a case involving a car wreck I had witnessed. As a result, I missed several days of school. When I finally got back to school I learned (much to my disappointment) that I had been scheduled to take geometry. I knew that I was in trouble because I'd had no background in math that could have prepared me for the rigors of plane geometry. Unfortunately, my eighth grade math teacher had been bone lazy and totally inept. Students were expected to solve problems in the textbook working on their own. If students were to go to the teacher's desk and ask for help, he would help them. But if you got to, say, page 85 and were confused and asked for help he would then say, "You should have learned that on page 26." Then he would force the student to go back to page 26 and start over doing all the problems through the pages. In ninth grade we took Algebra I and our teacher was no better than what we'd had in the eighth grade. She would get frustrated because we didn't grasp what she was trying to get across; then she would cry, stomp the floor, and throw the chalk across the room. Some of the more mischievous boys would purposely push her buttons just to watch her throw a tantrum. She was rather homely, staring old maid hood in the eye, and probably wanted to be anywhere in the world other than in that classroom with us.

Naturally the plane geometry class was a disaster, and I didn't learn a thing. In fact, I got a grade of "F" during one grading period and a "D" the next period, with a final grade of "D." Once again I was short changed in math by an ineffective teacher. My lack of math skills is something that has held me back all my life. I could have earned my doctoral degree if I had been able to meet the math requirements for subjects like statistics.

For the most part, I had good teachers in high school but—unfortunately—I was never pushed (or even encouraged) at home to earn better grades in school. Consequently, I just wandered along and didn't really work to my ability until I was in my senior year. In fact, I could have probably even dropped out of school all together if I had wanted to. The class that broke the cycle of my laziness was Mrs. Doris Webb's English classes. They were the exception to my—up to that point—mediocre education. When I arrived at Marsh Fork, older kids warned me, "Don't get in Mrs. Webb's class, she is hard." By that age I had heard more than enough people murder the English language with poor grammar (i.e., double negatives, etc.), and I didn't want to embarrass myself by being one of them. For this reason, I went out of my way to make sure that I was in Mrs. Webb's English class from grade ten to twelve, as well as in a class that she taught only for seniors. I worked hard in her classes because I wanted to learn and because she expected and demanded that I truly work. Decades later, I became a high school principal for 19 years and I never met an English teacher I thought was better than she.

In my senior year, I finally woke up and realized that school had not been designed just for me to have a place where I could play basketball. We had an outstanding coach, Dewey Romine, at Marsh Fork High who coached all the sports the school offered: baseball, basketball, football and track. He was one of the best coaches I have ever known at motivating and encouraging his players. But—at six feet two inches and 160 pounds—I was not a football player. My mother was adamantly opposed to any of us boys playing football because she had been in the hospital (or visited a hospital) when a lady there told her about a very bad football injury that her son had suffered. For me, that story was a clincher! Because I could not play football the coach would not let me play basketball. No 16-year old boy is going to tell his coach that, "Mommy won't let me play football." Coach Romine told me at the end of my junior year that if I didn't go out for football in my senior year, there would be no use for me to go out for basketball. I didn't go out for the football team, but I did go out for basketball which would prove to be a mistake.

Practice usually ended well after dark in the winter and there was no transportation provided for student athletes to get home safely. I lived thirteen miles from the school and had to hitchhike home in wintry weather every night after practice. Looking back, I can't believe that the school officials allowed that to happen. Some nights I actually had to keep walking so that I wouldn't freeze. One night it was snowing hard--there were no cars coming along, so I just kept walking. I would stomp my feet on the road to knock the cold off my feet—I was getting really concerned that I might not get a ride home at all and might have to knock on someone's door to ask for shelter. I don't remember who picked me up or where I was, but I made it home and got some good hot food inside me. Finally, I realized that I was wasting my time going to practice every day, hitchhiking home every night, only to ride the bench at every game. So, I quit the team and decided to get serious about my classes. When I became a high school principal in 1980 I made sure no kid was treated that way.

During the closing days of my senior year, the senior class was called into Room 8—the classroom where (four years later) I would teach social studies. All 56 of us jammed the room with half of us standing and half of us sitting. The purpose of the meeting was to hear a college recruiter speak to us about the value of enrolling at Beckley College, a two-year private school. The speaker was John B. Van Dyke, Jr. who doubled as a professor and recruiter for the college. He spoke with us about the college and what it offered, then passed out 3x5 cards and asked us to write our name and address on the cards if we had even the slightest desire to go to college. I was seated in the back of the room with a bunch of other wise asses who dared me to fill out the card. In fact, I really did want to go to college, but I knew there was no chance in the world such a dream could be realized. Still, prodded by prankster peers, I filled out the card out anyway.

Perhaps my motivation to continue my education was the fact that my brother, Bee, had come out of the Navy and was already attending Beckley College. Bee was my role model; I thought that if he could do it maybe I could do it too. When Mr. Van Dyke read through the cards, he asked the person to identify him or her self, then he'd ask each student a couple of questions. Finally, he came to my card, on which I had printed "Dee Cantley." He readily told me that he knew my brother who was one of his students at the college. Mr. Van Dyke asked me a few questions then proceeded to the name on the next card. I thought that would be the end of my dealings with him. Not so--the next time I saw him he was the speaker at our commencement ceremony. I still remember the title of his speech, "Quo Vadis?" which (roughly translated from Latin) means "Where are you going, young man?"

After I graduated in June of 1958, it soon became abundantly apparent to me that there were absolutely no opportunities for work in Rock Creek, West Virginia or in any of the surrounding rural communities. Rock Creek had Charlie Jarrell's store, Rader's General Store, which housed the post office and the Rebecca Chapel. That was it! I had finished high school during the year of the so-called "Eisenhower Recession." The local men who had gone north to work in the factories and steel mills had been laid off and were returning to West Virginia. Occasionally I would pick up a day of work here and there by working for farmers (in corn and or hay) for 50 cents an hour. I frequently told my students how I got my start and I recommended the same dose of hard physical labor to them. Invariably, they looked at me—in shock—as if to ask, "What planet are you from?"

Academic achievements of Marsh Fork graduates have been fairly well addressed in this book, however, in my research there was no documentation of Bulldog athletic teams to be found. Apparently, no documentation was kept at the school of records set by any teams or individuals. Mac McKinnon, our athletic and activities director at Lake Worth High often said, "Sports and other extracurricular activities are the other half of education." Academic purists will probably disagree, but I believe Mac had a point. As a high school principal, I encouraged and supported all extracurricular activities: teams, music programs, clubs and all activities. In addition to offering the best dropout prevention program, sports and other extracuricular activities helped build confidence and character and develop leadership skills.

After discovering the school had no records of its athletic teams, I contacted athletes who played during my years, 1956--58, at Marsh Fork High and asked them what they remembered from their careers at their alma mater. Thanks go to Carl Bradford '56, Larry Cassell '55, and Larry Sarrett '57 for their input. Cassell and Sarrett provided newspaper clippings to support their stories.

To my knowledge, the only state championship team at Marsh Fork High School was the 1942 Class B basketball team. The only information available about that team was a list of the players on the team provided by Tex Williams, a Clear Fork High and Marshall University athlete. Tex sent me a picture of the sign on the basketball court dedicated to the team at the Marsh Fork High School Park listing the names of the players. Team players of the 1942 championship team were: Daryl Acord, Orville Carr (brother of Marsh Fork Coach Virgil Carr), Richard Everett, Azel Farley, Jr., Dean Jarrell, Jack Kyle, Don Lamb, Dewey Romine, Bobby Tabor, Glendale Tabor and Coach Carl Jarrell. Coach Jarrell eventually left teaching and purchased the grocery store at Dry Creek; he also served on the Raleigh County Board of Education.

As a sophomore, I remember playing in a basketball game at Trap Hill High when Larry Sarrett, a junior and normally one of our top scorers, was held scoreless in the first half. In the locker room at half time Coach Virgil Carr was chewing Larry out big time. Larry told me he was scared to death listening to Carr's tirade. Very early into coach's "presentation," our principal said, "You boys haven't played any ball since...." That was as far as he got when Coach Carr jumped in and said, "Hold it right there. I am still coaching this team." Coach Carr went on to say other things which I have forgotten. Coach Carr later apologized to the team for his remarks to the principal and, as I recall, the principal was present. Coach Carr was gone in two weeks, selling cars in Charleston and Dewey Romine took over as coach. Larry scored 26 points in the second half of that Trap Hill game but we lost 81-85. Larry told me, "If Coach Carr had yelled at me before the game I might have scored 50." Although mostly known for his basketball game, Larry was selected as honorable mention as an end on the Class B All-State Football Team his senior year, 1956-57.

Sarrett sent me a clipping stating he scored 47 points in one game against Pax at home to set a school record. I remember playing in that game when Larry said, "Give me the ball, Dee. I'm trying to break the school record." We beat Pax 82-74. He also told me Carl Bradford was second with 41 points but Larry Cassell sent me a clipping reporting he (Cassell) scored 44 in a 98-71 win over Sherman. Sarrett also said Carl Bradford scored the most points in one season, 609 and that he (Sarrett) was second with 560. Cassell said he scored, "Between 550 and 650."

Our biggest rivals were Clear Fork and Trap Hill High Schools. Any contest between Marsh Fork and either of those schools was sure to draw a packed house. Jim White, one of my assistant principals at Lake Worth High, was a proud graduate of Clear Fork High where he lettered in all sports offered there. He and I use to engage in friendly banter about our respective schools. I told our coaches that when we played Clear Fork on their home turf we could expect to encounter a tree cut across the road forcing our bus to turn around and take the long route over the mountain to get back home. However, I stated, when they played at our place our Mothers would cook a meal and say a prayer for them before they left.

Dick Sellards was an outstanding athlete at Marsh Fork High, starring in all sports. In one home basketball game against Clear Fork we beat them 67-85 with Dick scoring 27 points aided by Percy Jarrell with 20. Larry Casssell who provided the clipping scored 13 points and said this game in his junior year was the best team performance of his career.

Larry Cassell is arguably one of the best all-round athletes to play at Marsh Fork. He was valedictorian of his 1955 class and was nominated first alternate to West Point by Congressional Representative Robert C. Byrd. He married Carole Scarbro, one of my classmates and a cheerleader. He says he is probably the only valedictorian in his class at Marsh Fork and maybe in the state and nation to throw five touchdown passes in one game, score 44 points in a basketball game and pitch a shutout in baseball.

Larry was captain of the football and basketball teams and the students voted him best athlete in 1954 and 1955. The baseball team did not have a captain. He looked forward to baseball season in his senior year with what he said was a loaded Marsh Fork team; however, the principal and Coach Carr said the school could not afford to fund the team. Larry still harbors hard feelings over this; he felt his team could have gone far in the playoffs. Cassell threw five touchdown passes in a 50-20 win over Baileysville in 1955 and scored 44 points against Seth in an away basketball game, going 20 for 22 at the foul line, claiming the school record. Usually a shortstop on the baseball team, he pitched a shutout against Van in 1954. He told me that he and his brother, John, were the only brothers to lead their basketball teams in scoring--John in 1945 and Larry in 1953, 1954, and 1955. He was catcher and played third base for the Montcoal mine team, and he also played third base as well as catcher for the Whitesville American Legion team.

After graduating high school, Cassell enrolled at West Virginia Wesleyan where, as a freshman, he started as quarterback and as a catcher on the baseball team. He caught for Wesleyan when they beat WVU and were the unbeaten champs of the WV Conference. His clippings show he was highly regarded by Wesleyan coaches and showed great promise for a career at Wesleyan. However, Larry decided to leave Wesleyan and go to Cleveland, OH to work in steel mills.

Carl Bradford played basketball all four years at Morris Harvey College (now University of Charleston) and is in the Hall of Fame there. He, Tex

Williams and former Morris Harvey team mate, Bruce Hewitt, played in the Senior Olympics until 2008. Carl told me that he and Tex played only one season together when they played in Tucson, Arizona, beating favored California in the semi-finals before losing to New York for the gold medal by one point on the last shot of the game. Tex told me when he played with Carl, Carl would pick a fight with the biggest, strongest, meanest and ugliest player on the opposing team, get four fouls on him and then he (Tex) would have to guard the guy. They won several gold medals in 3X3 and 5X5 basketball. Carl played with Portland, Oregon when they won gold in the 2002 Melbourne Australia World Games. Carl is retired and lives in Santee, South Carolina where he plays golf two or three times a week.

Scott Jarrell was an outstanding running back who graduated in 1956. He married one of my classmates, Carol Johnson. I heard lineman Johnny Johnson say, "If you didn't make a hole for him he would run right up your back." Scott went to Marshall University on a football scholarship and retired as football coach and guidance counselor at Wayne High School. Sadly, Scott was murdered in his home by one of his former football players on New Year's Eve, 2010. His attacker was sentenced to life in prison without possibility of parole after the jury deliberated only 40 minutes. He was lured into the prison kitchen by a small group of inmates, knocked to the floor and held down while scalding water was poured on his head. He was taken to a hospital where he was pronounced dead.

Larry Cassell told me the best basketball teams we had were coached by L. G. Daniel in the late 40's when Tom Jarrell, Dick Darby, Stanley and Benny Larabee, Cebert and J. D. Bradford, Sharkey Byrd and Carl Bawgus played. Bob Milam told me that veteran teacher Bernard Green told him that Darby was the best all round athlete to graduate Marsh Fork High. I don't know why but Marsh Fork once played the big powerhouse Woodrow Wilson High in Beckley where the enrollment was probably five times that of Marsh Fork. I have spoken with several people who saw that game. Both Marsh Fork fans and people who didn't have a dog in the fight told me Marsh Fork was robbed in losing that game. Carl Bradford told me the starters of that 1948 team were his brother Cebert, Dick Darby, Tom Jarrell, John Rutledge and E. Griffith. The score of the game was Woodrow Wilson 41, Marsh Fork 36.

A telephone conversation with Jimmy Farley, who grew up in Rock Creek, provided me a good synopsis of the basketball career of Bill Jarrell at Marsh Fork High School. Bill was the son of Lantie and Betty Jarrell of Rock Creek. Betty was an elementary school teacher at Mr. View Jr. High School, also located at Rock Creek.

Jimmy said that Bill was big and strong and very difficult to stop from scoring. Bill was a rare starter in his freshman year and grew to be 6' 6" by his senior year when he frequently scored 30-40 points a game. Jimmy said Bill was a special player as he controlled the boards and could also score from the outside corner.

Jimmy saw Bill play during his senior year and said that Bill was highly recruited by college coaches. Bill was honored as the First Team All Starter in West Virginia and was named an All American High School player.

Although scoring records were not available, Jimmy said that Bill Jarrell would be, in his opinion and the opinion of several others with whom he has spoken, the highest total scorer to ever play basketball at Marsh Fork High School, especially since he was a starting player four years—as a freshman, sophomore, junior and senior.

In October 2019 Bill was inducted in the recently established Hall of Fame at Liberty High School, the consolidated high school that includes Marsh Fork, Clear Fork and Trap Hill high schools. Bill was the first and to date the only basketball player from Marsh Fork High School to be inducted in the Hall of Fame. There will be more basketball players inducted in the upcoming years, but Bill Jarrell will be remembered as the first one to be honored.

As stated in Coalfield Baseball, Maynard Daniel was a very effective pitcher for the Bulldogs, winning both games of a double header under Coach L. G. Daniel. There are many other great Marsh Fork athletes, most of whom I am not aware or have forgotten. I apologize for those I have overlooked.

Any Marsh Fork alum will tell you that they have fond memories of their high school years. Athletes, band members, majorettes (my wife Kay was one) and cheerleaders put on quite a show for the people of Coal River. Our cheerleaders always started a cheer by asking the fans, "Are you ready, Bulldogs?" The fired-up pep club and other fans would reply in unison, "Bow Wow!" The cheerleaders would then go into an arousing cheer. In the days before television, residents from the hills and hollers crowded the venue when every game was played.

Who could forget the closely contested basketball game when our local constable thought the refs were cheating sufficiently to justify him going onto the floor and pulling his hawk-billed knife on them. Sarrett remembers getting into a scuffle in a home game with Buddy Hensley of the Sherman team. Larry says that the constable came onto the floor and positioned himself between him and Hensley whereupon he announced to Hensley, "I'm gonna take you to jail." Larry Cassell reminded me of the time when we lost a home game and the constable blamed the refs. He waited for them at Pettus and before they crossed into Boone County he stopped them and gave them a ticket for speeding. Whether true or not he was quoted as saying, "I knew that anyone who would cheat like that would have to break the law before leaving the county."

If you haven't already done so, go to MarshFork.com and take a walk through Bulldog history by reading the yearbooks.

Chapter photo: Marsh Fork High School located at Montcoal, West Virginia. The original school was built in 1922 as Montcoal High School. That building burned and the modern school was built in 1945 and closed in 2003. After the school was closed, it was burned by vandals. *Photo courtesy of Charles Bradford.*

COLLEGE YEARS

Struggling through the summer after graduating high school, I did whatever possible to make a dollar while simultaneously praying for something to come along that would give me an opportunity to build a better life for myself. Sometime in late July, prayers were answered. As I walked from the farm to the store or post office, I saw this little two-tone green '52 Chevy coupe approaching the bridge that spanned Coal River separating our farm from Rt. 3. Both the car and its driver were familiar to me-- It was Mr. Van Dyke, the Beckley College recruiter and professor. I thought, "Now, how am I going to graciously get this guy out of my hair and back on the road to Beckley". Little did I know that my conversation with him on that little bridge was to have an impact that would forever change my life and provide experiences beyond my wildest dreams.

Mr. Van Dyke asked if I still wanted to go to college; I replied with an emphatic, "Yes!" I told him, however, that it would not be possible because my dad was a disabled miner, thus our family did not have the money to pay for my college education. Then Mr. Van Dyke said what many of my teachers had told me, "If you set your sights on a goal and are willing to work for it, you can become anything you want to become." He also told me that our family name was well-known at the college because Eustace, Bee and Donna had all graduated from Beckley College--name recognition would be to my advantage.

He said, "The squeaky wheel gets the grease and if we squeak loudly enough we can get you some grease." For some reason he made me want to believe all that he was saying and I had confidence in what he told me. Mr. Van Dyke told me to come to the college on a specific date in early August to speak with Dr. Shroyer the college president about getting some financial help. He said he would help me by talking with Dr. Shoryer prior to my arrival, saying Dr. Shroyer was currently on vacation in Florida and would return in early August. Mr. Van Dyke told me I needed to be on the campus at a stated date to discuss the possibility of financial aid.

Today, I shudder to think of what my life would have been like if this determined man had not followed up on a card I had filled out—in jest—back on that day in Room Eight. Until I met Mr. Van Dyke, I had no skills, no money and no hope.

Since my only mode of transportation was my thumb I crossed that bridge, stepped to the edge of Route 3 on the appointed date, and hitch hiked a ride to Beckley (a distance of 25 miles.) I then walked two miles across town to where I understood the college to be, the enormity of what I was doing didn't hit me until I neared the entrance of the college. I said to myself, this man is going to think I am crazy coming into his office with no money—and no way of getting any, to ask that he allow me to enroll in his college.

Dr. Shroyer was the most unforgettable person I had ever met. He had a loud booming voice, wore contrasting colors and patterns in his clothing, and had an office full of exotic souvenirs that included two large totem poles which stood behind his desk. Dr. Shroyer started the conversation, "Boy, I understand you want to go to college. You got any money?" I explained that I not only did not have any money, but that my dad was a disabled miner. He said, "You are tall. Have you ever played any basketball?" I answered, "Yes, sir." Then I told him that while I had played, I'd quit the team in my senior year. He said, "Hell, we'll give you a basketball scholarship," and then he started making out my class schedule. When he asked me what I wanted to major in, I told him I wanted to major in business. (I chose business because I was a good typist.) He then started checking off the classes I would need to take. "Hell," his commentary went on "here is a class that is easy, and here's a damn good one. You can pass this one." That went on until he had completed my schedule. When he finished creating my entire schedule, he handed it to me and said, "Here. Take this across the hall to Dean Hartman, and tell him you're going to college." That is how it all started.

I literally strutted out onto the sidewalk and onto Harper Road to hitchhike a ride home. I couldn't wait to get home to tell my parents the good news; when I told them I was going to college I sensed they were a little skeptical about my going to college. Years later, my brother, Bee, told me that when my mother told him that she couldn't see how I was going to go to college, he told her, "Whatever you do, don't tell him that."

Later, I hitchhiked a ride to my high school to tell whomever I could find that I was going to college. The principal was sitting at his desk, chewing tobacco, spitting into a coffee can, and reading a paperback book. When I told him that I was going to Beckley College, here's the encouragement I got: "Well, Dee, I don't know how you are going to go to college. I know your dad doesn't have any money." That made me even more determined than ever to find a way to not only start, but to finish college.

The new school year started, and I hitchhiked a ride to Beckley. All the details escape me, but I somehow ended up living with three other basketball players in a home owned by an elderly lady on Paint Street. The college must have funded that room and board as part of my scholarship because I certainly didn't pay anything for it. It was free, but it was not a good experience. When we sat at the table it was dangerous to reach for a dish because you just might pull back a bloody stub. Forget about someone "passing" a dish to you—that just wasn't going to happen. That was probably the first time I really appreciated my upbringing.

My nephew, Ike, was living in Beckley with his maternal grandmother, Mrs. Cavendish, and was attending Woodrow Wilson High School. He came to visit me, saw what a difficult situation I had on Paint Street and went back to talk with his grandmother about the possibility of me staying with them. It would be an understatement to say that I was thrilled to get out of that boarding-house-like environment. Mrs. Cavendish graciously agreed to keep me for $30 a month, Ike and I shared the room--the $30 a month included breakfast, a lunch to take to school, and a good home-cooked dinner. I am willing to bet that she didn't even break even on the deal. Good thing for me that (years earlier) I'd saved Ike from drowning in the Jack Hole! Since I had no way of getting my hands on $30 I borrowed the money from my sister, Betty, and her husband, Bill.

My classes at Beckley College were enjoyable, especially the ones taught by Mr. Van Dyke. Other than Mrs. Webb, he was the first "blue chipper" teacher I'd ever had and he was the type of instructor who made you want to go to class. The lively stories and funny jokes he told in class are etched in my memory.

When basketball tryouts were held, I was cut from the team after only five days but I retained my scholarship. Every Friday night I hitchhiked home—taking my dirty laundry with me—and then hitchhiked back on Sunday evening. My Mother would wash my clothes and hang them on the line to dry on Saturday. During the winter—when cold weather would not permit outdoor drying—she would hang them on curtain stretchers that she set up around the pot-belly stove in the dining room.

By the end of my first year of college, the economy had improved, so I went to Cleveland, Ohio and got a job in a steel mill. My sister, Barbara, and her husband, Bill, lived in Cleveland; I was fortunate to be able to live with them while I worked to save money for the next year at Beckley College. I was paid an unbelievable $4.50 an hour which was unheard of back in 1959. On my first weekend trip home, I went over to Charlie's store. When I told the locals how much money I was making, no one would believe me. Paul Doss, who had worked in a coal mine and made a good living looked at me askew and said, "Cantleeee!" When I got my second pay check, I paid my debt to Betty and Bill. Years later Bill told me he had thought he would never see that money again, but it was OK because the money was going to a good cause.

In the fall of 1959, I went back to Beckley College with enough money saved from the steel mill job to pay Mrs. Cavendish the $30 each month for my room and board. When basketball tryouts were announced I went out

187

for the team again. This time I was cut after four days. This was fine with me because the economy had improved and I was able to get a part-time job working at the W. T. Grant store in town. I made 85 cents an hour as a stock boy and custodian. This enabled me to tell my students that I had had many jobs, even cleaning toilets, while I was getting my education.

Shortly after the basketball season began, I was approached by the new basketball coach, Joe Cook, who told me that one of the players, the thirteenth player, was unhappy. This player had complained that I had a scholarship and didn't even have to attend practice. (He had been practicing every day in hopes of being the twelfth player on the team, so he could get a scholarship.) Cook asked me what I thought we should do. I told him that I was not giving up my scholarship because without it I would be forced to drop out of college. He then suggested that we take the problem to Dr. Shroyer and let him settle it.

When I went to Dr. Shroyer's office, he opened the meeting with, "Boy, what are we going to do about this?" I explained that without this scholarship, I would have to leave college. He told me to go back to class.

That response seemed to settle the problem — for a couple of months. Coach Cook approached me again to tell me the thirteenth player was still complaining. Again, I was sent to see Dr. Shroyer and again he said, "Boy, what are we going to do about this?" I told him—a little more emphatically this time—that this was my only way of getting an education; I reminded him what I had told him back when he'd given me the scholarship—that my dad was a disabled miner. I ended my spiel by saying, "It is up to you, Dr. Shroyer. If you want me to go back home, I will go home." My heart was in my throat because I knew my fate was about to be decided. He looked at me and said, "Boy, go on back to class. If anyone says anything to you, tell them to see me. I'm still running this damn place."

That was it, no one ever spoke to me about my scholarship again. I graduated Beckley College in two years, and I hadn't spent a cent on anything including tuition, books, fees or anything else. Another huge regret I have is, unfortunately, I never contacted Dr. Shroyer later in life to thank him. Dr. Shroyer and Mr. Van Dyke were the determining factors in setting me on the path to a future that would provide opportunities and take me to places beyond my wildest dreams.

One day, from my desk at Lake Worth High School, I called Mr. Van

Dyke and reminded him of that day on that little bridge at Rock Creek. I thanked him profusely, as I didn't want to repeat the mistake that I made with Dr. Shroyer. I stay in contact with Mr. Van Dyke via phone calls and letters. He celebrated his 95th birthday October 28, 2019. He lives in Scott Depot, West Virginia, where Kay and I have visited him..

After graduating from Beckley College in June of 1960, I again went to Cleveland to work in a foundry, and—one more time—I stayed with Barbara and Bill. I made a lot of money, but not nearly enough to enroll at Morris Harvey College in Charleston, now the University of Charleston. (President Eisenhower initiated The National Defense Student Loan which was continued by President Kennedy. This program was established to both bolster teacher ranks and to allow financially needy students to get a college education.) I fit the mold! I applied for the loan and Miss Stella Cooksey, who administered the program at the college, granted me the loan for both years I was enrolled at Morris Harvey. Possibly, the fact that two years earlier both Bee and Donna had graduated from Morris Harvey helped me get the loan. Miss Cooksey probably also knew that Eustace was a part-time student there while he worked in a coal mine during the day. I called and reconnected with her sometime in the 1990's to thank her for that much-needed loan long ago.

Life at Morris Harvey was a whole new experience for me, living in a dorm felt a lot more like college life. My first year (I was a junior), I roomed with Gerald Dickens and Raymond Domingues. Gerald and I had been in the same class from grades one through nine at Mt. View, grades ten to twelve at Marsh Fork, and for two years at Beckley College. We would graduate Morris Harvey together, work the same part-time jobs, and teach at Marsh Fork High School for three years before Kay and I moved to Florida. Sadly, Gerald passed away in 2013. My other close friends at Morris Harvey, were Bill Alexander, Birdeye (Jesse) Richardson, Bob Backus, Carlos Hurst, Tony Rinaldi, Gerald, Gary Miller and Ted Ellis. Bill and I became fast friends mainly through our love of country music and our "pickin'" and singing sessions in the dorm. Bill and I would later hook up again when Kay and I moved to florida in 1965. Sadly, Bill passed away in July of 2019.

Thanks to my summer job in Cleveland and the college loan, I was able to buy a '52 Ford—six-cylinder engine with a stick shift transmission—from my brother, Hubert Jr. for $250. The six cylinder engine was not powerful. Once I parked on the unpaved college lot one night when the only vacant spot was muddy. That night the temperature dropped and the mud froze around all four tires. The next morning I tried to move the car but it wouldn't budge from the frozen mud. I had to wait until the afternoon when the sun came out and warmed up the mud.

I needed that car as the college was 50 miles from home. Gerald and I would go home every Friday, get some home cooking and clean clothes, then head back to Charleston Sunday night. As stated in a previous chapter, Noel drove an auto transport rig and was usually home on Sunday nights. We would make a stop in Whitesville at Noel's house, back my Ford up to Noel's truck, and siphon gas with a five-foot Coal River credit card from it into my car. That free tank of gas would take us through the entire week and was a big help because gas was getting expensive—39¢ per gallon.

A part-time job was a must for me while I was at Morris Harvey College, the best-paying job I had was a union job working on the docks for McLean Trucking at their Bell, West Virginia terminal. My pay was $24 for eight hours—enough for meals and spending money, especially if I could get two shifts per week. The temperature inside those trailers was extremely hot in the summer and freezing cold in the winter. Eventually, I managed to get Gerald a job at McLean. The terminal manager liked to schedule Gerald and me to work as much as possible because we were good workers. A small number of the full-time workers were protected by the union and they goofed off a lot.

My senior year at Morris Harvey was to be one of great joy and satisfaction. My dream of a college diploma was nearing reality; little did I know that I was about to face one of the worst events in my life. My nephew, Larry, had graduated Trap Hill High School in 1961, and he had enrolled at Morris Harvey. He roomed with me, and I was looking forward to enjoying a great year with him, however, on Halloween weekend he went home and was killed in a car wreck within sight of his family's home. His death was devastating for our entire family; it certainly put a damper on my enthusiasm for college life.

Because we had graduated Beckley College some of our credits were not transferable. Consequently, Gerald, Birdeye, Raymond and I were required to go to summer school to earn the credits we needed to graduate

Morris Harvey. Since Bird Eye only needed to complete one class to meet requirements, I suggested that he go see the professor and ask if he could go home and complete the course requirements via mail. He didn't think the professor would go for that, but I disagreed and told Birdeye I would go plead his case with the professor.

I went into the professor's office, pleaded Bird Eye's case, and told him that my friend could not afford to spend the summer in the dorm because he had no money for food. The professor understood and Bird Eye was able to go home where he completed the course by mail. (A note to the younger set: This was an unusual situation because we did not have computers in those days and "online classes" did not exist.) Birdeye drove his '48 Chrysler back to Charleston and we all graduated together at the end of the summer session.

While I was in college, my Aunt Lou told me that "Hubert (my dad) ought to sell that timber over there and help you go to college." Betty, Barbara and Noel all helped me in different ways; I am glad that my dad did not sell his timber. He did sell the timber years later when he and my mother really needed the money. During my four years of college, he was only able to buy me two pairs of pants. While I was at Beckley College, we had a winter that was brutally cold; the temperature was below zero and it stayed there for a week. Daddy ordered two pairs of wool pants for me—one pair was brown, the other was charcoal. They were wooly and scratchy, but they sure felt good when it was freezing cold outside—when I had to walk two miles to school or hitchhike home and back.

Spring Break 1961—the six of us came to Orlando. Here we are at Betty and Bill's home. L-R—Tony Rinaldi, Joe Kinder, me, Birdeye Richardson.

Top picture: Spring Break 1961. Pictured L-R—Ron Rexroad, Ray Goode, Bill Alexander.

Center picture: One of the many golf tournaments that Bill and I played in together over the years.

Bottom Photo: Bill Alexander, Ray Goode and me at DeeAnne's wedding, April 1990.

Chapter photo: Morris Harvey College buddies. Standing: Birdeye Richardson, Gerald Dickens. Seated: Raymond Domingues, David D. Cantley.

MY FIRST TEACHING JOB

In spite of what—at times—had seemed like impossible odds, finally my dream of completing my college education was a reality. The road had definitely been rocky, but I was determined to make it happen. Many people had told me an education was something that no one could take from me. Upon my graduation, that began to take on a special meaning for me. Now, it was time to start applying for a teaching job. Gerald, Birdeye and I all managed to get jobs at Marsh Fork High. Raymond went back to his alma mater Mt. Hope High where he taught social studies and later became principal. Birdeye taught English. Gerald, whose major was social studies, taught the lower level social studies courses such as freshman civics. I taught the upper level social studies classes—World History and U.S. History. It was difficult to understand why I wasn't given the civics classes and Gerald given the upper-level classes. After all, he had majored in social studies and it had only been my minor.

Another first-year teacher at Marsh Fork High that year would have a big impact on my life. Gweneth Kay Jones Pollock, a Marsh Fork grad, class of '56, graduate of Concord College, was introduced at the first faculty meeting as a new Business Education teacher. She immediately began to shine her eyes on me and pursue me until I finally agreed to go out with her in the fall of 1962. We would be married December 27, 1964. As previously stated this was the best thing that ever happened to me.

My internship had been at Charleston High School where I learned a great deal—not only about how to teach social studies and my major, physical education, but I was also able to observe a big school with innovative programs. When I went back to teach at my (small) alma mater, I was disappointed with what I saw. There had been no changes or improvements to the curriculum since my graduation four years earlier. In fact, there were no new programs nor any signs of willingness on the part of the principal to entertain any suggestions for change of any kind. He was perfectly content to wait for retirement; he didn't want to hear any ideas that would alter the routine he had established back in the 1940's when he had become principal. This "keep 'em under your thumb" style of leadership helped me to be a better principal when I went to Lake Worth High School in 1980. I knew Marsh Fork did not have enough students to support the curriculum of Charleston High, but some effort could have been made to implement at least one innovative program.

As stated earlier, I met my wife, Kay, who was divorced and had a two-year old daughter, Beth, when I taught at Marsh Fork. We were married in the Baptist Church at Whitesville on December 27, 1964. The Baptist preacher refused to marry us because Kay had been divorced, so we used the Methodist minister from Rebecca Chapel. My brother, Bee, was my best man. Before the ceremony, he told me, "Now I don't know this preacher at all, but I want you to watch him when he gets here. I guarantee you he will be right in the face of the first woman he sees." When the preacher walked in, Bee and I were located near Kay's mother, Mary Elizabeth, and two or three other people. As I introduced people to the preacher, I didn't look at him; instead I looked at the people I was introducing to him. Bee elbowed me and nodded his head toward the preacher. Sure enough, he was right up in Mary Elizabeth's face completely ignoring me.

Our reception was held in the Appalachian Electric Power Company Social Hall. The fare was weak punch, cake and cookies. When we returned from our honeymoon, Kay's grandpa, Blaine Daniel, (who was known to occasionally "take a little drink") told us that Hubert (my dad) had told him at the reception, "Blaine, if this punch had about a quart of good liquor in it, a man could drink it." When we next saw Daddy, he said, "Blaine told me that if that punch had about a quart of good liquor in it a man could drink it." We were never able to figure out who had told the truth!

As I stated earlier, marrying Kay was to be the next big game changer in my life and the best thing that ever happened to me. Without her I don't know where I would be today. There was an elderly congressional statesman from north Florida named Claude Pepper who used to say, "Any man who has had a good mother and a good wife has nothing to complain about." I have had both!

The population of our homogenous community was totally white and Protestant. The term WASP (White, Anglo-Saxon, Protestant) would have described the Coal River area. The majority of our students' parents either worked in mining or mining-related jobs. They were, for the most part, God-fearing people who had a strong work ethic which made for good strong students. Many Marsh Fork High students went on to become college graduates who majored in business, education, law, medicine and other fields. In a school board meeting, one Raleigh County Board Member stated that Marsh Fork High School had graduated as many doctors and lawyers as any school in the county.

The only regret I have regarding my three years teaching at Marsh Fork was my use of corporal punishment. Being a rookie teacher, I thought it was the thing to do as that was the modus operandi at the time. I have apologized to a few students but they seemed to have not been offended. Danny Cole at the 2015 school-wide reunion even bestowed upon me the dubious honor as being, "The best paddler in the school and Dewey Romine was second." Danny was well qualified to make that assessment.

It was difficult to live on a teacher's salary in West Virginia during the 1960s. Kay and I taught there for three years and during our last year,

1964-65, we only made $3,800 each. Lyndon Johnson was president, and he initiated his Great Society Poverty Program. It went like this: If you earned less than $3,000 per year, you were considered poverty-stricken and were entitled to certain government benefits such as commodity foods, medical and dental benefits, etc. We looked at that and said, "Here we are with four years of college (as well as three years teaching experience each), yet we are only being paid $800 above the national poverty level." It was painful to think that was all we were worth. Additionally, Kay had "gotten herself pregnant" and would not be allowed to teach during the 65-66 school year because she would be "showing." We were making monthly payments of $65 on a new Ford Fairlane, and our rent was $55 per month.

Together, we decided that we had to do better than this. I left for Cleveland to live with Barbara and Bill so that I could work with Bill for the summer in a factory building Army tanks to be sent to Vietnam. Meanwhile, Kay was sending application letters to Orange, Palm Beach and Monroe Counties in Florida. On one of my weekend trips home, she and Beth came back to Cleveland with me. One day we got a call from Kay's Aunt Louise, whom we had asked to pick up our mail at the post office. She told me that I had received a letter from Palm Beach County Schools; she asked if I wanted her to open the letter and read it to me. Of course, I did!

The letter was from Jim Pigott who had recently been hired as the coordinator of physical education for the school district. He offered me a job teaching elementary physical education. I called him, told him I was definitely interested in the job, and realized that I would have to fly down for an interview. He said, "No, you have already been cleared for employment, we will consider this the final interview." I did wonder why he would offer me the job sight unseen. Wisely, I did not question him on the matter.

When I arrived in Palm Beach County, I learned why I'd been given the job. Ike and his wife, Pat, had already been to Palm Beach County; Pat had been offered a job teaching art, but she would not accept the job unless Ike also got a job. The new itinerant elementary physical education program had been approved late in the summer, and now Pigott had to scrape up teachers to fill the slots. When the program was finally approved the director of personnel, Charlie Wilson, told Jim that he could get a guy

Cantley up in West Virginia. He explained that John I. Leonard High principal, Mel Adolphson, wanted to hire Pat, but she would not come unless Ike—whose field was also physical education—got a job as well. Jim then went to the files, came to "Cantley," and proceeded to pull "David," which came immediately before "Glenn" (Ike's given name). That is how Kay and I got to Palm Beach County. Tell me there was not a higher power at work here!

Freshmen basketball team 1963. I coached all three
years I taught at MFHS-- from 1963-65.

Chapter photo: A photo of Kay and me used in the 1964 Marsh Fork High School yearbook.

26

FLORIDA, HERE WE COME

While we packed for the move to Florida, Jim and Ellie White came to our house. (They had gone to Concord College with Kay. Jim would later be one of my assistant principals when I became principal at Lake Worth High in the spring of 1980.) They had arrived at Kay's mother's home across the street to see Kay. Mary Elizabeth told them that Kay was now married, lived across the street, and was packing to move to Florida. When they walked in, they asked where we were moving to in Florida; when we replied, "Palm Beach County," they said, "That's where we live."

Jim and Ellie asked which school I would be teaching in, and I explained that I would have three elementary schools: "Belle Grade, Canal Point and some Indian name town." When they asked if it was Pahokee and Belle Glade, I said, "yes." They looked at each other in a way that told me there was more to the story, so I asked if there was a problem with the area. "Oh no," they said. "*There are good people out there.*" The "out there" concerned me. Once I got to Florida, I would hear that phrase repeated a few more times.

Ike, Pat and I left Beckley on August 12, 1965 headed for Florida. Ike hoped there would be a job for him when he got there. As it turned out, there were still slots to fill in the elementary physical education program. So, he had no problem getting hired. Kay's doctor said that she and Beth could come with us as long as we stopped to let her walk periodically. Wisely, Kay's mother and Aunt Louise did not like that option. They— and I—convinced Kay to wait until I got settled, then she could fly to Florida with Beth.

Our long drive to Florida was a real challenge! Ike drove a '62 Ford convertible and towed his beloved '36 Ford which he refused to leave behind. He could have left it in Mrs. Cavendish's basement where it would have been perfectly safe, but "Noooooooo;" he had to drag it along. He couldn't drive over 45 miles per hour because the '36 would start to fishtail. Meanwhile, I was driving our '65 Fairlane and pulling a U-Haul trailer that contained our bedroom suite, a baby bed, Beth's youth bed, a table model black and white Zenith TV, a piece of green carpeting, assorted kitchen wares and other miscellaneous stuff. It was a hot summer, our cars weren't air conditioned, and there were no interstate highways. In those days, we travelled U.S. Highways 301 and 601; we didn't get on any modern roads until we got to the Florida Turnpike. As I recall, we spent two nights in motels along the way. Now, when we travel interstate highways to West Virginia, we only spend one night on the road. We have even driven straight through a couple of times in our younger days.

As we came closer to our Lake Worth exit on the turnpike, I decided to search for some serious music on the car's AM radio. I came across WSWN "In Busy Belle Glade," which was broadcasting all the country music a man could ever want to hear. The emcee was Jimmy Sims; I thought, since we hadn't had any all-country stations in West Virginia, this will be my kind of place. When we rolled into Lake Worth, we went to Pat's cousin's home; the first thing they told me was I needed to call home. When I phoned, Kay's grandpa, Blaine, answered and said, "Hey, we've got a big baby girl up here, four pounds and one ounce." Big baby girl, four pounds and one ounce? I said, "Let me speak with Mary."

When Mary got on the phone she explained that DeeAnne had been born two months prematurely on Friday, August 13, the day after we'd left West Virginia. The day after DeeAnne was born, her weight had dropped to only 3 pounds and 11 ounces. She would be in an incubator for two weeks and was touched only to change and feed her. The hospital staff could not even let Kay hold our daughter during this time. And I would not get to see my baby until five weeks later when I picked up Kay and the girls at the Palm Beach International Airport. The plane was scheduled to arrive at 6 p.m., but I was there at 3 p.m. anxiously waiting for that plane to touch down. (In those days, passengers had to walk down the steps from the plane onto the tarmac.)

As I happily drove home with my family, headed west on SR 80, a highway patrol officer pulled me over. When he got to my window, Beth (who was five years old) was standing behind me with her arms wrapped around my neck and crying hysterically. The officer silently took a look at that situation and walked away without saying a word. Thanks, Beth!

When I first arrived in Lake Worth, I stayed with Jim and Ellie in an efficiency apartment that was on one side of a duplex apartment they owned. This was only a temporary arrangement (i.e., just a few days) until I could find a place in the Glades. While I filled out the proper employment forms in the school district office, I asked about housing in the Glades. The secretary replied, "We don't know anything about housing out there, but there are good people out there." She advised me to call CTA, The Classroom Teachers' Association, but when I called they said, "We don't know about housing availability, but there are good people out there."

My schools were located in western Palm Beach County on the eastern shore of Lake Okeechobee. I finally managed to rent a house in Canal Point where one of my schools was located. It is an agricultural area that grows sugar cane as well as winter vegetables, getting two crops of corn during the winter months. South Florida summers are too hot, too rainy and full of too many insects to grow crops. The area's soil, called muck, is very rich and soft; bodies cannot be buried in it because coffins would rise to the surface. One day I was the only person on the athletic field at one of my schools, and I could feel the ground vibrate. I looked around me and saw the reason—a dog was trotting across the field, and his weight was causing the ground to shake. Although she was glad to be in Florida, Kay was very disappointed on her first day in the Glades. Her comment was, "I didn't think there was a place in the world more remote than Whitesville, West Virginia, but I was wrong."

Glades folks didn't seem to be very friendly or welcoming to outsiders. The white people didn't welcome me because I was an outsider, and the black people didn't trust me because of my accent. They'd ask, "Are you from Alabama?" I answered that I was not from Alabama and let them continue just to see where this would go. I then heard "Mississippi?" Again, I said "No" and told them that I was from West Virginia. They then would want to know if I'd gone to college in Alabama or Mississippi. I'd heard of "outsiders" who had eventually had been accepted by Glades folks, but I didn't plan to hang around long enough to receive that honor.

At that time, teachers were in great demand in Palm Beach County, especially in the Glades. When my three elementary principals heard that Kay was a certified teacher, all of them wanted to hire her, even though she was a secondary teacher who was certified in business education.

In late October, Kay took a job teaching second grade at Gove Elementary in Belle Glade; she was the ninth teacher those kids had had in a little over two months. The original teacher had left her keys on her desk the day before school started with a note telling the principal that she had accepted a job as an airline stewardess and wouldn't be back. Kay felt unqualified to teach second grade, but a good teacher can teach any grade level and Kay was just that—a good teacher. For the remainder of the school year, she brought warmth and stability to her students' lives. When the school year ended, we went to Lake Worth and stayed with Pat and Ike until we bought a home. When we closed on the house, I went back to Canal Point with a truck and a friend, Eric Danny, to move our furniture into the new house. Kay didn't go back until some 20 years later—to attend a funeral.

We did meet one couple in the Glades, Charlie and Barbara Poole, who have remained our friends since 1965. Jim Pigott told me (once I arrived in the Glades) to look up Charlie Poole, a long-time resident of the area. I later heard a legend that Charlie's family had lived around Lake Okeechobee so long that the gators had to check with them to find a place to bed. Charlie was locked into the area and did not want to leave his homeland, but his wife was a city girl from Miami, and she longed to move to the coast. They moved shortly after we did and Charlie bought a home on a good-sized piece of land with mango trees on it. He continues to tend his trees and harvest a large crop of mangoes each year. He also helps me by grafting different varieties of mangoes onto my trees.

We left Canal Point at the close of the school year in 1966 and went to stay with Ike and Pat in Lake Osborne Estates. While we were exploring the neighborhood we saw a house on High Ridge Road that was for sale. We purchased the home and I rented a U-Haul truck and went to Canal Point to get our possessions.

As I was placing furniture in the house a man appeared through the back yard to help. It was John I. "Jack" Sanders, known otherwise as "Sandy." Jack and Jeannette became a part of our family immediately.

The Sanders family had two daughters, Tina and Jeanne. Angela would be born a year later. They had just lost a baby, Julie, and were still grieving when we moved in next door to them. When Jack found out we were having problems finding day care for DeeAnne he asked Jeanette about taking care of her while Kay and I worked. She said she would try but was not making any promises. It was a match made in heaven; Jack and Jeanette needed DeeAnne, and we needed them. Years later, they both also took care of DeeAnne's baby, Taylor, while DeeAnne taught.

Meeting the Sanders family was a blessing for our family. We shared many happy (and some sad) life events with the Sanders as we raised our families. When I was principal at Lake Worth High Jeanette was always ready to lend a helping hand. She was instrumental in establishing the Court of Flags Memorial and tracking down grads for the Alumni Directory.

Jack has passed away but we remain close with Jeannette and the girls.

TOP LEFT: Christmas 1965 with family in West Virginia: Beth (L) is 5, and DeeAnne (on Kay's lap) is 4 months. **TOP RIGHT:** Jack and Jeanette Sanders at DeeAnne's wedding. **BOTTOM:** Jeanette, Jeanne, Tina Angela, Beth, DeeAnne and Kay at Angela's wedding.

Chapter photo: Here we are in Canal Point, FL. Although we miss the mountains of West Virginia, we have never regretted our move.

ROYAL PALM SCHOOL

After I had completed my four years of teaching (three in West Virginia and one in Florida), it was time for me to satisfy my National Defense Student Loan. A new ruling allowed teachers who taught migrant or special needs students to write off their loan each year taught. I had taught mostly migrant students in the Glades, and I went from there to a school for special needs students, which satisfied my two-year student loan without any out-of-pocket expenses. Thank you, Presidents Eisenhower and Kennedy.

Kay and I left the Glades after one year, we both got jobs on the coast. She taught business education at John I. Leonard High School, and I taught physical education to special needs students at Royal Palm School. My principal was Madge Edwards, a good 'ol Georgia gal, and I have enough stories about Madge to fill a separate book. Madge had no children of her own--the students at Royal Palm were her life. She insisted that "trainable" students should be taught to read. Most of the teachers (including myself) disagreed, believing that (a) it was a waste of resources, and (b) the students could be better served by vocational skills instruction. I have since come to believe that Madge was right, as I have watched Kay tutor our grandson, Jackson, who has Down syndrome. Jackson can read just about anything he wants to read.

My classes didn't begin until about 30 minutes after the classroom teachers started. During that time, Madge wanted me to come into her office and talk. She would close the door and reach down into her bottom right-hand desk drawer. It was smoking time! She had a Planters peanut can with a snap on plastic lid that she used for an ashtray. We would talk about the hard times in our childhood, and how we had been raised. No matter what I said, she would always find a way to top it. One day we were on the topic of life in farm houses. I told her that I remembered those cold winter mornings when I would get out of bed, hit that cold linoleum, and head for the fireplace. "Linoleum hell," she said. "We didn't even have linoleum, all we had were bare boards that let the wind blow up through the cracks." I can still hear Madge complaining about her, "damn arthuritis."

Madge and the other faculty smokers would put their cigarettes in the mailboxes in the lounge which doubled as the teachers' lunch room. It was a small school and there was room for only about a dozen teachers to sit for lunch. Looking for excitement, one day I decided to take a cigarette or two from Madge's pack and secretly flush them down the toilet. I did this for a few days and when I didn't hear anything from Madge about it, I then took six out one day and flushed them. A teacher's aide, Edna Selberg smoked the same brand as Madge and I happened to be in the lounge when "the fit hit the shan." Madge said, "Selberg, you have been smoking my cigarettes." Mrs. Selberg answered, "I have not been smoking your cigarettes. I have my own cigarettes." Madge countered with, "I have been missing cigarettes all week, I counted them this morning and six are missing. You are the only person here that smokes my brand." This heated discussion went back and forth until I became afraid that the two of them were going to come to blows. I let the situation cool down for a couple of weeks before I put a prank cigarette load in one of Madge's smokes. I wasn't there when she lit up, but those who were present said she nearly jumped through the ceiling when the cigarette exploded. When someone explained to her what a cigarette load was she said, "That has to be Mr. Cantley." She called me "Mr. Cantley" when she wanted to get on my case about something—otherwise, I was "Little David." Every time she saw me talking with a young single, female teacher she would bark out, "Mr. Cantley, how are Kay and those little girls doing?"

I gained a lot of valuable experience while teaching special needs children, and I know that my time at Royal Palm made me a better teacher. Exceptionalities at Royal Palm included students with emotional, mental and physical challenges. During the summer months I taught hearing impaired and blind children. Many of our students could have been educated in their neighborhood schools with just a modicum of extra assistance from the classroom teacher or an aide. One such student, David, who was confined to a wheelchair and needed assistance with his personal needs, was very bright and definitely should have been in his neighborhood school. A few years later, I was on the campus at Florida State University where I saw David, who was in his senior year and was looking forward to graduating. Unfortunately, Royal Palm School became a dumping ground used by traditional schools to rid their school of students who should not have been in Royal Palm. Federal legislation (Public law 94-142) that required students to be educated in the least-restrictive environment would be just a few years away. Later, as the principal at Royal Palm, it would become my job to enforce that legislation and place students in their neighborhood schools.

The school had very little means with which to purchase equipment for teaching physical education. I soon learned that it was easy to get civic organizations to donate materials, money and their time to help the school. I became a member of the Southboro Civitan Club, which was especially generous. I designed an obstacle course that was made entirely of discarded galvanized pipe, tires, plywood, ropes and other materials. I called it a "confidence" course because "Our kids have faced enough obstacles." That was a big hit with the media, parents, educators and the public. Later, we received a grant from the Kennedy Foundation and—with matching funds from the school district—built a covered pavilion that included a teachers' office and equipment storage room on one end of the structure.

Eventually Royal Palm School became a demonstration school. We had visitors from all over the state visit us to observe what we were doing in physical education. President Kennedy's mother, Rose Kennedy, came for the dedication ceremony of our demonstration center.

In 1967 Madge and I went to Washington to attend a workshop for physical education teachers and recreation personnel who served special-needs children and adults. It was hosted by the American Association of Health, Physical Education and Recreation. Eunice Kennedy Shriver attended the workshop because it was being underwritten by the Kennedy Foundation—I would later get a scholarship from the Kennedy Foundation that enabled me to get my master's degree in special education. Mrs. Shriver spoke to our group about an idea she called Special Olympics. She told us about her sister, Rosemary, who was intellectually challenged and lived in a private facility for her care. Mrs. Shriver said that Rosemary was inactive and spent most of her day sitting or sleeping. Then she told us that she thought there should be programs for students and adults like Rosemary. There were 25 people from around the country sitting at the table. Together we worked out the plan for Special Olympics. A year later I would take two boys on a train to Columbia, SC to compete in the Southern Regional Special Olympics. The next year I organized the first Special Olympics competition in Palm Beach County, which (ironically) was held at Lake Worth High School. Eleven short years later, I would become that school's principal.

Every job I ever had in the Palm Beach County School District was, I thought, the most important job in the district--I worked very hard at whatever that job might be. The students at Royal Palm always challenged me to search for innovative methods and programs to meet their needs; their enthusiasm made my job very rewarding. As I stated earlier, they forced me to become a better teacher. After seven years, however, I needed a change because I no longer really enjoyed what I was doing, and it was beginning to affect my health.

Kay and I had a neighbor, Dr. Ronald Hansrote, who was our family doctor. Ron and his wife Mitzi had a daughter, Linda, who was one of my Royal Palm students. One day, when our daughter, Beth, was in second grade, she was struck by a car in front of our house. Ron had just happened to come home early that particular afternoon, and he "just happened" to be sitting out on his patio when he heard the impact. He told Mitzi that he was sure someone had just been struck by a car! He had heard that sound before; it was a sound he could never forget. Luckily, he "just happened" to have his medical bag with him. He rushed two blocks to where Beth was lying on the pavement. She had been knocked into some garbage cans that were by the road. Ron said that when he got to Beth she had already stopped breathing. Thankfully, he was able to revive her. When the EMT personnel arrived, he continued to work with her in the ambulance. When they arrived at the hospital, he basically dismissed the ER doctors, ordered treatment, contacted her pediatrician as well as other specialists to treat Beth's injuries. Without Dr. Hansrote, we would not have a beautiful daughter, a son in-law, and three wonderful grandsons today.

Ron had a doctor friend, Bernard Chong, who also had a daughter in Royal Palm School. When Mrs. Chong learned that the Hansrotes were friends of mine she arranged for Mitzi to invite Kay and me to dinner at her home. Mrs. Chong cooked a beautifully prepared meal and everything was delicious. At the conclusion of the meal the ladies retreated to the living room while Ron, Chong and I remained at the table. Ron complimented Dr. Chong on the meal asking what the ingredients were in a certain dish. Chong began with water chestnuts, bean sprouts, rice, two or three other things and CAT MEAT! I had eaten two extra helpings. I knew Ron had done that for my benefit but I showed no reaction. When we got home I told Kay what we had just eaten and started walking the floor and belching while my stomach was turning. I told her before we went to bed, "If I wake up tonight meowing and trying to lick my rear please get me outta here and take me to the hospital." When people ask me if I like cats I reply, "I do indeed like cats, they taste like chicken."

But I regress, I began to have health issues (not related to the cat meal) that alarmed me enough to schedule an appointment with Ron, who immediately diagnosed my problem. He said, "Mitzi and I were talking about you the other day; we both have seen a change in you. You need to either get out of Royal Palm School or adopt an 'I don't give a damn' attitude. Since I don't think you are going to adopt an 'I don't give a damn' attitude, you need to look for another job."

Once again, Kay was about to come to my rescue.

Southboro Civitan Club

honors

DAVID D. CANTLEY

for

SUPERB PERFORMANCE AS CHAIRMAN
PALM BEACH COUNTY SPECIAL OLYMPICS

Presented this 22nd day of APRIL, 1976

President

Chapter photo: I am boarding a train with two students (Roy and John) from Royal Palm School headed for Columbia, SC to participate in the Southern Regional Special Olympics. This was the first time a Palm Beach County had participated in Special Olympics.

28

LANTANA JUNIOR HIGH

In 1969, Kay had transferred from Palm Beach Gardens High School to Lantana Jr. High where she implemented their new Business Education Program. In 1972, Kay became aware that a vacancy for an assistant superintendent for the south area would soon be advertised; she spoke with her principal, Ken Schrimsher, and told him that I was unhappy as well as frustrated at Royal Palm and needed a change. Kay asked Ken what he thought about me applying for the position of assistant superintendent for south area, which is a job that principals spend years preparing for and hoping to achieve. Ken smiled and replied, "I don't think he is ready for that; however, I may have something coming up that might be of interest to him." The job he had referred to was a new position originally called Community School Director and was later renamed Assistant Principal for Adult and Community Education.

Community Education, originated in Pontiac, Michigan, was a relatively new idea to South Florida. Basically, the Community Education concept advocated keeping schools open during evenings, weekends, and summers when the K-12 classes were not in session. Course offerings included General Education Development (GED,) Adult Basic Education (ABE), and general interest classes in subjects that ranged from art, bridge, cooking, dance, dog obedience, furniture repair, sewing, and many other subjects. The community education program was known as "Program and Process:" the "program" was made up of various class offerings, and the "process" advocated ways to help solve community problems by involving citizens in the identification of community problems and finding solutions for them. The community school director's responsibility was to facilitate the process.

When Kay asked me if I would be interested in the new position, I jumped at the chance for an interview. Ken, an Oklahoma farm boy with a long drawl in his speech, and I hit it off from the first day. When he offered me the job, he told me that the position required the Lantana Town Council to contribute $6,000 toward my salary. He then added that the council had voted 3-2 to fund the program for the coming year. Ken explained that (a) if I wanted the job next year, I would be working on a 3-2 vote; (b) it was up to me to make the program work; (c) he would stay out of my way and let me do my job; (d) he would be there for me if I needed him. What a far cry from my first teaching position at Marsh Fork High! In our final interview, he also told me that if he had a disagreement with Kay, he didn't want me to get involved, and if he got into a disagreement with me, he didn't want to see Kay enter the fracas. I told him that if he got into a disagreement with Kay, I would be in his office to help him. I thought his laughter would never stop! When he finally stopped, I told him that she was hell on wheels—and then the guffawing started all over again.

This new program was not without its opponents—primarily from teachers who did not want anyone "coming in here at night and using my classroom." It helped greatly that the principal had said, "This is what we are going to do." Also, it helped that Kay was highly respected by the faculty. Since I had funds to purchase equipment and supplies for teachers (and allowed them to take classes free of charge), I eventually won over converts to our cause.

To advertise our programs, we mailed out a newsletter (called "The Mullet Rapper") two times per year to explain what we were about and what we planned to do. We published pictures of people who were involved in classes, and asked readers for suggestions about possible course offerings. Almost immediately, "The Mullet Rapper" was a big hit with citizens, teachers and other community school directors. At that time, *The National Enquirer* newspaper was based in Lantana and I approached them about funding the cost of printing the newsletter. They readily agreed; "The Mullet Rapper" became a big part of our early success. Dr. Michael Robbins, the County Director of Adult and Community Education, brought in a marketing consultant to evaluate how we were promoting our programs. In our meeting, the consultant said that he had looked over all our materials, and, in his opinion, "The Mullet Rapper" was a good example of how to effectively market community education. He said it was written like most newspapers on a fifth-grade level and was easy for people to read. When I proudly told Kay what he had said she replied, "Did you tell him that you could only write on a fifth grade level?"

When we started the program at Lantana in 1973, there were only five or six schools designated as community schools. We hit the ground running and opened with a full slate of class offerings sooner than any other school. In addition to the night classes, we also offered after-school activities and classes for elementary and jr. high students. Math and reading classes were both available as well as dance and baton classes. The town of Lantana had no recreation department which allowed us to increase our program by offering leisure activities for adults and students alike. Our summer recreation program for students rivaled any similar offerings in the county. I called upon my old friend from the Glades, Charles J. (CJ-5) Poole, to head up the kids' summer program. He selected three or four guys each summer to assist him. We were so successful that churches were forced to close their Vacation Bible School camps because kids preferred to attend our recreation program instead.

I only worked for Ken one year, 73-74, but I learned a lot about leadership from him. His philosophy was, "Hire good people, give them what they need to do their job, support them, and then leave them alone." He didn't look over anyone's shoulder unless—as demonstrated through sub-par job performance—he needed to look over their shoulder. Ken transferred to another middle school in the northern end of the county closer to his home and, after serving a short time, he became Assistant Superintendent for Personnel. He later became Assistant Superintendent for Maintenance and Construction where he came under unrelenting fire from *The Palm Beach Post* newspaper. He probably brought a lot of that on himself because he refused to be intimidated by the reporters. Eventually, the paper alleged that Ken had misappropriated funds; vicious-attack editorials appeared four or five times a week. He knew that his colleagues, family and friends were reading those editorials, and he agonized through each one of them until he eventually suffered a fatal heart attack. A subsequent investigation into misappropriated funds resulted in no charges being filed. None of the allegations proved to be true. A good man lost his life because he refused to kowtow to newspaper reporters, and I lost a dear, dear friend.

Ken was not only a close friend; he was also my professional mentor. Soon after he saw what I was doing to get the community education program off the ground, he told me that I needed to go to Florida Atlantic University to get certified in administration and supervision. Ken told me there would be no problem to be absent from my duties while *I took the needed classes.* Five years later when the principalship opened at Royal Palm, I was officially certified to become a principal and he advocated for me to fill that vacancy. After I had been there three months short of two years, he again called and asked, "Dave, are you ready to take over Lake Worth High?" He's the one who made that move happen as well.

After Ken left Lantana, Bill Goode became principal, I enjoyed the same close working relationship with Bill that I'd had with Ken. Bill was very much involved with the community; he secured their support in raising funds to both air condition the school and purchase much-needed equipment.

West Virginia was well-represented on the Lantana Jr. High faculty. Assistant Principal Jack Christie (who would follow Goode as principal) was from Princeton, Doris Welsh (the choral music director) was from Preston County, Kay and I were from Rock Creek and Whitesville, respectively, Jerry Jenkins (physical education teacher who also coached football and basketball) was from Wyoming County, and Pat Cantley (the art teacher) was from Beckley. The entire faculty was totally dedicated, loved their jobs, and seemed to effortlessly work well together.

Spearheading community education was the most carefree and enjoyable job I have ever had! There were no problems with discipline or motivation, and everyone was there because they wanted to be. I worked at night, but I lived close to the school and could go home to have dinner with my family each night.

We gave every student a "Completer Certificate" at the end of each course. It stated that the student had completed a course in whatever the subject was, and it bore the signature of the principal, the teacher and me. One night at the end of a semester, an elderly gentleman kept waiting for everyone to leave the office lobby. When they had all left, he approached me and said, "This little piece of paper is the only thing I own that proves that I have been to school." He told me that when was young, he had been forced to drop out of school to help support his family. He said he planned to frame our certificate and to hang it on a wall in his home.

In June of 1978, when Madge Edwards retired as principal of Royal Palm, she called me to say that she wanted me to be her replacement. I was headed "back home to Royal Palm."

Chapter photo: Charlie Poole, Lantana Jr. High School Summer Recreation Director, receiving the "Workhorse Award".

BACK TO ROYAL PALM

When young aspiring assistant principals ask me how they can best prepare to qualify themselves for a principalship, I always tell them that they have to work for a principal who will push their candidacy. I also tell them they first have to win that principal's confidence and respect by working hard, volunteering for extra duty, and supporting their principal's goals. Ken Schrimsher was such a principal for me, and I hitched my wagon (as General George Patton once said) to his star. He believed in me as his community school director which gave him confidence that I could handle the job at Royal Palm School and, later, the job of principal at Lake Worth High.

Returning to Royal Palm—where I had been a teacher only five years earlier—was a little awkward. It wasn't easy being the boss to teachers I had worked with for seven years. When I arrived at Royal Palm in 1978, I learned that the school had many needs—including a copier for office and teacher use. My friend from Pineville, West Virginia, Ray Goode, was vice president of the Ryder System based in Miami. He helped by writing a check for the copier (which delighted the teachers), carpeting for the offices, as well as a chair for my desk. (Someone had confiscated the original chair from the principal's office and replaced it with a metal folding chair.) School Board member Susan Pell's father, whose hobby was woodworking, was kind enough to build equipment for the use of our physically handicapped students. To the delight of our students, the art students from neighboring Forest Hill High School painted Disney-themed murals on classroom walls, the halls, our clinic, and even the cafeteria.

As stated in a previous chapter, before I became principal, federal legislation (specifically Public Law 94-142) ensured that special needs students would be educated in the least restrictive environment. This meant that students could no longer be "put away" or segregated in a special school when they could, with minimal assistance, be educated in their regular neighborhood schools. Madge Edwards loved her students and refused to send them out into the cruel world for fear they would not be accepted in traditional schools.

Midway through my first year (78-79) as principal we began the process of identifying students whom we felt could succeed in their neighborhood schools. To ensure a proper and successful placement, evaluation and input was provided by classroom teachers, psychologists, therapists, parents and others. One teacher, Mrs. Stetson, came to me in tears and begged me to not, "Send our kids out there where they are not wanted and will be mistreated." Later, that same teacher would call me at home to tell me how well our former students were faring in their neighborhood schools: "Johnny is at Conniston Jr. High, and he is doing very well, Susie is at Forest Hill High and she is very happy there, Fred is at Lake Worth High and he loves it." The process received Mrs. Stetson's stamp of approval, which meant it had worked.

Royal Palm had been started back in 1942 by Mrs. Marjorie Crick who had convinced the superintendent to allow her to teach seven polio victims in a back room of the Crippled Children's Society Building in Palm Beach. It was a monumental move because, up to that point, special needs students were not considered worthy of an education. From that first class a very large program grew that—ultimately—educated students of all exceptionalities. The program did, however, eventually hold some students back because they should not have been enrolled in a protected environment like Royal Palm.

By the end of 1979-80 school year we had transferred all the students who met the criteria to their neighborhood schools, and I was headed to Lake Worth High School which had more faculty members than Royal Palm had students.

As stated previously, I always considered every job I held in Palm Beach County to be the most important job in the school system—and my time at Royal Palm was no exception. I always believed special needs kids were being short-changed by the school district, and it would be several more years before a new Royal Palm School (with updated facilities we had only dreamt of) was built and fully staffed.

I was frustrated that—when it came to facilities—too many people were satisfied with the status quo. One day, while I was principal at Royal Palm, a 12" x 12" pane of glass in an exterior door broke—and a student's arm protruded through the window pane. Luckily the student was not injured, but the shards of glass could have severed an artery. When the maintenance department was called to repair the door they replaced the pane with a safety glass that was reinforced by wire. I asked them to replace the glass in all of our doors with safety glass, but they replied that they were not allowed to replace them until they were broken. So, the next day I arrived at school long before anyone except the custodian, Doug. We went through the school and he held a wastebasket over the inside of the door while "an anonymous someone" took a baseball bat and broke the glass out of all the doors. From then on, all the exterior doors had safety glass—without questions or comment.

Chapter photo: Mrs. Marjorie Crick (L) and Mrs. Madge Edwards (R). Mrs. Crick was the first special education teacher in Palm Beach County and first principal of Royal Palm School. She later became the school district's first Director of Special Education. Mrs. Edwards was the second principal of Royal Palm School.

Two Royal Palm School teachers, Mary Elizabeth Watts (left) and Wendy Petrovich (right), at my retirement dinner.

LAKE WORTH HIGH

When Ken Schrimsher, then Director of Personnel for the Palm Beach County School District, asked if I was ready to "take over Lake Worth High," I told him that there were more things I wanted to accomplish as principal of Royal Palm. After all, I was only nearing the end of my second year at the school for special needs students. Ken's reply was, "Dave, wherever you are, there will always be more you want to do."

Lake Worth High was considered a "rough school" with an enrollment of 2,600, a reputation for student fights, and continual teacher complaints about a lack of discipline. I accepted Ken's offer for an interview for the job and became one of six applicants. I told my brother, Bee, (who was superintendent of our school system in Raleigh County, West Virginia) about the school's problems and the fact that I had been interviewed. One of the things he told me was that it sounded as if the only way for Lake

Worth High to move was up. When I told him that I had been appointed principal at Lake Worth High he replied, "Now, we are going to see what you are made of." His words served as a big motivator for me to accept head on the challenges that Lake Worth High presented.

When Ken called two weeks later and told me that I had the job, he said I couldn't tell anyone until 3 p.m. that day because he said he had to call the "losers" and tell them who got the job. Because I had to tell someone, I called Kay at Lantana Jr. High to share my good news. She waited until exactly 3 p.m., then Kay told our dear friend, her principal, Jack Christie. Jack and shop teacher, Bill Morehead, were fishermen. Jack asked Bill how much fish he had in his freezer. Between the two of them they came up with enough fish for a big celebratory fish fry at Jack's home that very night.

Superintendent Mills transferred me to Lake Worth High with five weeks remaining in the 1979-80 school year. At the time, I questioned the soundness of that decision, but it was the right one because it gave me five weeks to see what we needed to do to begin the new school year.

I became the fifth principal in the '79-'80 school year. The first principal was Curt Woodall who had been at Lake Worth for a number of years before being promoted to the south area administrative office. The next principal was Byron Steinbaugh, who was terminated. Charles "Peck" Perry, the south area superintendent, then became acting principal. Peck simultaneously juggled his regular job with being principal at Lake Worth High. The next principal, Fess Wallace, became interim—and I succeeded Fess.

I was introduced at a specially called faculty meeting. Mrs. Betty Pitchford, a science teacher, stated, "Mr. Cantley, we have had a rough school year--you are the fifth principal we have had this year. Now, how long do you plan to stay?" Everyone in attendance laughed. I answered, "Ma'am I am like Johnson grass and country music, I am here to stay." (Any farm boy who has ever hoed corn will tell you that—in truth—Johnson grass never really goes away.) I fulfilled that promise by staying for 19 years—I retired at the end of the 1998-99 school year.

When I arrived at Lake Worth High, Jim White was a dean at the school and had a good history of the problems at the school. He had not been satisfied with the administration's lack of discipline. He genuinely wanted to establish law and order, but could not get approval to make the needed changes.

Lake Worth High had several students who were two years or more behind in the pupil progression plan which meant that (at a minimum) these troublemakers were "frequent flyers" in the dean's office for causing disruption in the classrooms and on campus. They blatantly showed disrespect to teachers and often used profanity and threats without fear of punishment. Students were frequently out on campus, unchallenged, during the day when they should have been in class. There was a certain hard-core group of boys who only came to school to sell drugs, hit on girls and cause disruption.

At the time, Lake Worth High was on double sessions, which meant that seniors and juniors attended the first session (from 7 a.m. until noon), and sophomores and freshmen came in from 12:15 p.m. to 5:15 p.m. We had a 30-minute break mid-way through each session when what little order had been established would be suspended. During these "breaks", students drove their cars off campus, went to fast food restaurants where they sometimes caused trouble. Some went to their cars (in the student parking lot under I-95) where whatever you want to imagine occurred. Conditions at the school had been so bad for so long that relatively few teachers actually thought those conditions could be reversed. One faculty member (an outstanding English teacher) resigned and told me that she wished me well, but she felt that I was fighting a losing battle. She even wrote a letter to the editor of the Palm Beach Post to that effect.

When the school year began in August of 1980, Jim and I had a plan that we introduced with mixed reviews. We began by initiating a program—well thought out and led by Jim—to either suspend, expel or place in an alternative school those students who were known to (a) constantly cause disruptions, (b) interfere with the teachers' job to teach, or (c) compromise the students' right to a safe and orderly school environment conducive to learning. When the worst offenders were swiftly removed from the school, it sent a message to the borderline students that they would be dealt with similarly if they didn't get in line with the new plan. Removing the high-profile mischief-makers also sent a positive message to both the majority of students who wanted an orderly school and to faculty members who wanted their classrooms to be free of disruptions.

We eliminated the 30-minute breaks which brought a howl of dissatisfaction from the students. They thought they would starve by attending five straight classes without a break. But our reply to their complaint was that they should eat a hearty breakfast or lunch and bring a piece of fruit or a candy bar to eat while changing classes. Both my daughters, Beth and DeeAnne, graduated from Lake Worth High--Beth in 1978 and DeeAnne in 1983. DeeAnne was a freshman when I arrived in 1980, with five weeks left in the school year. We put the changes into effect at the beginning of her sophomore year which caused her to be on the receiving end of much criticism of "What your Daddy is doing . . .". One afternoon after school, I was sitting, reading the paper at home and noticed that DeeAnne kept walking back and forth in front of me. I knew something was on her mind so I said, "OK, DeeAnne, what is bothering you?" She then jumped into my lap and said, "Daddy, I don't like it when they talk bad about you." She still remembers all those rough days she had to endure, but will happily admit that it had it advantages as well. Over the years I have been invited to speak at the reunions of some of those early classes where I take great delight in telling them, "What we were trying to do back then was to give you the school that you want for your kids today." That always gets a big round of applause.

The school ran smoothly after the '80-81 school year. We enjoyed getting compliments from parents and the media who were supportive of what we were doing. Fortunately, I had a strong superintendent in Tom Mills who supported our efforts. Three of his own children attended Lake Worth High which gave him extra incentive to set the school straight.

In the early 1980's, the school system was beginning to enter the age of technology. This resulted in reports provided to principals with data on students' test scores, grades, attendance, etc. On one of the reports I noticed that Lake Worth High had a very high dropout rate plus a low graduation rate. When I asked Bill Mowry, an assistant principal who had been in a high-profile position at the school for several years, what was the reason for this, he and the guidance coordinator, Dick Cahill, replied that it was caused by a lack of academic success. I knew that kids didn't drop out of school if they had a 4.0 GPA, so I asked why they were not having academic success. Bill and Dick repeatedly placed the blame on everyone and everything—from the district's middle and elementary schools to the parents.

When I asked them if they had looked at the reading scores of dropout and at-risk students, they replied that they had not. So, I told them to check the reading scores and come back to share what they had found with me. Bill came back in only a few minutes and said, "You are right, Mr. Cantley, the problem is that these kids can't read." When I told him that we needed to get some reading teachers on staff, he replied that it would be a waste of resources because, "research shows that if a kid can't read by the time he reaches high school, he will never learn to read."

I have always been careful around people who say, "research shows" because if you want to support a position or if you take on an issue, you can always find "research" to support your point of view. In this case, I knew that Bill was wrong--people in their 80's were not only being taught to read, but some were even earning their high school diploma and going to college. So, we started adding reading teachers—as our budget would allow—and saved a lot of kids from becoming dropouts.

Before Bill went to check on the reading scores, I knew what he would find. My biggest regret of being a principal for 19 years is that I failed to convince my superiors including area superintendents, superintendents, and school board members that if a kid is to graduate high school he or she must know how to read. One superintendent would even tell a fellow principal that I was living in the 1950's because I was lobbying for reading! My strongest ally in the push for reading was Penny Beers, the county reading director.

My continuing fight to support reading never stopped! I tried, without success, to get other high school principals to support my position of hiring more reading teachers. At one high school principals' meeting Dr. Art Johnson (who would later become superintendent) was the Chair, when he came to the topic of reading on the agenda he said, "OK, the next item for discussion is Dave's reading". I replied, "What do you mean, 'Dave's reading' this should be everyone's reading problem."

After Art retired, he ran for the school board and one day we were discussing his campaign. He said that he would stress discipline and reading. Adamantly I answered, "What the hell do you mean by 'reading'? All those years when I preached reading I couldn't get your support." Art smiled and said, "That's right, and now I am going to get elected on your platform." When he became superintendent a few years later, he called me out of retirement in 2002-03 to serve as supervising principal at Forest Hill High.

My supervisory assignment was to help the principal get the school off the state-assigned "F" list which the state had assigned to Forest Hill High. Art introduced me at a principal's meeting and stated that I had tried for years to tell everyone that our schools' main problem was a lack of reading skills. He added, "It looks like we should have listened to him." I was elated when Art increased the number of reading teachers in the school district.

During the late 1980's, I noticed a slow change in Lake Worth High's demographics. There was an increasing "white flight" from the city of Lake Worth caused by deteriorating housing quality and increasing crime. We were losing students who would have been third-generation graduates; this "white flight" was causing the school to wither and die right before my eyes. The magnet school concept would turn out to be the solution to our problems.

The student parking lot at Lake Worth High is under interstate 95 on the west side of the campus. The parking lot is huge with space for several hundred cars. Frank Kohl, the executive director of the Lake Worth Chamber of Commerce kept telling me that the chamber and the school should operate a flea market in the parking lot during weekends when the lot is vacant. Frank offered to operate the market, the school would provide the venue, and we would split the profits fifty-fifty. I finally agreed, and the market was started in January of 1987. The market took off like gangbusters, earning more money than we ever expected. Ralph and Betty Milone took over management of the market after Thanksgiving of 1992 when Frank's health failed. Shortly after Betty and Ralph assumed management of the market, the school became the sole proprietor of the market. The Milones greatly expanded the business by advertising. Betty passed away in February of 2006 and the management duties were assumed by Ralph and his wife Consuella. The Lake Worth High School Flea Market is the most successful school fundraiser in the Palm Beach County School District, earning the school a net profit of $150,000 annually.

Wayne Beckner, Ken Schrimsher and me . Ken was my mentor and good friend. He hired me at Lantana Jr. High as assistant principal and recommended me for LWHS.

Chapter photo: This photo was taken in the early 1990's during class change.

TOP: At an academic breakfast in the early 1980's. Seated at my right is Les Akers. Les awarded a top senior the use of a new Mustang for 9 weeks each quarter.

MIDDLE: Awarding my daughter, DeeAnne, her diploma in 1983.

BOTTOM: (L-R) Larry Brown, me, and Herb Score at the rededication of Dick Brown Field. Larry and Herb were outstanding major league baseball players and LWHS graduates. Larry played for the Kansas City A's when they won the World Series. They both played for the Cleveland Indians where Herb set a record for strike outs for a rookie in a single season. I played first base for the Rock Creek Boy Scouts.

TOP, LEFT: Meredith Johnston "arresting" me as part of Senior Take Over Day.

TOP, RIGHT: I am standing in front of the old auditorium, also known as "The Mole Hole". This building was constructed in 1926.

MIDDLE: In a cherry picker when LWHS mascot, the trojan, was being painted on the side of the building, facing the I-95 overpass.

BOTTOM: Jim White on a return visit to Lake Worth High School after his retirement.

TOP: I am pictured here with Miss Kitty Wells, the Queen of Country Music. Backstage at the South Florida Fair. (photo taken by Mr. Sam Hamilton, a father of one of my former students) **MIDDLE AND BOTTOM:** I love attending LWHS reunions to see my former students and catch up with them. Kay and I attend whenever possible.

MAGNET PROGRAMS

Dr. Joseph A. Orr, Assistant Superintendent for Instruction for the School Board of Palm Beach County, was a brilliant educator with an eye for innovation. During the 1980's, The Palm Beach County School District was recognized nationally for its curriculum and Joe Orr was its architect. He brought The International Baccalaureate (IB) Program to Suncoast High School, enabling the school to attract "cream of the crop" students and to be recognized annually as one of the top high schools in the nation. IB programs would later be added to other county schools.

Dr. Orr also introduced the magnet school concept to Palm Beach County Schools. Its two aims were (a) to offer students an intensive program that allowed them to study in-depth subjects that they planned to pursue in college (or which would prepare them for a job right out of high school), and (b) to racially balance a school by attracting students to a magnet school. I was initially opposed to the idea of magnet schools, and jokingly referred to them as "Maggot schools." It didn't take long for that to travel through the system like wildfire all the way to the top.

Also, it didn't take me long to realize that for our high school to survive I needed to get on the magnet bandwagon. In the summer of 1981, Dr. Orr called a meeting of high school principals who might be interested in having Junior ROTC in their schools. I was on vacation at the time of the meeting, but I sent two assistant principals, Carol Shetler and Roger Pelser, to attend in my absence. When I returned, Carol and Roger told me that we could get Army JROTC immediately, but they recommended we go on a waiting list for Air Force JROTC because of their emphasis on leadership and education. We chose Air Force and we were told that we were second on the waiting list.

Within a few months, we were told that the school that was first on the list had rejected the offer. That's how Lake Worth High became the first school in the district to have JROTC in 1982. Our students who wore the uniform drew considerable interest from teens in other schools. However, it was not feasible for them to transfer to Lake Worth High. In 1989, we were able to obtain magnet status for JROTC. This resulted in our enrollment to dramatically increase with academically stronger students. Palm Beach County is the largest county, geographically speaking, east of the Mississippi River, but we were attracting students for JROTC from one end of the county to the other. One student actually rode his bike two miles from his home in The Acreage, a mid-county rural area, to get to his school bus stop. There was such a demand for our program that the district had to set up a lottery system to determine who would attend Lake Worth High, previously known as "that old ghetto school." We were on our way, but we didn't stop there.

Medicine and Allied Health had also been a very popular program at our school, especially for the limited number of students who wanted to study nursing after graduation. I saw an opportunity to provide a more in-depth program for our students if we could elevate the Medicine and Allied Health Program to magnet status, expand the curriculum, and add teachers. When we finally succeeded in gaining magnet status for the Medicine and Allied Health Program in 1991, we again attracted a whole different group of students, many of whom went on to become doctors and nurses. The program received state and national awards under the direction of Department Head Barbara Alexandro who never ran out of ideas to expand the program. Our magnet offerings were new to the district, and we constantly sent personnel in the district offices into a tizzy with our ground-breaking ventures. The one that really got them upset, especially the lawyers, was when we announced our plan to teach kids in the medical program to draw blood.

A very popular part of the medical magnet program was the clinical experience which the students took in the second semester of their junior year. In "The Clinics," students were placed in clinics, doctors' offices, hospitals, and other medical facilities two afternoons per week to gain practical experience. This assisted students to choose the area of medicine they wanted to study or to determine if they wanted to study medicine at all. One student told me that she decided she did not want to pursue a career in medicine because of an experience she had in a hospital on her first day there. She had been asked by a nurse to help her take the body of a 10-year old boy to the morgue. The young student decided to switch to our Criminal Justice Academy. She became a lawyer.

Before students could qualify for clinical experience, they had to be checked off on a list of 100 skills that ranged from medical skills to appropriate dress and when—or when not—to speak. Medical personnel were very impressed with the ability of our students and were happy to involve them in their work.

A certain segment of our student population did not have the grades to qualify for entrance into The Medicine and Allied Health Program. We, through the assistance of the school board, contracted with an outside company, Practical Nursing and Health Occupations, to come on campus and train those students to become Certified Nurse Assistants (CNA). They were also taught the skills needed to pass the state-mandated FCAT test required for graduation. We had a very high success rate with this program and the students graduated high school certified by the state to work as a CNA. These students had their feet in the door of medicine with the opportunity to advance to higher level jobs.

Lee Reese was Chief of Police for the city of Lake Worth and, as a transplant from Diamond, West Virginia, became my dear friend. Lee and I used to get together and talk about how poor we had been back in the hills and—just as with Madge Edwards—I could never one-up the chief.

Lee loved to tell stories about hopping a coal train to roll off coal that he would later pick up to heat his family's home and fuel his mother's cook stove. He told me that he had to give some of the coal to the engineer so he would run the train slowly enough for Lee to knock the coal onto the ground.

Chief Reese called me one day and said, "Dave, I know this is short notice, but they are going to swear me in as Chief today at 5 p.m., I would like for at least one person from West Virginia to be there." Of course, I was happy to attend. I later took him a West Virginia State seal that was mounted to a circular piece of wood. He thanked me but said, "I can't hang it on my office wall because someone will surely complain because it is the West Virginia—not the Florida—seal." The next time I visited his office, he had it prominently displayed on the wall.

One day, when the Chief and I were talking about the magnet programs we had in the school, he said, "Dave, you have JROTC and medical magnets. Why don't we have one in law enforcement? We could grow our own cops." That is how the Criminal Justice Academy came into existence at Lake Worth High in 1993 and, later, to other schools in the district. The program introduced students to a career in Law Enforcement and to a path that could enable them to become a Criminal Justice Attorney. Lee later became Chief of Police in Cleveland, Tennessee and attempted to establish an academy there but it failed after a short run of only two or three years. When I asked him why it didn't succeed he replied, "I needed a high school principal from West Virginia to make it work."

Students in both the medical and criminal justice academies received twelve college credits upon completion of the program. Initially, the Criminal Justice Department Head at Florida Atlantic University did not want to give our students college credit because it was hard to accept the fact that high school students could do the same course work that he offered on his campus.

Lake Worth High School served as a textbook example of what magnet programs can do to bolster enrollment in a school. In 1984, our enrollment had decreased to 2,200, but by 2008 the three magnet programs had boosted the enrollment to 2,979 students—1,151 of whom participated in magnet programs. AFJROTC became a magnet program in 1989 attracting top academic students from other schools. These students brought honors to our school by winning state and national drill competitions, and they were chosen by the Air Force as an honor unit eight years in a row. We were the second largest AFJROTC unit in America and Eastern Europe, and our students were regularly awarded appointments to the military academies. It was not uncommon for us to have students at West Point (Army), Annapolis (Navy), Colorado Springs (Air Force) as well as with the Coast Guard. In 1997, our students received nine military academy appointments. I have never heard of a school that had three academy appointments in one year, much less nine.

Many of our students received college scholarships from the Air Force which required the students to be in ROTC during college and to serve three years active duty in the Air Force after graduation. Our ROTC program was only a mediocre operation until Col. Karl Price arrived in 1988, and much of the credit for its success must be given to Col. Price, who headed the department. All the JROTC instructors were Air Force retirees, and their salaries were funded jointly by the Air Force and the School Board. When I interviewed Col. Price, he said, "Mr. Cantley, I don't need this job for financial reasons. I have a job in Washington, and it pays more than I could ever make here, but there is no satisfaction in that job. I have been blessed with a good career in the Air Force, good fortune in life, and I want to give back." He helped our kids in ways I never thought the program could. Hundreds of students benefited from the leadership of Col. Price and his staff. The high number of academy appointments and scholarships are attributable to the guidance sessions and classroom instruction generously provided by his staff.

Top Left: Secretary, Char Doran; Assisstant Principal Deloris Brown; me; Assistant Principal, Kathy Perry; and student, Dan Cane **Top Right:** with Dr. Joe Orr **Middle Left:** with Lee Reese, Lake Worth Chief of Police **Middle Right:** Criminal Justice Magnet. **Lower Left:** AFJROTC Magnet **Lower Right:** Medicine and Allied Health Magnet

THE MASTER PLAN

The first building on the Lake Worth High campus was built in 1922 and was known as West Grade Elementary School. The city had a North Grade, South Grade and West Grade which was built west of the city where, as critics pointed out, "there was nothing but scrub palmettos and sand spurs." West Grade would later be part of the high school campus when it joined the north building (built in 1922) and the junior high—aka South Building—built in 1928. At that time, air conditioning and heat were not available. When the temperatures dropped, students were taken to the roof to bask on the warm tar roof; if the thermometer dropped below 50 degrees, school was dismissed altogether.

The City of Lake Worth has always been known as a blue-collar working—class community whose residents paid their taxes, obeyed the law, supported their schools, and "did the right thing" while asking for little in return. As a result, the city's schools fell into disrepair as new communities were built west of the coastal towns where parents spoke up. Those schools were getting the board's attention with new and remodeled schools. Some officials even considered abandoning the Lake Worth High campus in the 1960's and selling the property to the state for an interchange for I-95. Mayor Dennis Dorsey convinced the board that the school was vital to the city. Lake Worth High would have been the first school built west of the coastal strip. Again, the idea came up during the time I was principal, but Superintendent Mills squashed it.

Jody Gleason, a Lake Worth High parent and Chair of the Palm Beach County School Board, was my only ally on the board working to get us the much-needed improvements at the school. She called me one day and said, "Dave, I don't think I am going to get support from the board to get anything done at Lake Worth High. We are going to have to shame them into doing it." She then asked me to get some students, teachers and parents to speak at a board meeting. I didn't like the idea of getting people to speak in opposition to the superintendent's agenda; I confided to Jody that I hoped to retire in a few years. She said, "Don't worry about the superintendent. I will take care of her. We have done it your way for years, and it hasn't worked." (Superintendent Mills had retired by this time.)

"My way" had been believing that eventually we would get our turn at the trough, and these broken promises we had endured for years would be fulfilled. I remember when I spoke of a master plan during an early faculty meeting, the teachers started laughing. Annoyed, I turned to Assistant Principal Bill Mowry and asked, "What's so damn funny?" He replied that the faculty had heard all that before.

Jody's phone call came in the mid 90's, it was a do or die time for Lake Worth High! Since I trusted Jody, I called a meeting of students, parents and alumni to plan our strategy. I coached them on what to say and how to say it in a way that would not offend the board. We had 100 Tee shirts printed that read **"Fund Lake Worth High Master Plan Now!"** All the speakers—students and adults alike—wore those shirts, did a great job, and spoke in a very positive (even pleading) way. One of our most persuasive speakers was Meredith Abrams, a senior. (She went on to become a teacher in a Lake Worth elementary school and a board member of our scholarship program, Dollars for Scholars.) And just as

Jody had predicted, we shamed the board into approving Phase I of our master plan. (At the same time, they also approved projects at John I. Leonard and Atlantic High Schools.) The Lake Worth High plan called for remodeling two of the original buildings and demolishing the East (West Grade) Building which was located on a remote corner of the campus. It also included a new three-story building (Hamblin Hall) that would house a new cafeteria, receiving area and classrooms.

Obviously, timing is everything! One week prior to our board appearance, I received a Sunday night call from Olivia Northern (one of our dedicated custodians) who told me that she had been to the school to see if the "mole hole" had flooded during a heavy extended rain. (The mole hole was our name for the basement in the north building.) Our campus is located on a hill, and when the north building was built flooding was not a problem. Construction that had been added around the north building in subsequent years, however, had forced the water to run to the footer of the building, and—eventually—into the classrooms. Olivia told me that the flooding was very bad; she wanted to know if she should call in the other custodians to pump the water out. I told her to not pump it, wait until the next day when I would call the TV stations in to give us some media coverage on it. My daughter, DeeAnne, who was visiting us overheard the conversation with Olivia and said, "I would call them tonight, Daddy." I called four TV stations and headed for the school. The TV crews filmed the flooded classrooms and interviewed me that night; the next morning they were back to do it all over again. One reporter, William Giles from Channel 12, was there two times each day on Monday, Tuesday and Wednesday. On Monday, I told the cameramen and reporters to turn their sound on because I was going to the office to make a public address announcement to the teachers and students about the flooding. I announced that this was the worst it had ever been, and they should follow the same plan we had done so many times before— use alternative spaces (library, cafeteria, etc). I ended by saying that I did not know how long it would take to get the classrooms dried out so classes could resume. The school board was meeting Wednesday night and the TV coverage gave them (and the entire community) a good look at what we had been enduring for years.

In 1998, the year before I retired, the board approved Phase II of the master plan. This included a new building later to be dubbed "Hansen Hall" in honor of Tommy Hansen, a 1935 alumnus, who donated $100,000 to the Lake Worth High School Alumni Foundation. Hansen Hall houses an auditorium, spacious band and choral suites, a TV production studio, classrooms and a culinary arts lab. A smaller building would house a child-care program that would qualify students to be state licensed child-care workers. Eventually, both culinary arts and child care became magnet programs. Phase II also included facilities for art, sewing and design, drafting as well as computer labs. The new facilities allowed our school to eliminate many of the portable classrooms on campus. Because of the many students who came to our school, we had a total of 63 portables—more than any school in the entire state of Florida. Word in the building department of the district office was that "Lake Worth High's classroom shortage is self-imposed because Cantley brought in all those magnet programs." But no one dared to try to stop me because Jody was squarely in my corner.

A few years earlier, Superintendent Mills had my back on whatever I wanted. If I needed to get something done by the maintenance department I would tell them, "Superintendent Mills is having a big meeting here next month, and we need to get the grounds spruced up." One time, when a maintenance supervisor didn't want to repair the pool heater because he didn't think "we need to be in the swimming business," I pointed to the Lake Worth Towers, a retirement home located just east of our campus. I said, "See that third window from the right end on the tenth floor? Superintendent Mills' mother lives there, and she called me last week to ask why the kids weren't swimming. She said she liked to have her morning tea and watch the students swim." He got in his truck, went to Sewell Hardware, bought a short piece of galvanized pipe and fixed the heater. I never got caught up in any of that, but I told Mr. Mills about it—after he retired of course—and he got a big laugh out of it.

I retired as principal of Lake Worth High School in June of 1999, and witnessed all the magnet programs I had brought to the school be duplicated at other schools around the county. This meant that the magnet concept at my school had been greatly diminished—if not completely eliminated. Students no longer needed to be reassigned to Lake Worth High School as a magnet student because they could now get the same program in their home school. Today, Lake Worth High—like all other district schools—merely reflects the socio-economic makeup of its community. In school year 2018-19, the minority population of Lake Worth High was 92%. Joe Orr is turning in his grave.

Left: Superintendent, Tom Mills speaking at my retirement dinner. I was blessed with having a very strong and supportive superintendent in Mr. Mills. **Right:** School board member, Jody Gleason, speaking at the Lake Worth High School 1999 commencement ceremony. Mrs. Gleason was, at times, my only ally on the school board. She was instrumental in bringing the Master Plan to fruition.

Chapter photo: Aerial photograph of Lake Worth Community High School after the Master Plan.

33

JETER BARKER

I first heard Jeter Barker's name—which was synonymous with Lake Worth High School and its football program—when we moved from the Glades to Lake Worth in 1966. The first time I met him was at a party at Jim and Ellie White's home about two or three years before I became principal at Lake Worth High. This would have been about 1977. The Whites had a group of teachers, coaches and football boosters over to their house after a Friday night game. I saw this man sitting in an easy chair with people gathered around him. Their mouths were agape as they listened to him speak as if he were a god. I asked Jim, "Who is that guy over there?" He replied, "Don't you know who that is? That is Jeter Barker." Jeter would later become one of my strongest supporters when I became principal at Lake Worth High and a dear friend until his dying day.

When I became principal of Lake Worth High in the spring of 1980,

Jeter saw to it that he was the first teacher I met. He came into my office unannounced, introduced himself, and said, "Mr. Cantley, I know you are from West Virginia. There is something I have wanted to get done here, and I know you can do it." He then went on to tell me that he had always wanted to get pinto beans and cornbread (a West Virginia mainstay) served in the teachers' line in the cafeteria, but he could never pull it off. He then said that the cafeteria manager, Virginia, could cook the beans and bake the cornbread, but that I would have to go tell her to do it. He went on and on and finally asked, "Now, do you want me to go tell her what you said?" I hadn't said a word but we would later have not only pinto beans, turnip greens and cornbread, but a teacher's dining room as well, all thanks to Jeter.

Jeter and Betty Cross, a biology teacher from Logan County, West Virginia, oversaw the construction and decoration of the "Trojan Den" which became a great morale booster for the faculty and staff. We served pinto beans, cornbread and turnip greens in the Trojan Den every day in addition to whatever else the school district mandated. We fed more adults than any school in the district because maintenance workers would travel halfway across the county to eat lunch at Lake Worth High. Thanks to pinto beans, cornbread, turnip greens, fried chicken, and ice tea, many repairs were made at our school, that may have never been done otherwise.

Jeter was born and raised in Bristol, Virginia; his first teaching job was in Big Stone Gap in the western mountainous area of the state around 1940. He taught math and coached football, track and baseball. His teams won state championships in both football and track. I came to know several of his football players, his "Big Stone Boys," who worshipped the ground "Coach" walked on.

Jim White and I flew with Jeter to Bristol, Virginia where we were met by one of Jeter's "Big Stone Boys" who took us to Buddy Barker's home in Big Stone Gap for a reunion with Jeter's former players and students. It was one of two such three-day events that I will cherish forever. Jim and I would later entertain the six Big Stone Boys in our homes; it was truly heartwarming to see both the love and admiration that these guys had for their old coach. They told us many stories about Jeter—who had been a very tough and demanding coach—and his style of coaching. After being drafted into the Army during WWII, one man, Jim Roy Noel, said,

"There's nothing the Army can do to me that hasn't already been done. I played football for Jeter Barker."

At another party at Buddy's home, one man said, "Coach, I have never forgiven you." Jeter asked what he had done to him that would cause him to say that. The man replied, "You left Big Stone Gap before I reached high school, and I wanted more than anything to play football for Coach Barker."

Another classic Jeter story is about a game where the "Big Stone Boys" were being beaten in the first half. When they went to the locker room for half-time, Jeter came down hard on them. When he asked one player why he had missed a tackle the player replied, "They had me double teamed, Coach." Jeter then asked another player who let the runner get past him why he hadn't made the tackle. The player replied that he, too, had been double teamed. Jeter put the discussion to rest when he said, "Hold it, hold it, I see the problem. We were out-numbered, they must have had at least 15 players on the field." He then looked at the captain of his team and said, "Hoyt Moore, there you sit six feet three inches tall and 175 pounds, captain of the Big Stone Gap Buccaneers; you couldn't stick your thumb in your hind end with both hands." The players told me they nearly choked trying to keep from laughing.

One particular Monday afternoon—after having lost a Friday night game and before school was dismissed—an announcement was made over the school intercom system informing the football team to meet Coach Barker in his classroom instead of reporting to the football field for practice. The players told me they were scared to death, not knowing what fate awaited them. Once they all had been seated Jeter said, "Boys, you played a good game Friday night. You did everything I asked you to do. I was proud of your play. We will not practice today. There is a box of Hershey bars on my desk. Take one as you leave." That was a real treat for them because chocolate was one of the items being rationed during World War ll.

During one baseball season, the Big Stone Gap senior class was scheduled to take a trip to Washington, D.C. The seniors on the baseball team came to Jeter, who was their coach, and said they wanted to go on the trip and wanted to know how this would affect their status on the team. Jeter told them that the trip was a good opportunity for them. He told them that he thought they should go, and that it would be a good experience for them, but the team would be playing two games while they were gone. If the team won while using the substitute players then they, the regulars, would lose their starting jobs if the team kept winning. The regular players agreed to the deal; upon their return they learned that the team had won both games during their absence while using the subs. The teams continued to win games, but the regulars rode the bench becoming agitated. One of the regular player's father was an influential man in town who went to the principal and asked him to force Jeter to let the first team play in place of the subs. When called into the principal's office and told that he must put the boys back on the team Jeter, being a highly principled man, refused. The principal said, "As your principal, I'm telling you to let them play." Jeter replied, "As the baseball coach, I am telling you that they are not playing." Threatened with being fired, Jeter told his boss that he would go to the local paper and tell the editor that he, the principal, had changed a boy's grade to an "F" so that he would not graduate and have one more year's eligibility for football. The principal asked Jeter to step out of his office for a few minutes. When Jeter returned, the principal told him that he was authorized to pay his salary for the remainder of the year if he would resign.

In those days, the principals wrote the teachers' salary checks at their desks. Jeter took the check, went to William and Mary on a graduate assistantship, and got his master's degree. He told me that while he was at William and Mary, part of his duties was to scout other college teams. He said one coach in particular he scouted had made a big impression on him. He said Art "Pappy" Lewis at West Virginia invited him to his hotel room, talked football with him, and even told Jeter his game plan. He said while talking, Coach Lewis would pop a cherry-filled chocolate in his mouth and chase it with Ancient Age Bourbon.

After he got his master's degree, Jeter coached at Saltville, Virginia High School, then he did a stint in the Navy. Jeter came to Lake Worth High in 1954 as the football coach and athletic director, a position he held for nine seasons, leading the team to a 9-0-1 season in 1960. Jeter was an innovator who brought his experience at William and Mary to the high school program. He even initiated a football feeder program known as small fry and large fry for seventh and eighth graders.

Jeter and local businessman Andy Andrews formed a football booster organization called "The Trojan 20," which was named for the school's mascot. Jeter went to Andy's office and asked him if he could get 19 men to join him in purchasing 50 football tickets which they would sell to boost game attendance. Andy reached into a desk drawer and took out a bottle of bourbon as well as two paper cups. After a few drinks, they had hashed out the plan for what would eventually become one of the oldest high school booster clubs in Florida, "The Trojan 20."

Andy said that Jeter was knocking on his door the next morning before he could even get out of bed. Jeter and Andy took to the streets visiting local businessmen asking them to donate $250 (this was later raised to $500) and get a number of tickets that they could sell or give to people in the community. Additionally, their donations could be used as tax write offs. Andy and Jeter called on 21 people before they got 20 members; the one who had turned them down later came around and joined. One member paid for his tickets but did not sell or give them away. Jeter and Andy went to his office, asked for the tickets, and the member was dropped from the organization. The Trojan 20 Booster Club became a very prestigious organization which sometimes caused hard feelings among men who were not asked to join. Sadly, as the demographics of Lake Worth changed, interest in The Trojan 20 died and the organization went out of existence in 2002.

A small number of Lake Worth coaches had developed a reputation of frequenting bars making no attempt to conceal their extracurricular activities--it eventually became a well-known "issue" throughout the community. The problem came to a head in 1963 when the school's principal, Charlie Stanfield, (a deacon in First Baptist Church of Lake Worth) decreed that all coaches must sign a pledge that they would not frequent any business that sold alcoholic beverages. The younger coaches, fearing for their jobs, signed the pledge while the two main offenders signed the pledge but continued to drink when and where they pleased. Jeter, being a highly-principled man, refused to sign. He told me that he hadn't signed it because if he had signed he couldn't have gone to a restaurant for dinner if alcoholic beverages were sold. Jeter said he had been bass fishing on Lake Okeechobee with Principal Stanfield the Saturday before the pledge was presented on Monday, but the principal had not mentioned it to him. He said that if Stanfield had asked him to curtail frequenting bars he would have complied. This stand ended Jeter's coaching career, but he remained as a work experience teacher until his retirement in 1987. He had been a *very* successful football coach and athletic director.

Jeter was the consummate fundraiser. He, along with Dennis and Doris Dorsey, raised funds to build the first high school swimming pool in Palm Beach County. He also raised money to build the athletic track at the school and talked John Couse, an air conditioning contractor, into donating the air conditioning for the newly-constructed band and choral suites. I have heard people say that Jeter had a way of asking you for a donation, making you feel it was "your duty' to contribute. One Lake Worth businessman, Hilliard Smith, once told me, "Every time I saw Jeter coming I reached for my checkbook. I turned him down one time, and I didn't sleep a damn wink that night. I called him the next morning and said, Alright, you S.O. B., come and get your damn check."

Jeter's *modus operandi* was to tell his prospective donor how much money he needed and what he needed it for. He would say, for example, that he needed $1,000 which would immediately scare the donor and he would then quickly follow it up with, "But I don't want you to give me the $1,000, I want other people to get involved. I only want $100 from you." The "victim" then felt he was getting off easy, and happily gave him the $100.

When we were planting trees and laying sod on school grounds in the mid-1980s, Jeter and Jim White went to see Doc Dolly, who owned a coconut palm nursery that specialized in a unique variety of coconut palm that was resistant to the blight that had taken all our Jamaican Talls on campus. When Jeter asked Doc to donate trees for our campus he replied, "Jeter, my wife and I were talking the other day, and we agreed that the Lord had been kind to us. I have never given anyone anything in my life. You are my best friend in Lake Worth and I haven't seen you in 15 years. Take all the trees you want." Our shop teacher, Bill Abel, took his truck, low-boy trailer, as well as his loader and made countless trips to the nursery. A number of the trees were removed during construction projects, but many are still growing on the campus.

I suppose I could go on writing non-stop about Jeter, his contributions to our school, and the good times we had. Every school needs a Jeter Barker, but I have never known of another school that had one.

Jeter and me standing on the football field where
Jeter coached in Big Stone Gap, Virginia.

TOP: I am pictured here with Jim White, Jeter and his, "Big Stone Boys."
Don Wax owned some property located in Cracker's Neck, a section of Big
Stone Gap, VA, where he developed a 5-hole golf course---Cow Chip Country
Club. **BOTTOM:** Jeter pictured, at his retirement celebration with his wife,
Alieen, and grandson, Jamey Blair.

Chapter photo: Superintendent Mills is presenting Jeter with a "Lifetime
Contract" with the school district, in jest.

RETIREMENT

My nineteen years as principal at Lake Worth High were both rewarding and challenging. I had the opportunity to build an outstanding team of teachers and staff who were loyal to the task of educating students. Gary Weidenhamer (who was our chemistry teacher, science department head, and athletic trainer) left the school to later be in charge of all instructional computer services in the school district. His work required him to visit all schools, make presentations to faculties, and work with academic departments and grade levels. He once told me that he had never seen a faculty as strong and dedicated as the Lake Worth High faculty. Mark Howard, who left with Gary to work in the county office, told me that when he taught at Lake Worth High he had actually looked forward to coming to work each day. I believe we had a number of others who felt as

Mark did. I often said—contentedly—that even in my absence the school could run smoothly.

After my retirement plans became public knowledge, parents often asked me, "Mr. Cantley, please stay just one more year until my son graduates." One mother asked me to stay one more year so that her daughter—who would be an incoming freshman—could have me as her principal for one year. I told everyone that I simply could not do one more year because I had done "one more year" twice. I was just tired! The school was running smoothly with great kids and a top-notch faculty. I had done my best and I needed to rest. Kay had retired in '98 so she could be of more support to me.

Looking back, as I have stated in a previous chapter, my only regret is I could not convince anyone except Mrs. Penny Beers (the County Reading Coordinator) that if kids are to graduate from high school, they must know how to read. I didn't really need to convince Penny—she already knew it!

In the spring of 1983, I made the biggest mistake of my career at Lake Worth High.. That school year Superintendent Mills told principals of a court ruling regarding separation of church and state. He stated that we should not allow religious clubs in schools nor were we to do anything that would indicate we were promoting religion in any way. When the 1983 yearbook was delivered, it included a picture of the Bible Club in the book. Since I had already told the yearbook sponsor to not allow the picture to be in the book, I ordered the page to be removed. This action was prompted both by the direction from the superintendent and by the frustration I had experienced by attempting to allow prayer at ball games and graduation ceremonies. At each event, I would ask the minister to deliver a nonsectarian prayer, explaining, "Preacher, I believe as you, do but I have families here tonight of many different faiths and I need to respect their beliefs. So can you please deliver a nonsectarian prayer?" The minister would agree, then violate the agreement by ending his prayer with, "in the name of our Lord and Savior, Jesus Christ." Other than, "Why a student didn't do his homework" and "Why he was innocent of a rules infraction," I was probably lied to more about religion issues than any other topic during my 19 years as principal. I finally took Superintendent Mills' advice when he told me "School is the place to practice your religion, not preach it."

Shortly after the "Bible Club Incident," I started receiving the most horrific hate mail from people proclaiming to be "Good Christians". One Saturday, while I was at school, Kay got a threatening phone call asking where I was. When she replied that I was at school the caller replied, "That's alright, we know where he is. We'll get him." The *Palm Beach Post* even printed one full page of letters to the editor that attacked me. I was surprised that the newspaper would print some of them—especially given the nature of the content. I wish Mr. Mills had given me that advice earlier.

During my years at Lake Worth High, I often called on Dennis and Doris Dorsey for financial assistance for various needs. While principal, I wanted to establish an alumni foundation that would provide scholarships for needy students. When Vivian Edgell, my secretary, retired in the mid-1990's, she left $450 of her retirement gift for the express purpose of establishing just such a fund foundation. I called Dennis and talked with him about establishing a foundation. He was all for it, and he told me that another alum—Al Elam—had also expressed an interest in establishing a foundation.

I called Al to discuss his ideas which resulted in the two of us flying to Indiana to attend a workshop at Richmond High School on the subject of establishing an alumni foundation. Richmond High School is over 150 years old and frequently hosts events to train other communities in establishing alumni foundations. While at the workshop, I noticed a table with information sponsored by Scholarship America about one of its programs, Dollars for Scholars. The representative gave me information on how to start a local chapter of Dollars for Scholars to help us in providing scholarships for financially needy students. Dennis, Al and I had envisioned establishing Lake Worth High School Alumni Foundation that would, in addition to traditional alumni duties, raise money and award scholarships. When I learned about Dollars for Scholars and the services they provide, I began to think that we needed to have two separate foundations. Why? Because I could foresee problems with members of the board of directors squabbling over whether we should spend our money on alumni projects or on scholarships. After much discussion, the decision was made to have two organizations and this proved to be the best way to go.

Dennis Dorsey is a self-made man. He started working for a funeral home right out of high school, eventually graduated from a funeral director college in Boston, and established his own funeral home. I always introduce him as, "Dennis Dorsey, the last man to let you down." Over 200 alumni attended the breakfast where we announced our plans and Dennis picked up the tab for everyone which helped draw a crowd. He would continue to do this for twelve years—two breakfasts per year—until I finally convinced him that it was time for everyone to pay for their own breakfast. This, naturally, prompted a decline in attendance.

On the last day of school in the year 2000, Barry Grunow, a teacher at Lake Worth Middle School, was murdered by a student in front of a classroom full of students. Shortly afterwards, I received a call from school board chairperson, Jody Gleason, who asked about creating a scholarship in Mr. Grunow's name. She, County Commissioner Warren Newell and other office holders donated leftover funds from their own campaigns to start the fund. We received donations from Palm Beach resident Donald Trump, soap opera star and Lake Worth High grad, Deidra Hall, and from many concerned citizens. The Barry Grunow Memorial Scholarship is available to any student graduating from a public, private, or parochial school as well as home-schooled students. The scholarship is for aspiring teachers who can demonstrate the ability to do college work and prove— like other Dollars for Scholars applicants—financial need. A total of $156,250 in scholarships has been awarded from the Grunow fund since its inception in 2001.

In 1999, our first year, Lake Worth Dollars for Scholars awarded $10,000 in scholarships. The class of 2019 was awarded $126,500 which brought our grand total since 1999 to $1,257,000. The main criteria for receiving the scholarship is financial need. Many of our recipients are the first in their family to graduate from high school, much less attend college. The majority of our recipients are immigrants who are trying to achieve the great American dream and they understand that the way to get there is through education. First-timers to attend our awards ceremony are impressed with the quality of our recipients who are well-dressed, polite and grateful to everyone for their scholarship.

It has always been my position that if we are going to allow immigrants to our shores, it is to our advantage to help them get a good education. I have been President of Lake Worth Dollars for Scholars since 2001, and it appears I'll be so for life. I would like to continue to be involved but in a lesser role. Since it is my philosophy that The Lord put us here to help make the world a better place than what we found it to be, I will continue to do my part as long as He allows me to.

The alumni foundation pays all overhead expenses incurred by Dollars for Scholars which ensures that every dollar donated goes to help a needy kid attend college. The alumni foundation also publishes a newsletter, "The Alumni News," which is mailed to alums twice per year. Our alumni directory, which is like a college directory, is printed every five years and is available for purchase by alums. Dr. Bill McGoun, Class of 1952, wrote "Lake Worth High School, a History" in which he covered—in great detail—the complete story of the school from 1922 to 2007. Bill generously donated proceeds from the sale of the book to Dollars for Scholars. Palm Beach County School District has twenty-four high schools, and Lake Worth is the only school that has an alumni foundation with a newsletter, a scholarship foundation, a published history of the school, and an alumni directory. There is probably not another school in the state of Florida that can boast of those achievements.

When you retire from a public job in Florida—whether it be in education, fire or police work—you must be retired for one year before you can return to work. After I had been retired the required one year, I was asked to fill in as principal on a temporary basis at one elementary school and two middle schools. The first school was Bear Lakes Middle School. I arrived on campus seven days before the students were to appear. The school had discipline problems—unruly students disrespected the faculty and refused to go to class. In the first faculty meeting, I gained the confidence of the teachers by telling them, "When the students get here next week, we will have a plan in effect that will nail their little asses down to where they can't bat an eye."

That statement shocked some of the teachers because they had been accustomed to a principal whose leadership style was far different from mine. The teacher's union, Classroom Teachers' Association (CTA), had made weekly visits to the school before my arrival to check on teacher complaints about unruly students. After my first week at the school, I didn't see them at all. The teachers were great; they needed a strong leader and asked me to stay but I was retired and Kay and I were anxious to hit the road for a fall trip in our motorhome.

I would later fill in at a middle school whose principal had cleaned out her desk and left in the middle of the night. I was only there for a few weeks until the end of the year. It was the same scenario at an elementary school the following year where the principal had been removed and I finished the year there. The real challenge would come next

At my retirement dinner (L-R) Lori and Bob Backus; Billie Jo Hurst; me; Bill Alexander; and Carlos Hurst. I was pleased to have my college buddies in attendance.

Left: This eagle was presented to me by the Air Force Jr. ROTC instructors. The inscription read: "To the wind beneath our wings." It is still prominently displayed in my home office.

Middle: At my retirement celebration with my grandchildren: Tyler Kaczmarek, Christopher Kaczmarek, Logan Kaczmarek and Taylor Feulner.

Left: Beth, Tyler, Christopher, Taylor, and Logan helping me clean out my office.

TOP: Mac McKinnon, Athletic and Activities Director, Emeritus, emceed my retirement celebration.

MIDDLE: Kathy Perry, AP of Curriculum, presenting me with my retirement watch. "KP" was a successful teacher, magnet coordinator and assistant principal at Lake Worth High.

BOTTOM: Dr. Jim Daniels was the Deputy Superintendent of Palm Beach County Schools. He was a coal miner in Pennsylvania before entering the field of education. Jim was known to be very approachable, and a friend and supporter of principals.

TOP:(L-R) Tony Benson, Beth, me, DeeAnne, Christy Benson, Lauren and Summer Benson (in front).

MIDDLE: Kay and me at my retirement celebration.Kay was always 100% supportive of me in the various positions that I held in the Palm Beach County School System.

BELOW: Jeff and DeeAnne at my retirement celebration.They live here in Atlantis. within 10 minutes of our home.As Kay and I grow older, DeeAnne and Jeff are a great help to us.

A special thanks to those who worked to ensure my retirement dinner was a success:Patty Mandigo, Eldene Spriggs, Betsy and Larry Lyon, Arleen Finkelstein, Kathy Perry, Bill Abel, Dede Dehon, Betty Cross, and Dr. Annette Gilbert. I am sure I have forgotten others involved, and for that I am sorry.

TOP: City of Lake Worth Fire Chief, Paul Blockson and his wife, Carla.It was a great day for the city when the Blocksons came to town.They continue to work to make Lake Worth all it can be.

MIDDLE: Jack Marcum, our Athletic and Activities Director. Jack was the pride of Delbarton, WV.He played baseball at Marshall University and held the record for triples when he graduated.He was one of the most successful high school baseball coaches in Florida.We were in the state playoffs four of the first five years I was principal at LWHS.He was inducted into the Palm Beach County Sports Hall of Fame and the Florida Sports Hall of Fame

Bottom: Me with Deloris and Clayton Brown.They drove from their home in South Carolina to attend my retirement celebration.

TOP: Pictured here with my granddaughter, Taylor Grace, after my last high school graduation ceremony, 1999. Taylor's middle name is in honor of my mother, Grace. I call her "Choodle-Cake"

MIDDLE: The marquee, made possible by assistant principal Jim White, in front of Lake Worth High, where I would end my career in education.

BOTTOM:(L-R) Walter Pierce (Exec. Dir of The Principals' Assoc.), Alan Carnahan, me, Don Chenicek, and Bill Fay at the Bomb Squadron celebrating the school board passing the Principals' Retirement Incentive Plan

TOP LEFT: Pictured here with Bill Goode at my retirement. **TOP RIGHT:** Here with DeeAnne, Kay and Taylor at my last high school graduation ceremony in 1999. **MIDDLE LEFT:** Calvin Taylor, Area 3 Superintendent of Schools. **MIDDLE RIGHT:** Buz Spooner, Dean of Elementary Principals at my retirement celebration. **BOTTOM:** My sister, Betty, and brother, Bee came from Orlando and West Virginia, respectively to attend my retirement shindig.

FOREST HILL HIGH SCHOOL

Not too long after my retirement, my friend, Superintendent Art Johnson, called me shortly before school started in August of 2002 asking me to meet him for lunch. Dr. Johnson explained that the School District faced seven "F" rated schools from the previous school year and he intended to fix the problem with reassignment of high performing teachers to be paid an additional $10,000. He also intended to create a "supervising principal" position. He wanted me to go to Forest Hill High School to serve as "supervising principal." The school had previously received a grade of "D" from the state two years in a row, and in 2001-2002 they became an "F" school. Dr. Johnson told me that if I would accept the offer my job would be to stand behind the principal and advise her on what to do to get the school in good standing with the state which was threatening to take the school over and manage it. He further stated, "If you take this job, and

I know you can do it given your track record bringing back Lake Worth High School. He also indicated that he would back me on transferring out anyone who did not want to cooperate with the needed work and that I could withdraw over-aged students with no credit and reassign them to adult education and/or alternative education. He indicated that FHHS could not remain an "F" school!

I accepted the challenge and reported to Forest Hill High. One of the first things I did after arriving was to see the report on reading scores. When I looked at the reading scores I immediately saw what we needed to do. The school population was primarily made up of Hispanic and black students, many of whom were reading on third grade level. Also, an alarming number of seniors had not yet passed the FCAT, the state-mandated test required for graduation. The seniors would have three more attempts to pass the test; if they didn't pass they would receive a "certificate of completion" instead of a diploma. I told the principal and one of the assistant principals that I had to go to West Virginia to attend my sister's funeral. While I was gone, I wanted them to identify ten non-essential positions that we could operate the school without. I also told Superintendent Johnson that I wanted to hire ten reading teachers to fill those ten vacancies. He approved my plan and told me that when he was principal at Spanish River High School, he put his lowest achievers in two reading classes. That was advice I would follow and implement in order to achieve the goal we needed to reach.

When I returned to Forest Hill we announced the transfer of the ten "non-essential" teachers and that was when "the fit hit the shan." Teachers were complaining about the transfers as well as about other changes we were implementing. They had been allowed to leave campus during their planning periods and go home, shopping, to the bank, or wherever. We put a stop to all of that which further infuriated the teachers. The reading teachers we brought in received a pay bonus which caused additional resentment among the ranks. We identified those senior students who were within reach of passing the FCAT test and assigned them to two reading classes taught by teachers that I'd hired—a retired army sergeant and a retired football coach. Test results at the end of the year showed that Forest Hill High had more seniors who passed the FCAT than any school in the county.

We had a vacancy for an assistant principal and I needed a strong person for that position. Walter Pierce was Executive Director of the Principal's Association and he told me he knew just the right person for the job. He said that Jon Prince, an assistant principal at Jeff Davis Middle School, wanted to get experience at the high school level. We brought Jon aboard and it would prove to be the best move I made all year. Jon was the "total package;" he was strong in all areas. Jon is now the Deputy superintendent in St. Lucie County. I look for him to be appointed as superintendent somewhere in the near future. To round out the administrative team, I brought Charity Martin in to fill another vacancy. Charity was a gutsy person who would not be intimidated by anyone. She and John made a great team and were very effective in both maintaining discipline and working with teachers.

There was a group of incorrigible primarily overaged male students from rival housing projects in West Palm Beach who were constantly being referred to the dean's office for major discipline problems. I told Jon and Leonard Coleman, a teacher on assignment for discipline (who had also been one of my former Lake Worth High students), to look at the discipline and academic records of these students to determine if they stood a chance of graduating. Furthermore, I told Jon and Leonard that if the students had frequent referrals and were behind schedule to graduate, they should withdraw these students and refer them to alternative schools. The next report on suspensions in the *Palm Beach Post* showed that Forest Hill High had the fewest number of suspensions of any high school in the county. Like the Lake Worth High students I had encountered upon my arrival in 1980, these students only came to school to cause trouble. They were—quite obviously—making no effort to graduate.

As the opening weeks of the school year went by, I continued to make more changes that irritated a certain group of teachers who fought any deviation from the way they wanted things to be.

The faculty at Forest Hill High had been accustomed to, in effect, running the school. A friend on the staff, assistant principal Willie McCoy, told me that certain teachers were saying, "Cantley doesn't know about the Forest Hill tradition." That "tradition," as it turned out, was that "the county office has its way of doing things, and Forest Hill has its way of doing things." When they decided that they didn't want to do things

"Cantley's way," they asked the CTA (Classroom Teachers Association) Executive Director to meet with them and listen to a list of 21 complaints against me. They filed a grievance procedure with the school board; however, not a single complaint qualified as a grievance. They were all basic things that any good classroom teacher does on a routine basis.

One teacher in particular was especially negative & resistant when it came to expressing her displeasure with "the new way" we were doing business. One day I was walking down a corridor when I met her, whereupon she turned her head away from me and looked upwards. I reached over and touched her on the arm-- This turned out to be a Big Mistake! She went to the State Attorney's office, accused me of assaulting her, and reported the incident to the school police. Several days later, she showed them a large bruise on the inside of her left arm and claimed that I had brushed her breast and pinched her arm. When the police failed to file charges, she took her fight to the CTA, which had probably been advising her from the beginning. The CTA Executive Director requested an internal investigation prompting Superintendent Johnson to send me home for a month during the investigation. When the inquest was completed, I was found innocent of the charges and after the Thanksgiving break I returned to the school to resume my duties as supervising principal.

During the investigation, I had been represented by Scott Richardson, a high-profile criminal attorney on retainer by the Principal's Association. After I was cleared to return to work, Superintendent Johnson told Walter Pierce and me to ask Richardson if I had grounds to sue for defamation of character. The next time Walter and I were in the lawyer's office, we asked him about the possibility of a suit. Richardson was at his desk with his head down, writing notes. He replied that he didn't think I had a case because I would have to prove that someone had lost confidence in or respect for me because of the accusations made against me; he didn't think I could do that. He added, "I don't want to offend you, but you will be asked very personal questions—like if you have sex with your wife as often now as you did before the case." Immediately, a joke that my brother, Bee, once told me came to mind. I told Richardson, "Almost every night." His head raised up and his jaw dropped. I closed the subject by adding, "Almost Monday, almost Tuesday, almost Wednesday." Walter Pierce, an Irishman who loves a good joke, nearly fell off his chair laughing. He must have told that story one hundred times by now.

As we began our second semester, conditions and faculty attitudes remained the same. The reading teachers were doing a good job of preparing the students for the FCAT, but they were working under constant harassment from the same minority of teachers who resented change and anyone who was working hard.

As we approached the end of the school year, Jon and I determined that if the principal was to be in charge of her school after I left, some changes in personnel were needed. We identified 27 teachers that we felt needed to leave Forest Hill High. Some of them were the dissidents who would fight change until their dying breath, while others were—or had once been—good teachers who merely needed a change of venue. When I approached the superintendent with the idea, he said, "Dave, our lawyers tell me there is not a court in the land that will uphold me in this." I have always felt that most school board lawyers would rather run than fight, so I told him, "The teachers' contract only says they have a job. It doesn't say the job will be at Forest Hill High—it could be at Belle Glade, Jupiter or Boca Raton." I told him that we needed to make a stand on this; he finally agreed to "zero base" the school, which meant that every teacher had to apply and be interviewed for his or her job. Those teachers who were not rehired were given transfers to other schools.

As expected, CTA filed an unfair labor practice complaint against the school board, the superintendent and me.

I dreaded going to the courthouse to give a deposition in the unfair labor practice complaint. The CTA lawyer was tough, and I had been up against him before. To my surprise, as soon as I arrived, he complimented me on my career and told me he had Googled me and knew the jobs I had held during my career. He even congratulated me on being elected to the Atlantis City Council. We talked baseball (namely Pete Rose's ban) and other sports before we got down to business. The questioning was going very well, but I kept waiting for the axe to fall; it soon became clear that he was actually on my side. The hearing was held within a week, and it went the same way—only this time with CTA representatives and the teachers who had brought the charges were present to hear it all. The lawyer, just as he'd done during the deposition, demonstrated his support of me—and at the conclusion of the hearing he wished me well and told me to enjoy a well-deserved retirement. One month later, the school board attorney would receive a letter from the state hearing officer dismissing the complaint.

State test scores for schools were released before I departed Forest Hill High in early June, 2003. In those days, the media got test score results before the schools received them. I actually got the good news from a reporter with the *Palm Beach Post*, which had been my strong ally throughout the whole school year. Forest Hill was a "C" school and was finally off the state's "bad" list. This big monkey was finally off the backs of the superintendent and school board!!!

Dr. Johnson had kept his word to give me whatever I wanted as part of the agreement that sent me to Forest Hill High. During the second semester I told him that we needed to have an International Baccalaureate Program in order to attract high-achieving students. He made that happen. I later told him that we also needed a vocational program to prepare students who were not college bound for a job after high school, so he added a cabinet-building shop to fill that need. Those programs continue to thrive today and are helping to keep Forest Hill strong.

Those two programs were the bookends that we needed to (a) cement a strong curriculum and (b) ensure the school would remain vibrant. However, I'll never forget what we did for those seniors who finally passed The FCAT. I often wonder what they are doing now and what their lives would have been like without the reading classes that enabled them to pass the FCAT and get their high school diplomas.

TOP: Dr. Art Johnson, former principal, area superintendent, school board member, and ultimately Superintendent of Palm Beach County Schools.Dr. Johnson was very supportive during my tenure at Forest Hill High School.

Bottom: Willie McCoy, assistant principal for adult and community education at Forest Hill High, was an invaluable ally.

RIGHT: I hired Jon Prince as assistant principal shortly after I arrived at Forest Hill High. Walter Pierce told me Jon wanted to move to the high school level from Jeff Davis Middle School. This proved to be the best move I made during my year at Forest Hill. Jon was "the total package." I predicted big things for him. Dr. Jon Prince is now the Deputy Superintendent, under Wayne Gent, in the St. Lucie County system.

EPILOGUE

Through the grace of God, my family continues to thrive enjoying good health and prosperity, during the COVID-19 pandemic that has paralyzed the country and claimed thousands of lives during the year 2020. Our daughters, Beth and DeeAnne, and their families are a source of pride for Kay and me. Beth and Walt currently live in North Carolina where Walt is CEO of a pharmaceutical firm. DeeAnne and Jeff live near us in Atlantis. Jeff is self-employed in the ENT surgical instrument business, and DeeAnne teaches English at Christa McAuliffe Middle School in Boynton Beach.

Christopher Blaine Kaczmarek, Beth and Walt's first son, is an attorney and lives in Maryland. Chris is my most intelligent, most handsome and favorite grandson. He and Maegan Reese, were married on November 24, 2017 in Phoenixville, PA. They welcomed their first child, Elise, January 14, 2020.

Tyler Michael Kaczmarek, Beth and Walt's second son, is my most intelligent, most handsome and favorite grandson. He earned a Ph.D. in computer science with an emphasis on security at the University of California Irvine. He and Tara Martinez were married in Laguna Beach, CA on June 25, 2017, and live in Burlington, MA. They have a son, Oliver, born on April 10, 2019 which made Kay and me great grandparents!

Logan Daniel Kaczmarek, Beth and Walt's youngest son, graduated from St. Louis University with a degree in finance and works in Phoenix as a financial analyst.. "Yogan" is my most intelligent, most handsome and favorite grandson. Logan and Jessica Cannata were married November 9, 2019 in Scottsdale, AZ.

Taylor Grace Feulner, DeeAnne and Jeff's daughter, is beyond a doubt my favorite granddaughter. She is pretty, intelligent and is as goal-oriented as my grandsons. Taylor chose to take a year off her studies at the University of South Florida to study in Japan; she then returned home and graduated from USF on May 3, 2019 with a major in mass communications. She returned to Japan in August, 2019 and is teaching English to Japanese students in Kyoto, Japan.

Jackson David Feulner, DeeAnne and Jeff's son, is my favorite grandson-- he is very smart and handsome just like Papaw. He graduated from Park Vista High School in June of 2020. Jackson brings happiness and laughter to all with whom he comes in contact; he is a hard worker and loves to help others.

I continue to enjoy retirement. I am president, probably for life, of Lake Worth Dollars for Scholars, a scholarship program we started during my final year as principal of Lake Worth High School. We have awarded 1.5 million dollars to needy students from 1999-2020.

The scholarships would not have been possible without persistent efforts by alums Dennis and Doris Dorsey and other graduates who donated many hours of their time and made monetary donations to help many students realize their dream of a college education. Many of our scholarship recipients are first in their family to graduate high school. Much credit must be given to the Lake Worth School Alumni Foundation which pays all overhead expenses of Dollars for Scholars ensuring that every dollar that is donated to or raised by DFS goes directly into a scholarship fund for needy students.

We lost a valued member of Dollars for Scholars Board of Directors in October of 2019. MaryAnne Hedrick was a teacher at Lake Worth Middle School when teacher Barry Grunow was murdered in his classroom by one of his students on the last day of school in 2000. We established a scholarship endowment in Barry's name and MaryAnne worked tirelessly to raise funds for scholarships in Barry's name by conducting the annual Barry Grunow Memorial Golf Tournament. She had just finished the 2019 tournament two weeks before her passing. It is my hope that the DFS Board of Directors will endow a scholarship in MaryAnne's name. Despite being confined to a wheelchair due to a car accident she had a very positive outlook on life, working constantly to help others. I never saw her without her big trademark smile.

Neuropathy is slowing me down a bit in my 82nd year, but I try to keep on keeping on. I continue to be blessed by my wonderful wife who encourages and nags me to take my medication and to exercise. Ray Price sang my song when he recorded, "You're the Best Thing That Ever Happened to Me."

As the aging process continues to creep up on me, I recently contacted several college buddies to see how they were doing health wise. I called Carlos Hurst, originally from Covel in Wyoming County, WV, now living in Coconut Creek, FL, to check on him. He informed me that his wife, Billie Jo, another Morris Harvey College grad, had passed away. When I told him that I had also spoken with Jim Summers (Mt. Hope, WV, now living in Orlando) the day before, Carlos exclaimed, "Jim Summers? I thought Jim Summers was dead." I replied that Jim had told me he thought we were all dead, and he was the lone survivor. We have reached the age (78-84) where we talk non-stop about our ailments. I lost a dear friend in Bill Alexander in July of 2019. Bill and I met at Morris Harvey College in the fall of 1960 and remained close friends until his passing. When I lose a friend I think of what Jim Boyd, an older teacher at Royal Palm School told me. "Dave, wait until you start losing friends, that's when it is really going to hit you."

Thank God, I am not affected by dementia or Alzheimer's disease which impacted the lives of four of my siblings. I was hoping they would name a disease after me. "Dave Cantley Disease" has a nice ring to it. If I do become afflicted with cruel Alzheimer's Disease, I want my family and friends to know that I will still love you, but I won't miss you!

TOP: Kay and me touring Seattle with the Dorseys, Doris and Dennis.After the Seattle stop over, we did an Alaskan cruise.

MIDDLE: Tommy and Helen Hansen presenting me a check for $100,000 for the LWHS Alumni Foundation.

BOTTOM: Group shot at one of the reunions for the LWHS Faculty and Staff from 1980's and 1990's.We gather once ayear at John Prince Park.I was fortunate to have many amazing teachers and administrators in my years at LWHS.

Top Left: DeeAnne and Jeff. **Top Right::**Beth and DeeAnne.
Middle: Kay, me, Taylor and Jackson.
Bottom Left: Jessica and Logan. **Bottom Right:** Me and Kay

Top Left: Beth and Walt. **Top Right:** Christopher, Maegan and Elise. **Middle Left:** Me, Logan, Christopher, Tyler and Kay. **Middle Right:** Tara, Tyler and Oliver. **Bottom:** Taylor, Jackson, DeeAnne and Jeff.

My 80ᵗʰ birthday party in September of 2018—

TOP: (L-R) Ulysses Smith (Smitty), LukeThornton and me

MIDDLE: (L-R) Betsy Lyon, Meryl Preston, Me, Arleen Finkelstein, Chris Hart, Dede DeHon (all former LWHS teachers)

BOTTOM: Me with my nieces--Jessica Bodtman, and Susie Sayre

TOP: Family picture at my birthday party. I was blessed to have several of my family members travel from West Virginia, New Jersey, Georgia and Texas to celebrate with me.

MIDDLE: Jane Whitaker, Marien Guzzetti, Ed Whitaker (all former LWHS teachers) and me

BOTTOM: Dancing with my wife, Kay, to Roy Clark's, "If I had to do it all over again, I'd do it with you".

Party photos taken by my nephew, Byron Cantley

ACKNOWLEDGEMENTS

It took me years to complete writing this book. My goal was—especially in Part One—to tell the story of my family in depth and, to the best of my ability, make sure that all my facts were correct. In that section, I wanted to recount the lengthy history of the Cantley family. I felt it was important to capture the feeling of what it was like to grow up on the family farm at Rock Creek, West Virginia and to share what life was like on Coal River back in the 1950's. Part Two was much easier, because it was primarily straightforward information about my professional life as an educator.

A variety of individuals from Rock Creek have gone on to lead remarkably successful lives. They provided for their families, paid their taxes, and made positive contributions to society. I included stories of people who had been particularly successful—in fact, outstanding—in the fields of education, engineering, law and medicine. When Marilyn Murray Willison (my "Book Doctor"), read the chapter about Doctor Jim Wills she asked, "How did so many smart people come from that little place?" I would like to thank Jim Wills; Bobbie Farley; my cousin, Nelson; my nephew, Glenn Cantley; and my niece, Mary Jo Broyles for submitting their memories of growing up at Rock Creek. They added a different—and valuable—perspective to the story.

Since coal mining camps have become a thing of the past, I wanted to include information about them so that the younger—and particularly the future—generations might have a better understanding of what they were like, especially the many coal camps that were located on Coal River, in Raleigh, as well as in the surrounding counties. John Vergis graciously allowed me to include the story he had written for *Golden Seal Magazine* about life in a coal camp. Take it from me, John "nailed it" when he described life in his hometown of Edwight. My gratitude also goes to Larry Cassell and Maynard Daniel for their contribution to the chapter about Coalfield Baseball. Larry Sarrett, Carl Bradford and Larry Cassell provided valuable information on Marsh Fork athletics.

I will be forever grateful to my wife, Kay, for tirelessly editing my manuscripts, going over everything time and again and keying the genealogy section. As a business education major, she can sniff a foot-high stack of copy and accurately tell you how many typos lie within.

Special gratitude goes to my daughter DeeAnne for framing the book. She spent countless hours scanning, sizing and placing pictures where I wanted them.

Also, thanks to Chris Hart, one of my Lake Worth High teachers, for proofreading the manuscript. Chrissy, you did a great job!

Many thanks to Rick Bradford for allowing me to use information from his books written about Coal River, Edwight, Hazy and other areas of Raleigh County. If interested in his work, he can be reached by calling him at 304-854-3943. Also, many thanks to Rick's brother, Charles for the pictures he graciously provided.

Last, but not least, I want to thank Marilyn Murray Willison for her expertise. She is an accomplished editor, journalist, and author of six non-fiction books. She worked on newspaper and magazine staffs in London and hobnobbed with British royalty. When we began working on this project together, I asked her what title I should give her, and she answered, "Just think of me as your Book Doctor." That is a very appropriate title for her because no matter how careful I was with what I wrote, she could always find a way to make my words sound better.

ABOUT THE AUTHOR

When David Cantley asked me to write about him for the autobiography on which he was working, it took me about three seconds to say, "Yes." I consider him to be one of the most extraordinary people I have ever met and felt honored to be able to share my thoughts with others.

In *The History of Lake Worth High School*, I wrote this about his two decades as principal, "Without his guidance, the school might very well have been shut down." I believed that strongly then, and I still believe it as strongly today.

In May of 1980, Cantley became Lake Worth High's fifth principal during the 1979-80 school year. He took charge of a school that had deteriorated tremendously in the quarter-century since my class had graduated. The campus was overcrowded, and plagued with disorder. White students were fleeing, and academics were lagging.

The first thing he did was restore discipline. After that, he instituted magnet programs to arrest the white flight. Finally, he spearheaded efforts to get the campus rebuilt and enlarged. By the time he retired in 1999, the school was a model for how things should be done in secondary education.

Along the way, he worked to help the less fortunate achieve an education. He had known hard times as a youngster, and he never forgot his roots. He was instrumental in founding the flea market held beneath I-95 that provided scholarships, school supplies and other aid to those in need.

The year he retired, he was a key figure in organizing the Lake Worth High School Alumni Foundation and Lake Worth Dollars for Scholars. The latter has distributed over $1 million in scholarships as of 2017.

I can't say anything about David Cantley before his Lake Worth High years, because I didn't know him then. But this book fills in the gaps and gives me a better feel about how he became the outstanding man he is.

William E. "Bill" McGoun, Ph.D.

Printed in the United States
By Bookmasters